International Socialism 149
Winter 2016

Contributors

Anne Alexander is the co-author, with Mostafa Bassiouny, of *Bread, Freedom, Social Justice: Workers and the Egyptian Revolution* (Zed, 2014). She is a founder member of MENA Solidarity Network and a member of the University and College Union.

Shaun Doherty is a member of the Socialist Workers Party in Hackney and a teacher of English Literature at a Sixth Form College.

Martin Empson is the treasurer of the Campaign against Climate Change Trade Union group and the author of *Land and Labour: Marxism, Ecology and Human History*.

Iain Ferguson is Honorary Professor of Social Work and Social Policy at the University of the West of Scotland.

Pete Green is a retired activist in the UCU and member of Left Unity.

Jane Hardy is Professor of Political Economy at the University of Hertfordshire. She is the author of *Poland's New Capitalism*.

Rob Jackson teaches political theory in Manchester, and recently co-organised a conference at King's College London called Past and Present, on the thought of Antonio Gramsci.

Nikos Lountos writes for the weekly *Workers Solidarity*, published by SEK in Athens, Greece.

Allister Mactaggart is a lecturer in art and design at Chesterfield College where he is UCU branch chair, and he is a member of Chesterfield SWP.

Paul McGarr is a teacher in East London, and editor of the *Education for Liberation* magazine within the National Union of Teachers.

Dave Merrick is a long standing active member of Bristol SWP. He is the author of *Social Work and Child Abuse: Still Walking the Tightrope?* (Routledge, 2006).

Richard Morgan is a member of Coventry SWP and a long standing workplace activist.

Tony Phillips is a member of the SWP based in Walthamstow in London and is a Unison trade union branch secretary working in the fire service.

Brian Richardson is a barrister based in London. He is a member of the steering committees of both Unite Against Fascism and Stand Up To Racism and has just published a biography of Bob Marley.

John Rose is currently studying the roots of the failure of communism in the 20th century.

Terry Sullivan is an active member of the SWP and the National Union of Teachers in London. He is also the author of *Genes: Just How Important are They?*

Mark L Thomas is a national organiser for the Socialist Workers Party.

Resisting the long war

Alex Callinicos

In May 1970 a group of prominent Harvard academics with considerable government experience, led by the game theorist Thomas Schelling, went to the White House to meet their ex-colleague, Henry Kissinger, then national security adviser to president Richard Nixon. They were there to protest against the recent invasion of Cambodia by the United States and its client regime in South Vietnam—supposedly to attack "safe havens" used by Viet Cong guerrillas. The invasion provoked a massive wave of protest on American campuses and led to the fatal shooting of four students at Kent State University and two more at Jackson State. The historian Greg Grandin explains:

> Kissinger's former colleagues weren't aware that Nixon and Kissinger had already been secretly bombing Cambodia and Laos for over a year... They knew only about the invasion, and that was bad enough. "Sickening," Schelling said. Today in the United States, a shared and largely unquestioning assumption, irrespective of political affiliation, holds that Washington has the right to use military force against the "safe havens" of terrorists or potential terrorists, even if those safe havens are found in sovereign countries we are not at war with. This assumption was the premise of George W Bush's 2002 [sic] invasion of Afghanistan and Barack Obama's expansion of drone attacks in Somalia, Yemen and Pakistan, along with his most recent military operations against Islamic State militants in Syria and Iraq. This reasoning was not widely held in 1970. Schelling's Harvard delegation rejected Kissinger's attempt to

justify the invasion by citing the need to destroy communist "sanctuaries". As one reporter summed up the group's objections, violation of a neutral country's sovereignty "could be used by anyone else in the world as a precedent for invading another country, in order, for example, to clear out terrorists".[1]

So what in 1970 was exceptional and reprehensible has become normal in the course of the following near half-century. Moreover, Grandin argues that Kissinger, in attempting to justify his crimes in Vietnam, Cambodia, Chile and elsewhere, "provided a new generation of politicians a template for how to justify tomorrow's action while ignoring yesterday's catastrophe":

> History is affirmed, since it is America's unprecedented historical success that justifies the exceptionalism. Yet history is also denied, or at least what is denied is understanding of the past as a series of causal relationships. That is, the blowback from any given action…is rinsed clean of its source and given a new origin story, blamed on generalised chaos that exists beyond our borders.

> This evasion has been on full display of late, as the politicians who drove us into Iraq in 2003 tell us that decisions made at the time that facilitated the rise of Islamic State militants shouldn't hinder America from taking bold action in the future to destroy Islamic State militants. "If we spend our time debating what happened eleven or twelve years ago," former vice president Dick Cheney today says, "we're going to miss the threat that is growing and that we do face".[2]

But this whole ideological syndrome—both the normalisation of military intervention on the territory of sovereign states and what Grandin calls the "dodge" pioneered by Kissinger of imperialist powers ducking responsibility for the catastrophes to which their interventions are supposed to be responding—is no longer a US monopoly. European social democratic politicians seem especially keen on following in Kissinger's footsteps.

French president François Hollande reacted to the Paris atrocities of 13 November by pledging "pitiless war" against ISIS, without pausing to consider whether the killings might not be blowback from France's military

1:    Grandin, 2015, Kindle loc. 58. The contrast with Niall Ferguson's account of the meeting in his apologetic biography of Kissinger, which accuses the Harvard academics of running scared in the face of "campus radicals", is telling—Ferguson, 2015, pp15-16. Thanks to Joseph Choonara, Judith Orr, and Camilla Royle for their comments on a draft of this piece.
2:    Grandin, 2015, Kindle locs. 2007, 2015.

interventions in Libya, Mali and Syria. This evasion of historical responsibility was as evident in the Gadarene rush by right wing Labour MPs who had voted for the invasion of Iraq in March 2003 to give David Cameron the support he needed in the House of Commons on 4 December to authorise British participation in the US-led bombing campaign against Syria.

James Meek commented on the performance of the most ineffable Labour imperialist:

> listening to the speech of Hilary Benn, the pro-bombing Labour foreign affairs spokesman, was like hearing one of Churchill's 1930s lonely-voice-warning-against-the-dangers-of-Hitler speeches, but made in 1941, by which time, it seems safe to assume, everyone really got Hitler. It was bizarre to hear Benn adding his voice to the many who criticised Cameron for branding those opposed to bombing Syria "terrorist sympathisers", only for the Labour man to launch into a superfluous and detailed recap of the worst IS crimes. "All those who oppose air strikes are decent and honourable men," he was effectively saying, "even if, unlike myself, they prefer to do nothing while gay men are being thrown off buildings, and Yazidi women deemed too old for sex slavery are murdered and thrown into mass graves".[3]

US imperialism and the Middle East

Morally and politically responsible action is therefore inseparable from critical historical understanding. And here it is impossible not to be struck by a contrast. It's plausible to see recent moves over Syria as the latest stage in a long war that has been waged since 1990-91 by the US and the other Western imperialist powers in what's sometimes called the Greater Middle East—stretching as far west and south as countries such as Mali, and north and east as far as Afghanistan, but centred on the historic Arab world, in the Mashreq and Maghreb.

Before then, however, in the period 1945-90, the era of the Cold War, there were plenty of wars in the Middle East, above all between Israel and the Arab states, in 1948, 1956, 1973 and 1982. But direct imperialist military intervention primarily took the form of defensive wars waged by the declining colonial powers, Britain and France—for example, the disastrous Suez expedition of 1956 or the terrible Algerian war of 1954-62. Thanks to Suez in particular, the US established itself as the dominant imperialist power in the region—crucial as a source of the "strategic commodity"

3: Meek, 2015, p5.

oil—during this period.[4] But aside from a couple of brief military interventions in Lebanon (1958 and 1982-3), the Pentagon's muscle was visible in the Middle East mainly in the increasingly generous military aid the US supplied its two most important allies, the odd couple of deeply antagonistic confessional states, Israel and Saudi Arabia.

1979 clearly marked a turning point. First, the Iranian Revolution toppled a key US ally, the Shah of Iran, and stimulated a new political and ideological challenge to Western dominance in the shape of radical Islamism (most visible in the rise of Hizbollah during the Lebanese civil war). Secondly, the Soviet invasion of Afghanistan marked an escalation of the Cold War in which the Greater Middle East was now very clearly established as a terrain of superpower competition. President Jimmy Carter, who had already stepped up US arms expenditure to match what was (deludedly) represented as the growing military and economic strength of the USSR, declared in January 1980:

> The region which is now threatened by Soviet troops in Afghanistan is of great strategic importance: It contains more than two-thirds of the world's exportable oil... The Soviet Union is now attempting to consolidate a strategic position, therefore, that poses a grave threat to the free movement of Middle East oil... Let our position be absolutely clear: An attempt by any outside force to gain control of the Persian Gulf region will be regarded as an assault on the vital interests of the United States of America, and such an assault will be repelled by any means necessary, including military force.[5]

The Carter Doctrine is widely seen as the beginning of US military intervention in the Middle East. But clearly Carter was preoccupied with the danger that Moscow would seek to exploit the Iranian Revolution. Thus he issued Presidential Directive 59, which authorised the use of tactical nuclear weapons against a Soviet military advance into the Gulf.[6] The Rapid Deployment Force, from which developed Central Command, the organiser of the past quarter century's wars, was set up under Carter. As Lawrence Freedman puts it, "although both the doctrine and the force were triggered by concerns about potential Soviet actions, they eventually derived their importance through enabling later responses to threats from within the region".[7]

4: Bromley, 1991.
5: Carter, 1980. See, on the so-called "Second Cold War", Binns, 1983, and Halliday, 1983.
6: Halliday, 1983, pp226-227.
7: Freedman, 2008, p104.

Nevertheless, the Reagan administration (1981-9), for all its tough talk and increased military spending, after dipping its toes into Lebanon and losing 241 marines in a suicide bombing in October 1983, rapidly pulled out again.[8] Its most important intervention in the region was to back the Iraqi dictator Saddam Hussein after he attacked Iran in September 1980. The resulting protracted struggle, the longest conventional war of the 20th century, lasting eight years and costing a million lives, failed to strangle the Iranian Revolution. But it preoccupied two powers whose ambitions might otherwise destabilise the region; when Iran looked like winning, US naval and air power was selectively used to tilt the balance in Iraq's favour.[9] And indeed the new era of intervention was precipitated when Saddam, the eventual victor in this long contest, got greedy and grabbed Kuwait in August 1990.

But it's crucial to grasp the change in context here. In the first place, the 1991 Gulf War waged against Iraq by the US and a coalition of Western and Arab states occurred as the Cold War drew to a close. On the one hand, the collapse of the rival imperialist bloc gave the US much greater room for manoeuvre, removing a major inhibition on the use of military power. As Freedman puts it, "in contrast to Vietnam, the Americans did not have to worry about provoking a Great Power that might enter the war on the enemy's side".[10] The Gulf War, unlike the invasion of Iraq in 2003, was authorised by the United Nations Security Council because a prostrate Soviet Union, on the verge of disintegration, was too weak to oppose it. But, on the other hand, the dissolution of the superpower blocs could open up a new era of more fluid inter-imperialist rivalries. The easy defeat of Saddam's Iraq underlined US military supremacy, but America's economic position was being eroded by the expansion of other capitalist powers – Germany and Japan within the Western bloc, and, of course, China, the great outsider.[11]

Since the end of the Cold War, successive administrations have sought to defend and entrench US global hegemony. This has involved, firstly, the drive, particularly marked during Bill Clinton's presidency (1993-2001) to generalise neoliberalism, levering open all the world's states

---

8:   Freedman, 2008, chapter 7 (entitled "In and Out of Beirut").

9:   Hiro, 1989. The reality was much bumpier that this summary suggests: the revelation in November 1986 that the US and Israel had been supplying arms to Iran, to counter-balance Iraq (and, for the former, to help fund the right-wing Contras in Nicaragua) nearly brought down the Reagan administration. The tangled tale of the US and the Iran-Iraq War can be followed in Freedman, 2008, chapters 8 to 10.

10:   Freedman, 2008, p235.

11:   For an early attempt to make sense of the new conjuncture, see the essays by John Rees and myself in Humber, 1994.

to US capital and commodities.[12] Secondly, American military power has been used repeatedly to maintain US hegemony over the Middle East, and therefore allow it to control the access of other states (including possible or actual rivals) to what remains the key source of the "world's exportable oil". This undertaking peaked in a particularly aggressive and hubristic form under George W Bush (president 2001-9), but Obama has continued it, albeit in a much more cautious and selective manner.[13]

A crucial dimension in these wars has been the US relationship with Saudi Arabia and the other Gulf states. In February 1945 president Franklin Roosevelt stopped off on the way back from the Yalta summit with Churchill and Stalin for a meeting in the Canal Zone with the Saudi King Ibn Saud and two other Arab monarchs. On his return to Washington, Roosevelt told the British ambassador, Lord Halifax: "Persian oil…is yours. We share the oil of Iraq and Kuwait. As for Saudi Arabian oil, it's ours." (In the event, the US shoved Britain aside in Iran and the Gulf as well.) A State Department memorandum that same year called the oil resources of Saudi Arabia "a stupendous source of strategic power and one of the greatest material prizes in world history".[14]

Some 40 years later, it was Iranian attacks on Kuwaiti oil tankers that precipitated the deployment of US naval power in the Gulf in 1987-88.[15] After Saddam seized Kuwait in August 1990, the US first responded by sending troops to defend Saudi Arabia—a move that, in a nice piece of double blowback, provoked Osama bin Laden to develop the contacts he had built up when the US and Saudi Arabia encouraged Islamist militants to fight the Soviet occupation of Afghanistan into Al Qaeda as an organisation of struggle against the American presence in the Islamic world. The Gulf has become a major hub of global capitalism, where dynastic regimes preside over companies that are investing the profits of oil production and related activities such as construction elsewhere in the Middle East and indeed world-wide.[16] This is an important reason for the US to maintain its dominance of the region, even though it is now self-sufficient in oil and gas thanks to the shale revolution.

But the net result of these successive military interventions has been little short of disastrous, for US imperialism, but more importantly for the

---

12: Gowan, 1999, and Panitch and Gindin, 2012.
13: Callinicos, 2003, and Harvey, 2003.
14: Gardner, 2009, pp26-27, 32.
15: Hiro, 1989, chapter 9.
16: The economics of Gulf capitalism (though not the politics) is well explored in Hanieh, 2011.

people of the Middle East. The denunciation of the Roman Empire put into the mouth of a British leader by the ancient historian Tacitus, "*Solitudinem faciunt pacem appellant*"—they desolate and call it peace—applies fully to what Western imperialism wrought in the Middle East. Not simply was the US defeated in Iraq, but the form in which it was able, briefly, to stabilise the country—reliance on a sectarian Shiite government closely aligned with the Islamic Republic regime in Iran—created the conditions in which ISIS could emerge as a coalition of jihadis and ex-army officers enjoying at least passive support from Iraq's disaffected Sunni Arab minority.

Then came the revolutionary wave that swept through the Arab world in 2011, toppling the Tunisian and Egyptian regimes, and threatening to bring down many others. Eventually the risings were contained, but in forms that have further fractured political structures. At a regional level, Saudi Arabia and the other Gulf states orchestrated the counter-revolution—underwriting renewed military dictatorship in Egypt and (while targeting the Muslim Brotherhood) promoting Salafist (ultra-orthodox Sunni Muslim) jihadi movements. In Syria this collided with the efforts of Bashar al-Assad's regime to defeat the revolutionary uprising by provoking a sectarian civil war.

After some dithering over whether or not to intervene against Assad, the Obama administration opted to stay out, content that the war would paralyse the Arab state that under Assad—father and son—frequently sought to block or sabotage US initiatives. This reflected what George Friedman of the Stratfor strategic intelligence website calls a "double strategy" of divide and rule rather than direct intervention:

The first layer is to keep its distance from major flare-ups in the region, providing support but making clear it will not be the one to take primary responsibility. As the situation on the ground deteriorates, the United States expects these conflicts to eventually compel regional powers to take responsibility…

The second layer of this strategy is creating a balance of power. The United States wants regional powers to deal with issues that threaten their interests more than American interests. At the same time, the United States does not want any one country to dominate the region. There are four such powers: Turkey, Iran, Saudi Arabia and Israel.[17]

17: Friedman, 2015.

Political disintegration, inter-imperialist rivalry, and ISIS

The effect of this strategy has been as disastrous as Bush Junior's attempt to use military power to reshape the Middle East. The state collapse that was one of the main results of the overthrow of Saddam Hussein has spread much more widely. Iraq and Syria—the two core states of the Arab East—have disintegrated.[18] So too have Libya, where a NATO bombing campaign tipped the balance against Muammar Gaddafi in 2011, and Yemen. All these countries have become the sites of proxy wars between local powers.

The principal antagonists at a regional level are Iran—the main backer of the Iraqi and Syrian regimes—and Saudi Arabia, which since the accession of King Salman in January 2015 has been pursuing an aggressive external policy, refusing to cut oil production in order to smash the competition from American shale producers and launching a bloody war against what it regards as Iranian-backed forces in Yemen. Other major players are Turkey and Qatar, both of which have been promoting jihadi groups in Syria and underwriting the Islamist coalition claiming to rule Libya from Tripoli (the rival secularist government based in western Libya is backed by Egypt and the United Arab Emirates).

Some people on the left imagine that this chaos favours the interests of Western imperialism, or even that it is part of some cunning plan hatched in Washington. The reasons vary: some espouse a version of Naomi Klein's conception of "disaster capitalism", arguing that US capitalism today pursues a "bomb and build" strategy, encouraging wars that will allow American corporations to profit from the reconstruction of shattered countries.[19] This involves a basic misunderstanding of the structure and interests of US capitalism.

The top ten of the Fortune 500 list of major US companies in 2015 were, in descending order, Walmart, Exxon, Chevron, Berkshire Hathaway, Apple, General Motors, Phillips 66, General Electric, Ford, and CVS Health; Boeing, the biggest company involved in defence production, comes in at number 27.[20] Only the three energy companies in the top ten belong to Klein's "disaster capitalism complex", and dubiously so since their business remains extracting, refining and selling oil and gas, not rebuilding disaster

---

18: An interesting report details how the war is causing economic as well as political disintegration in Syria, as investment shifts to coastal regions and to the oilfields controlled by ISIS and the Kurdish PYD, and away from the capital Damascus, and the old industrial hub of Aleppo: Alami, 2015.

19: See, for example, Bieler and Morton, 2015, and the critique in Callinicos, 2015.

20: Go to http://fortune.com/fortune500, companies are ranked by total revenues.

zones.[21] Despite the continuing weight of the arms sector in US capitalism, American corporations make their profits primarily in civilian markets. They rely on the Pentagon to guarantee their access to these markets and to investment sites worldwide. This isn't helped when oilfields are shut down or seized by jihadis, as they have been in Syria and Libya.

Others argue that the US set out to destroy Iraq and Syria, the Arab states controlled for decades by rival wings of the Arab nationalist Ba'ath Party that were thorns in the side of America and Israel. Although this overstates the anti-imperialist credentials of Saddam and the Assads, it's undeniable that the US wanted to get rid of them. That's not the same as seeking the disintegration of Iraq and Syria as states, though this was the unintended consequence of the policies pursued by Washington.

In a characteristically brilliant response to the Paris atrocities, the philosopher Alain Badiou argues that these state collapses are part of a wider imperialist practice he calls "zoning", the emergence of "infra-state zones which in reality are areas of non-state pillaging"; ISIS, he argues, typifies how "certain kinds of savage, armed capitalist firms occupy the spaces left empty where the state has disappeared".[22] Badiou captures a real phenomenon here, whose main cause is probably the weakening of the state produced by the neoliberal "reforms" enforced under the Washington Consensus.

Zoning has to be seen as an extreme consequence of what Michael Mann called after 9/11 "ostracising imperialism"—"most of the world's poorest countries are not being significantly integrated into transnational capitalism, but are 'ostracised' by a capitalism which regards them as too risky for investment and trade".[23] But this malign effect can react back negatively on the imperialist core itself. Spreading political disintegration in the Middle East now threatens a region economically vital to world capitalism. Moreover, the contribution the mass exodus from Syria has made to the European refugee crisis and the recent terrorist incidents underline that the European Union, one of the core zones of advanced capitalism, can't be immunised from the chaos across the Mediterranean.

Like the sorcerer's apprentice, the US faces aghast the monster made possible by its handiwork. Out of the chaos in Iraq and Syria, ISIS has morphed into a major challenge to Western domination of the region. Despite the conspiracy theories, ISIS is not the creature of US imperialism, either directly or via the intermediary of its regional allies and clients. The

---

21: See Klein, 2007, pp381, 424.

22: Badiou, 2015, pp11, 15.

23: Mann, 2001, p54.

lavish support that Saudi Arabia, Qatar and Turkey have given Sunni jihadi groups undoubtedly facilitated the rise of ISIS. But, as this journal has consistently argued, ISIS is a sui generis political project that, thanks to the destruction wrought by the occupation of Iraq and the Syrian war, and to the defeat of the Arab revolutions, has been able to build a proto-state deep into the Mashreq, and attract recruits from all over the world on the basis of the reactionary utopia of restoring the Muslim Caliphate as a transnational polity. Its theatrical violence is perfect social media fare, while the selective destruction of non-Islamic artefacts (many others help to fund the Caliphate on the international art market) offers a jihadi version of the Khmer Rouge "Year Zero" in which the profane past is spectacularly cancelled.[24]

The catastrophe wrought by the Western imperialist powers in the Middle East created the conditions for ISIS's rise, but its leaders in their own brutal way have creatively seized on the opportunities these conditions offered to pursue their own sectarian and counter-revolutionary undertaking. Anne Alexander further develops her path-breaking analysis of ISIS elsewhere in this issue, but it's worth underlining one point. Adam Hanieh writes that ISIS "does not represent any kind of anti-imperialist response, or plausible route to a Middle East free of domination or repression, whether foreign or local".[25]

This is true from an objective point of view, in two senses. First, as Alexander shows, it's far from clear that ISIS is capable of constructing a stable state that is not based primarily on plunder and spectacular violence.[26] Secondly, were the ISIS project of state-building nevertheless to succeed, then sooner or later the rulers of the new state would have to come to terms with the capitalist world system, compromise their utopian ideals, and even negotiate with the dominant imperialist powers. We have seen precisely this trajectory followed by the Islamic Republican regime in Tehran in the decades since the 1978-9 Revolution, most recently in its nuclear deal with the "Great Satan" of the US and other "world powers".

But, as the example of Iran also shows, these objective constraints don't prevent ISIS from *projecting* itself as an anti-imperialist force. One of its first spectaculars was to tear down a border post between Iraq and Syria, proclaiming the end of the 1916 Sykes-Picot agreement that partitioned the Arab provinces of the Ottoman Empire between Britain and France. In a situation where the Arab revolutions have been defeated, marginalising not

---

24: Alexander, 2015, and Callinicos, 2014, pp30-34.
25: Hanieh, 2015.
26: On ISIS finances see, in addition to the sources cited in Alexander's article in this issue, Lynch and Francis, 2015, and the *Financial Times* investigations at www.ft.com/inside-isis-inc

just the secular left but also the reformist version of Islamism represented above all by the Muslim Brotherhood in Egypt, ISIS's formidable record of military success can attract many who want to strike back against imperialism. This is critical to understanding the appeal of ISIS to a small minority of the Muslim population in the advanced capitalist countries.[27]

There is a final dimension to the Middle Eastern catastrophe. Interwoven with the rivalries among regional powers is inter-imperialist competition. One of the main aims of US Middle East policy during the Cold War was to keep the USSR out of the region. Among its major successes were the overthrow of the nationalist military regime of Abd al-Karim Qasim in Iraq in 1963 and Egyptian president Anwar Sadat's 1972 abandonment of the alliance struck with the Soviet Union by his predecessor Gamal Abdel Nasser to secure military and economic aid against Britain and Israel.

In October 1973, Kissinger, by then secretary of state, and acting on behalf of a president incapacitated by the Watergate scandal, reacted to Soviet leader Leonid Brezhnev's threat to send troops unilaterally to enforce a ceasefire on Egypt and Israel, by placing the US military on DefCon III, the highest level of peacetime alert. "We were determined to resist by force if necessary the introduction of Soviet troops in the Middle East regardless of the pretext on which they arrived", Kissinger explained. Brezhnev backed down.[28] The Ba'athist regimes in Iraq and Syria continued to manoeuvre between the two superpower blocs, but Saddam (a participant in the 1963 coup) was lured westwards in the 1980s and isolated after the 1990-1 war, leaving the Assads as Moscow's sole reliable ally in the region.

That connection has now turned toxic for the US. The Russian bombing campaign in Syria announced by president Vladimir Putin on 30 September 2015 marked a turning point. His motives were, in all probability, twofold—first, to force the Western powers to end the policy of isolating Russia that they adopted in response to the seizure of Crimea in March 2014, and secondly to ensure Assad's survival. The rhetoric of "fighting terrorism" served as an all too see-through cover for the use of Russian airpower against the forces fighting Assad. But, not for the first time, Putin exploited Obama's caution, representing his dramatic intervention as a decisive move to confront ISIS.

27: Badiou has some interesting things to say about the "reactive" and "nihilist" form of subjectivity he attributes to young jihadi men, though he is quite mistaken to describe ISIS and the like as fascist (a view criticised in Alexander and Cero, 2015): Badiou, 2015, pp16-22.
28: Dallek, 2007, pp529-531.

In a compelling analysis of contemporary Russia, Perry Anderson recently described "Putin's belief that he could build a Russian capitalism structurally interconnected with that of the West, but operationally independent of it—a predator among predators, yet a predator capable of defying them", as "always an ingenuous delusion".[29] Certainly Russia's ability to rival the US is much more limited than that of the old Soviet Union, despite its nuclear arsenal and revamped military—both because of the shrunken Russian economy's chronic dependence on energy exports and its integration in global financial markets (which has helped the sanctions imposed by the US and the EU to hit home). But a series of developments—US defeat in Iraq, the financial crash, and Chinese economic and military expansion—have weakened American imperialism and made it more vulnerable to peer competition. China represents the big long-term threat to US hegemony, though so far both Washington and Beijing cautiously manoeuvre around each other (literally in the contested South China Sea). But the net effect is both to make the US much warier of taking on military commitments and to give Russia more openings to seize the initiative.[30]

The Western powers have now been goaded into promising a concerted military campaign against ISIS. Their prospects of success seem very poor. This is for both military and political reasons. Politically, very few of the players, Syrian or foreign, seek primarily to fight ISIS. Russia and Iran want to prop up the Assad regime in order to maintain their geopolitical influence in the Middle East (they might be prepared to ditch Bashar himself, as part of a deal with Washington, but not the order over which he presides). The priority for Turkey, Saudi Arabia and Qatar, whatever the conflicts between them, is to get rid of Assad. The different Syrian forces that have come out of the revolution form an incredibly complex mosaic of forces that, according to circumstances, cooperate or fight.

One study of the Syrian opposition lists 228 different groups and stresses the importance of Jabhat al-Nusra, which holds the local Al Qaeda franchise, for those groups actually fighting the regime:

> As Russian airstrikes intensify, Syrian opposition factions will likely seek the protection of a strong partner in the fight against the regime and its allies. The majority of the groups that may seek protection already cooperate militarily with Syrian al-Qaeda affiliate Jabhat al-Nusra out of necessity, and this trend is likely to increase as rebels come under greater duress... Groups that conduct

---

29: Anderson, 2015, p27.
30: Callinicos, 2014.

military operations with Jabhat al-Nusra do not necessarily share its vision, end-state, or values. Many rebel groups cooperate out of military necessity, because Jabhat al-Nusra [is] one of the most capable groups on the battlefield.[31]

Charles Lister of the Brookings Institution says:

Almost none of these groups will be dropping their fight against the Assad regime any time soon. Fighting Assad, Iran and now Russia is their foremost priority. Isis comes second... It is only the socially rooted, largely Sunni mainstream opposition that has the true potential to defeat ISIS in Syria. But they will not realise that potential with the Assad regime in power.[32]

The PYD, the Syrian wing of the Kurdish Workers Party (PKK), much lauded by the Western left, has had some success in fighting ISIS with US air support. But its aim is to carve out the beginnings of an independent Kurdish state, which will make it a liability in Arab areas. Its advances have produced a fierce reaction from the Turkish government, for which Sunni jihadi groups are an acceptable counterweight to the PKK. This example underlines the extent to which taking ISIS on doesn't figure on most players' radar screens.[33] The resolution calling for a ceasefire and talks that the UN Security Council passed on 18 December will most likely provide a framework for interstate bargaining rather than end the war.

In any case, defeating ISIS is a major military undertaking. It now deploys a substantial force of tens of thousands of well-equipped and highly motivated fighters, and has been tactically innovative—for example, integrating suicide bombing into battlefield tactics. Taking its strongholds in Raqqa in eastern Syria and Mosul in northern Iraq may be beyond the capabilities of any Middle East army, other than that of Israel (which is quite happy to leave Syria on the boil, preoccupying all its rivals). The *Financial Times* recently drew an apt parallel with the assault on the Iraqi city of Fallujah in November-December 2004, the bloodiest battle US troops have waged since Vietnam:

"The resources needed to do that were phenomenal," recalls Afzal Ashraf, a former RAF group captain who at the time was a senior counter-terrorism adviser at the multinational force headquarters in Baghdad.

31: Cafarella and Casagrande, 2015, p1.
32: Meek, 2015, p8.
33: Gardner, 2015.

"The city was leafleted for weeks beforehand to get civilians to leave. And then when we went in with the Iraqis, we went from house to house and room to room trying to clear it."

In total, 13,500 US, Iraqi and British forces in Operation Phantom Fury cleared a core of an estimated 500 al-Qaeda operatives from the city. The battle left 107 coalition soldiers dead—95 of them Americans—and 613 wounded…

Few, if any, policymakers in the west and Middle East seem willing to consider augmenting the aerial effort with the sort of immense ground campaign that many analysts think will be needed—on a scale far larger than the Iraqi "surge" instigated by the US in 2007 for which the earlier battle of Fallujah became the template—if the jihadis are to be destroyed.

"The air campaign has its limits," says Mr Ashraf.

If military planners are serious about destroying Isis, they need to think about what that will require on land. "Tackling one city at a time is not going to be effective in getting rid of Isis," he says. "You need to be hitting Ramadi, Tikrit, Mosul—and Syria too—simultaneously. That is a massive operation." At its peak, the "surge" saw about 140,000 US troops deployed in Iraq.[34]

There is absolutely no sign that Washington and its allies have the stomach for such a massive military undertaking. The US is gradually increasing the number of Special Forces operating on the ground in Iraq and Syria, but the fighting on the ground grinds away very slowly. Thus, *Foreign Policy* magazine points out, "Iraqi troops have been fighting at the edges of the Islamic State-held city of Ramadi for months, unable to push deeply into the city despite having up to 10,000 personnel—many trained and supplied by the United States—ringing the city. The Iraqi forces out-number the defenders 10 to 1, according to some Pentagon estimates".[35]

So Syria's agony will continue, as the country remains the object of intense manoeuvring among global and regional powers. Apart from the

34: Jones and Dyer, 2015.
35: McLeary, 2015. To add to the good cheer, a recent Pentagon situation report admits: "In the second half of 2015, the overall security situation in Afghanistan deteriorated with an increase in effective insurgent attacks and higher…casualties," Department of Defense, 2015, p1. Reneging on his promise to pull out of Afghanistan, Obama will keep 9,800 US troops there for most of 2016.

terrible suffering this will continue to cause for its people, this is a very dangerous situation, as different intervening states' air campaigns bump into each other. When Turkey shot down a Russian warplane in late November this was the first actual combat between a NATO member and Moscow since the alliance's foundation in 1949.

Rebuilding the anti-war movement

The left's response has been marked by widespread confusion. Of no one has this been more true than Slavoj Žižek. Over the past 20 years Žižek has managed to make Marxist philosophy exciting again, in the process giving encouragement to many movements and struggles. But in the past few months we have seen a dreadful decline, as he has found excuses for the Syriza government's capitulation to the EU, reiterated his sympathy for xenophobic reactions to migrants and refugees and, in response to the Paris atrocities, announced that the left must spring to the defence of Western values:

> The irony of anti-Eurocentrism is that, on behalf of anti-colonialism, one criticises the West at the very historical moment when global capitalism no longer needs Western cultural values in order to smoothly function. In short, one tends to reject Western cultural values at the very time when, critically reinterpreted, many of those values (egalitarianism, fundamental rights, freedom of the press, the welfare state, etc) can serve as a weapon against capitalist globalisation. Did we already forget that the entire idea of Communist emancipation as envisaged by Marx is a thoroughly "Eurocentric" one?[36]

On 19 November the supposedly radical-left Front de Gauche joined the overwhelming majority of the National Assembly in supporting a three month prolongation of the state of emergency declared by Hollande in response to the Paris attacks. It was left to three Socialist Party and three Green deputies to vote against this measure suspending some of the "fundamental rights" Žižek wants to defend: under it protests during the Paris climate negotiations were banned. Elsewhere more honourable stances have been taken by left wing parties—in the Bundestag Die Linke opposed the unprecedented step taken by Germany (which, for example, opposed the Libyan intervention) to deploy troops to the Middle East, albeit in non-combat roles.

But there are other forms of confusion. Activists from a Communist Party background have a significant influence on the European peace

---

36: Žižek, 2015.

movement. This dates back to the Communist parties' peace campaigns in the early phase of the Cold War. It helps to explain the resurgence of campism—support for the US's geopolitical rivals as supposedly more progressive forces—that we have seen on the left in recent years. Thus many in Western anti-war movements have expressed their sympathies for Putin's Russia in the Ukraine crisis and even the Assad regime in the Syrian war. This stance, as we have argued, represents a profound misunderstanding of the nature of imperialism, which is a *system* of rival capitalist states competing for domination, and therefore underestimates the importance of struggles against ruling classes South as well as North, East as well as West.[37]

Campism is therefore more than a theoretical error: it has negative political effects. In Britain the Commons debate over bombing Syria on 2-4 December became an opportunity for the two front benches to mount a concerted attack on Jeremy Corbyn's leadership of the Labour Party. Corbyn, despite the authority that his consistent opposition to Britain's participation in the long war has given him, found himself deserted by many in his own shadow cabinet and on the Labour back benches who—ignoring their own complicity in the wars in Iraq and Afghanistan—rallied behind the latest intervention. This reflects the fact that Labour—polarised between the Parliamentary Labour Party, the vanguard of neoliberalism and imperialism within the workers' movement, and Corbyn, with his massive support among the party membership—has become the lightning rod for the conflict in Britain over the Syrian war.

Mark L Thomas analyses the struggle for Labour elsewhere in this issue. But the intersection of the two antagonisms—Labour and the Syrian war—has put the Stop the War Coalition in the firing line, as its relationship to Corbyn (till recently its chair) has made it the target of a relentless barrage of attacks from the Labour right and the corporate media. These attacks are contemptible and self-interested. Stop the War can be proud of its record as the organiser of one of the greatest mass movements in British history, peaking with the giant two million strong demonstration against the invasion of Iraq on 15 February 2003, and its many counterparts around the world.

But decline inevitably came after this peak, when it became clear that the movement had failed to stop the war. As its support base shrank, and reflecting divisions on the revolutionary left, some in the Stop the War leadership increasingly adapted to the activists from a Stalinist background within its ranks. This led them to offer a platform to those willing to excuse Putin's military intervention in Ukraine, and to keep silent on the Assad

---

37: Callinicos, 2014.

regime's atrocities, antagonising Syrian supporters of the revolution. These errors have now been seized on by the right-wing campaign against Stop the War, which seeks to destroy it as a tool of anti-imperialist struggle as well to undermine Corbyn.

Stop the War's deviations from its original path do not in the least excuse those on the far left who have joined in the attacks and even supported the use of Western airpower in Syria. They have to explain how, if Stop the War were destroyed, they could build a better anti-war movement. It is to be hoped that the leaders of Stop the War will in future concentrate on its core mission of opposing Britain's participation in the West's wars in the Middle East. It will be particularly important, as during the movement's heyday, to involve the Muslim communities facing ever stronger waves of Islamophobia and repression.

One thing is clear, amid the chaos, confusion and bloodshed in the Middle East: imperialism is a key part of the problem there. The US, Britain, France, Russia and the rest, can do no good there. They should get out of the Middle East and leave its peoples to find their own way to the goals of democracy and social justice that inspired the revolutions of 2011. In the meantime, the task of the Western left is to rebuild the anti-war movement, and mobilise as many people as possible in a campaign to force our governments finally to end the long war.

References

Alami, Mona, 2015, "Syrian War Redraws Country's Economic Map", *Al-Monitor* (10 December), www.al-monitor.com/pulse/originals/2015/12/syria-war-impact-economy-division.html

Alexander, Anne, 2015, "ISIS and Counter-Revolution: Towards a Marxist Analysis", *International Socialism* 145 (winter), http://isj.org.uk/isis-and-counter-revolution-towards-a-marxist-analysis

Alexander, Anne, and Haytham Cero, 2015, "Fascism and ISIS", *International Socialism* 148 (autumn), http://isj.org.uk/fascism-and-isis

Anderson, Perry, 2015, "Incommensurate Russia", *New Left Review*, II/94, http://newleftreview.org/II/94/perry-anderson-incommensurate-russia

Badiou, Alain, 2015, "Our Wound is Not So Recent" (11 December), www.urbanomic.com/Badiou-Wound.pdf

Bieler, Andreas, and Adam David Morton, 2015, "Axis of Evil or Access to Diesel? Spaces of New Imperialism and the Iraq War", *Historical Materialism*, volume 23, issue 2.

Binns, Peter, 1983, "Understanding the New Cold War", *International Socialism* 19 (spring), www.marxists.org/history/etol/writers/binns/1983/xx/newcoldwar.html

Bromley, Simon, 1991, *American Hegemony and World Oil* (Polity).

Cafarella, Jennifer, and Genevieve Casagrande, 2015, "Syrian Opposition Guide", *Institute for the Study of War* (7 October), http://understandingwar.org/sites/default/files/Syrian%20Opposition%20Guide_0.pdf

Callinicos, Alex, 2003, *The New Mandarins of American Power: The Bush Administration's Plans for the World* (Polity).

Callinicos, Alex, 2014, "The Multiple Crises of Imperialism", *International Socialism* 144 (autumn), http://isj.org.uk/the-multiple-crises-of-imperialism

Callinicos, Alex, 2015, "Fighting the Last War", *International Socialism* 147 (summer) online only, http://isj.org.uk/fighting-the-last-war

Carter, Jimmy, 1980, "The State of the Union Address delivered before a Joint Session of Congress: January 23 1980", www.presidency.ucsb.edu/ws/?pid=33079

Dallek, Robert, 2007, *Nixon and Kissinger: Partners in Power* (Allen Lane).

Department of Defense, 2015, *Enhancing Security and Stability in Afghanistan* (December), http://tinyurl.com/zo73med

Ferguson, Niall, 2015, *Kissinger 1923-1968: The Idealist* (Penguin).

Freedman, Lawrence, 2008, *A Choice of Enemies: America Confronts the Middle East* (Weidenfeld & Nicolson).

Friedman, George, 2015, "Netanyahu, Obama and the Geopolitics of Speeches" (3 March), www.stratfor.com/weekly/netanyahu-obama-and-geopolitics-speeches

Gardner, David, 2015, "Turkey Still Sees Kurdish Nationalism as Bigger Threat than ISIS", *Financial Times* (1 December), www.ft.com/cms/s/0/58d22d1a-9845-11e5-9228-87e603d47bdc.html#axzz3u8AeSyR7

Gardner, Lloyd C, 2009, *Three Kings: The Rise of an American Empire in the Middle East after World War II* (New Press).

Gowan, Peter, 1999, *The Global Gamble: Washington's Faustian Bid for World Dominance* (Verso).

Grandin, Greg, 2015, *Kissinger's Shadow: The Long Reach of America's Most Controversial Statesman* (Henry Holt & Co).

Halliday, Fred, 1983, *The Making of the Second Cold War* (Verso).

Hanieh, Adam, 2011, *Capitalism and Class in the Gulf Arab States* (Palgrave Macmillan).

Hanieh, Adam, 2015, "A Brief History of ISIS", *Jacobin* (3 December), www.jacobinmag.com/2015/12/isis-syria-iraq-war-al-qaeda-arab-spring

Harvey, David, 2003, *The New Imperialism* (Oxford University Press).

Hiro, Dilip, 1989, *The Longest War: The Iran-Iraq Military Conflict* (Grafton Books).

Humber, Lee (ed), 1994, *Marxism and the New Imperialism* (Bookmarks).

Jones, Sam, and Geoff Dyer, "ISIS: Boots on the Ground?", *Financial Times* (25 November), www.ft.com/cms/s/0/364d0be4-9281-11e5-94e6-c5413829caa5.html#axzz3u11TQ6YW

Klein, Naomi, 2007, *The Shock Doctrine: The Rise of Disaster Capitalism* (Allen Lane).

Lynch, Colum, and David Francis, 2015, "The Billion Dollar Caliphate", *Foreign Policy* (15 December), http://foreignpolicy.com/2015/12/15/the-billion-dollar-caliphate

McLeary, Paul, 2015, "Obama's Pentagon Trip Highlights How Little Has Changed in ISIS Fight", *Foreign Policy* (14 December), http://tinyurl.com/zbyrzn3

Mann, Michael, 2001, "Globalization and September 11", *New Left Review*, II/12, http://newleftreview.org/II/12/michael-mann-globalization-and-september-11

Meek, James, 2015, "After the Vote", *London Review of Books* (17 December), www.lrb.co.uk/v37/n24/james-meek/after-the-vote

Panitch, Leo, and Sam Gindin, 2012, *The Making of Global Capitalism: The Political Economy of American Empire* (Verso).

Žižek, Slavoj, 2015, "In the Wave of Paris Attacks the Left Must Embrace its Radical Western Roots", *In These Times* (16 November), http://tinyurl.com/nssrq2j

ISIS, imperialism and the war in Syria

Anne Alexander

For the fourth time in less than a decade and half the UK is at war, and once again the vast majority of the victims will be Muslims. Bolstered by the votes and voices of the Labour right, on 2 December David Cameron finally secured the parliamentary majority he needed to extend military operations to Syria. The star performance that night was not the prime minister's however. The media's plaudits were reserved for shadow foreign secretary Hilary Benn, who invoked the memory of the International Brigades and their fight against fascism to build a case for war. Although opposition to intervention in Syria is growing outside parliament, with thousands protesting in the square outside as the debate took place, Benn's arguments are important because (not for the first time) they serve the interests of the British ruling class by translating Cameron's imperialist adventurism into a language that has a resonance far beyond the coteries of Labour MPs plotting to overturn Jeremy Corbyn and crush the unexpected resurgence of the Labour left.

The speech articulated a number of key arguments central to the case for war, including the claim that taking military action against ISIS is an effective solution to the "threat of terrorism" in the UK, and that this will also make things better for the people suffering under the group's rule. Failure to support British military action means complicity in ISIS's atrocities, Benn argued, claiming that ISIS is a "clear and present danger" to "international peace and security".[1]

In order to counter these arguments effectively, we need to show how they are based on a faulty analysis of what kind of organisation ISIS is, where it came from, and what its strengths and weaknesses are. In order to counter the accelerating drive towards imperialist war in the Middle East, and intensifying racism, Islamophobia and repression in Europe, we also need to do more than this. We have to make a clear and coherent case that the real alternative to imperialism, the Middle East's dictators and despots, and the vicious sectarianism of ISIS will be forged by the people of the region themselves, in their struggles from below for social justice and democracy. A left that despairs of this now, after witnessing millions take on the tyrants from Morocco to the Gulf in a popular uprising without precedent in the region's history, will not offer any alternative at all. A left that contents itself with mouthing apologetics for RAF bombing missions, or oscillates between one or other of the local powers and their global sponsors will be equally impotent.

This article will argue that there are three main elements to an analysis which avoids falling into the traps outlined above. First, we need greater clarity about the role of imperialism in the region (both the Western variety and the Russian version). Getting this question right means not falling into mechanistic analysis or conspiracy theorising, understanding the dynamics of competition and conflict between and within the states of the region and the global powers, and appreciating the uneven agency of the different actors in this process. Secondly, we have to get right our analysis of racism and Islamophobia in Europe, understanding that the ever-expanding battery of repressive laws dressed up as "counter-terrorism" may be rooted in the legacy of colonialism, but are an essential counterpart to the strategies of our rulers in their attempts to dominate the Middle East today. An analysis of the 13 November massacres in Paris or the killing of the *Charlie Hebdo* journalists which fails to set these acts in the context of the systematic social exclusion and political repression of Muslims in France, rooted in the history of a racist "civilising mission" dressed up in the universalist language of revolution against absolutism, risks not explaining anything at all.

Finally, we need to be clear and concrete about where the alternative for the region really lies and who can bring it into being. This means not only properly understanding the dynamics of revolution and counter-revolution that have gripped the Middle East for the past decade, but looking forward to debating strategies for the popular uprisings of

---

1:    Benn, 2015.

the future. A crucial part of that strategy, we will argue here, lies in correctly understanding the role of Islamism in the region. It requires an analysis which distinguishes between mass movements such as the Muslim Brotherhood, which in Egypt ended up reprising a similar role to social democratic reformists in the context of a revolutionary crisis, and armed jihadi groups. Failure to do this feeds into the despair that expresses itself either as apologetics for imperialism or various unpleasant regimes, or turns into paralysis.

Where does ISIS fit in? One of the key arguments advanced here is that all the different parts of this analysis are needed to understand the ISIS phenomenon properly: it is born out of the destruction caused by imperialism, out of the crushing of the hopes of revolution and feeds on the despair bred by racism and Islamophobia in Europe. But it is equally important to grasp that ISIS is only a small part of a much bigger picture. It is easy to be mesmerised by the horror of the battle over Raqqa, but we cannot forget that the more important frontlines are those still to be drawn.

Imperial hubris: The unmaking of Iraq

The catastrophe which engulfed US attempts to assert itself as the leader of the "new world order"[2] through the remaking of Iraq created the conditions for the rise of ISIS in more ways than one. As I have outlined in more detail in a previous issue of this journal, ISIS's direct predecessor, the group founded by Jordanian Islamist Abu-Musab al-Zarqawi, first coalesced in Iraq shortly after the US invasion.[3] It distinguished itself by its anti-Shia sectarianism and its brutality, leading eventually to a backlash from the Sunni communities where its fighters sought to operate. However, in the context of US policies which embedded sectarian competition at the heart of the weak and fragmented state, the Islamic State of Iraq rose again from the ashes of Zarqawi's defeat. Its resurgence was fed by the systematic marginalisation of Sunni political leaders by a deeply corrupt, authoritarian regime dominated by sectarian Shia parties and militias, such as the Da'wah Party of Nouri al-Maliki and the Badr Brigade of the Supreme Council for the Islamic Revolution in Iraq. Maliki's decision to send in troops to crush a protest movement which had mobilised thousands across Western and Northern Iraq during the winter of 2012-13 in largely peaceful demonstrations calling for an end to corruption and sectarian discrimination, was a particularly grim turning point. In a very direct sense, ISIS's leadership was

---

2: Bush, 1990.
3: Alexander, Anne, 2015a.

schooled in war in Iraq. Abu-Bakr al-Baghdadi passed through detention in Camp Bucca, and many of his second and third rank commanders are said to be former officers in Saddam Hussein's army.[4]

The impact of successive US interventions on Iraq through two decades of war, sanctions and occupation was little short of catastrophic. US policies took sectarianism to new heights, parcelling up what remained of the state between confessional militias and rapacious neoliberal corporations. Iraq's social fabric was torn apart through a process of ethnic and sectarian "cleansing" and civil war. By June 2007 four million Iraqis, one in six of the total population, had been forced to leave their homes. Two million had fled the country to neighbouring Syria and Jordan and two million were internally displaced.[5] The result was an Iraq which looked very similar to the maps of "ethnoreligious divisions" the CIA used to produce in the decades before the invasion of 2003, with their tripartite partition of the country into Sunnis, Shia and Kurds.[6]

The implosion of Iraqi society is often presented by apologists for Western intervention as somehow the inevitable consequence of pre-existing sectarian antagonisms. The West's mistake, according to this line of thought, was to leave "too soon" rather than to have invaded at all. There is a mirror image of this argument proposed by some who oppose intervention, on the grounds that "we" should have left the warring tribes and sects of the region to get on with the nasty business of killing each other. The huge efforts US officials went to in order to break cross-sectarian unity in the early phases of the occupation give the lie to the certainty of such claims. They pursued a scorched-earth policy in the largely Sunni town of Fallujah, the epicentre of armed resistance in Western Iraq, while drawing the Shia militias which had led the fighting against occupation in the South into a political process led by the sectarian parties to whom they promised the lion's share of the state.[7]

The disaster of US intervention in Iraq also created the conditions for the rise of ISIS in a number of broader ways. Although the US remained the most powerful global power in the region, its position had weakened both militarily and diplomatically. Regional powers, both allies of the US such as Saudi Arabia, Turkey and Israel, and its foes, such as Iran, gained room to manoeuvre as a result. In the case of Iran, the impact of US miscalculation

---

4:   See Naisse, 2015 and Atwan, 2015.
5:   *Forced Migration Review*, 2007.
6:   Go to www.lib.utexas.edu/maps/middle_east_and_asia/iraq_ethnoreligious_1992.jpg (from the CIA's 2003 Iraq country profile).
7:   Alexander, Anne, 2015a.

in Iraq was clear to see. The leadership of the Islamic Republic built on longstanding ties with Iraqi Shia Islamist opposition movements before the overthrow of Saddam Hussein, and benefitted from the installation of its clients at the heart of the reconstituted administration through US policies which deepened sectarian competition across state and society.

The destruction of Syria

Decades of US intervention in Iraq thus resulted in the interaction of three processes which were to have profound consequences for the fate of the Syrian Revolution. The embedding of sectarian competition in the neo-liberal post Ba'athist state created a number of important actors in Syria's conflicts, including ISIS itself and sectarian Shia militias which mobilised to defend the Assad regime. The sectarian polarisation also occurred at a regional level, becoming the general ideological cover for intensified competition between Iran and Saudi Arabia. This meant that the ambitions of both regional powers and the great powers which stood behind them flowed into and shaped the dynamics of counter-revolution and civil war. Finally the waves of mass displacement not only scarred Iraqi society, but placed enormous strains on Syria, which hosted millions of Iraqi refugees in the decade before the 2011 uprising. It is important to emphasise that the extreme brutality of Bashar al-Assad's revenge on Syrian people made the transformation of the revolution into civil war almost inevitable, and sectarian conflict highly likely. Combined with the devastation of Iraq, it created a catastrophe on a scale not seen in the region for decades.

Following the tactics honed by his father in crushing a localised rebellion in Hama in 1982, Assad's military strategy set in motion the vicious spiral of conflict which eventually overwhelmed the Syrian Revolution and the hopes of many who risked their lives to make it. Syrian government forces first laid siege to Deraa the small town near the border with Jordan where the arrest of children for writing anti-government graffiti had triggered protests in March 2011. As demonstrations spread the regime's troops moved in to encircle other towns, bombarding residential areas with artillery and using machine guns to mow down protesters. Banias came under attack in May, and by November Homs, one of the epicentres of the uprising was besieged.[8] Mutinies in the army and the defection of soldiers and officers led to the emergence of the Free Syrian Army in July 2011.[9]

Over the following months the uprising was transformed into an

---

8:   Marsh, 2011; Amnesty International, 2011; Bakri, 2011.
9:   Asharq Al-Awsat, 2011.

armed conflict: on the opposition side Islamist armed groups with access to funds, weapons and experienced fighters came to dominate, pushing aside other groups. Many of these groups had been successful in winning the backing of regional powers, particularly the Gulf states, which sought to influence the outcome of the conflict by providing arms and funding. An opposition offensive in July 2012 forced government forces to retreat from large areas of the country around Aleppo, Idlib, Deir Ezzor and Daraa.[10] This was followed nine months later by a government counter-attack, aided by Lebanese militia Hizbollah, which brought areas on the Lebanese border back under regime control. The ebb and flow of war displaced first tens, then hundreds of thousands. By June 2014 around half of the total population had been forced to flee their homes. The regime's tactics of encircling and bombing dissident population centres using barrel bombs, cluster munitions and chlorine bombs have created suffering on a massive scale.[11] The latest stage in the conflict has seen Russian forces take action in support of the Assad regime, aimed at preventing its collapse and ensuring a voice for Russia's geo-strategic interests in any future negotiations.

Some have argued that key elements in the regime's counter-insurgency strategy created a dynamic which led rapidly to sectarian civil war. According to Joseph Holliday's analysis, Assad's commanders deployed only trusted army units who were largely chosen on grounds of their confessional makeup, while other units were confined to barracks.[12] Lacking the manpower to deploy in much of the country (a fact that helps to explain why regime forces essentially abandoned large areas of the north east), the regime raised paramilitary forces, again from "trusted" communities and regions. Together regular and para-military forces engaged in "clear and hold" operations against opposition-held districts which were ostensibly aimed at "clearing" out opposition fighters, but quickly became "cleanse and hold" as large sections of the Sunni population either fled or were forced out by government troops. The pattern of selective deployment also accelerated the regime's adoption of a scorched earth policy towards areas it was unable to hold, with repeated use of barrel bombs and even ballistic missiles.[13]

10: See Charron, 2014, for a summary of the key events in the conflict and the impact on the civilian population.
11: See Charron, 2014 and reports by the UN Independent International Commission of Inquiry on the Syrian Arab Republic, 2011-2015, available online at www.ohchr.org/EN/HRBodies/HRC/IICISyria/Pages/IndependentInternationalCommission.aspx
12: Holliday, 2013.
13: Holliday, 2013, p56; see also International Crisis Group, 2014, p7 on the use of barrel bombs.

ISIS's success in Syria, as in Iraq, is predicated on appalling levels of social destruction.[14] However, there are also more specific factors at work. One of the key advantages that ISIS has enjoyed in Syria is that its military aims are different to those of the other major protagonists. Its commanders did not enter the Syrian conflict with the goal of either thwarting or accelerating the fall of Assad, rather their efforts were directed towards establishing and consolidating their caliphate. Their territorial strategy worked in symbiosis with that of the regime, in that ISIS wanted regions that Assad's forces had decided were impractical to hold, particularly the north eastern regions around Raqqa. Unlike for the opposition armed forces, this was not a staging point on the road to Aleppo or Damascus, but became an end in itself.[15] Another dynamic that aided ISIS's consolidation was the deepening of sectarianism, and in particular the growing polarisation between a "Sunni" northeast and the concentration of Alawite and Christian populations in regime controlled territories. As in Iraq, ISIS is no bystander in this process, but has reportedly carried out many acts of sectarian "cleansing". Finally, ISIS was much better placed than most other forces in Syria to benefit from the interaction between the conflicts in Syria and Iraq. As it had deliberately set itself the goal of breaking down the border between the two countries, ISIS could use each as a hinterland for offensive operations in the other, and could transport material, men and arms from one front to another.

Can ISIS build a state?

A year and a half after the fall of Mosul, there can be little doubt that ISIS's leadership are not only serious about building a state, but they have been relatively successful in beginning to do so (notwithstanding limitations which we will discuss in more detail below). This does not mean that their project will succeed but it does mean that we need to understand firstly why building a new state is so important to them, and secondly what are the resources they can draw on as they attempt to do this.

ISIS's state-building project cannot be separated from the devastation of Iraq and Syria over years of war, sanctions, occupation and counter-revolution. ISIS's leaders have concentrated the brutality of fragmented and violent societies into a form of government which could be directly compared with the

14: See Naisse, 2015, on this point.
15: Raqqa's strategic importance to ISIS lay in the fact that this provincial town could be combined with territory in Iraq, thus creating a stable centre for ISIS's state-building project across the existing border.

practices of organisations such as the Lord's Resistance Army in Uganda or the Khmer Rouge in Cambodia. Like ISIS, these groups emerged in the context of a long-running insurgency and in the Cambodian case, years of US bombing as a spill-over from the Vietnam War.[16]

In the Iraqi case, US occupation played a transformative role by framing the struggle over the post-Ba'athist state in sectarian terms, deepening existing grievances and creating the material conditions for the birth of new ones. The post-Ba'athist state failed to keep its citizens safe from either the US occupying troops or other bodies of armed men, it failed to provide adequate services and basic infrastructure, and its security forces repeatedly carried out sectarian killings under the direction of party-militia leaders. Meanwhile, in Syria, Assad's brutal attacks on areas liberated from government control have made the idea of returning to Ba'athist rule a horrific prospect for millions.

The document entitled *Principles of Administration* in the Islamic State, published by Aymenn al-Tamimi and the *Guardian* in December 2015 sheds interesting light on the ideology which underpins ISIS's state-building activities and how the group attempts to put this into practice.[17] The text provides a narrative of Sunni Arab loss and marginalisation which, far from being fleshed out with Qu'ranic citations or references to traditions of Sunni jurisprudence, articulates a case for statehood in surprisingly narrow terms. Chapter five deals with provincial administration. After decrying the role of the Sykes-Picot agreement in dividing up Sunni Muslims between the new states of the region, the author leaps forward nearly nine decades to argue that Sunnis have been systematically marginalised and oppressed:

> In Iraq, the separation of Sunnis from Shia was clear, along with the neglect of the administrative centres in every Sunni area, and indeed the appointment of officials from the filthy Rafidites [Shia] in areas of Sunni population. Meanwhile regions under the rule of Kurdish and Shia factions were entrusted with independence from the decisions of the ruling presidency, as we saw in Kirkuk and Arbil, and even in smaller areas such as Najaf and Kerbala which enjoyed undeclared "religious" administrative independence.[18]

The specific nature of the author's complaints against the Iraqi state, and the fact they express a narrative of exclusion from decision-making and

---

16: See Shawcross, 1979, on the US bombing campaign against Cambodia which paved the way for the rise of the Khmer Rouge, and International Crisis Group, 2004 on the LRA.
17: Al-Tamimi, 2015b; Malik, 2015.
18: The quotation and the two that follow are the author's own translation from the Arabic published by Al-Tamimi.

denial of state resources which sounds like the lament of a frustrated former provincial official is highly suggestive. The author paints a claustrophobic picture of the "Sunnis" hemmed in on all sides by hostile ethnic, religious and political forces: "All these divisions denied the Sunnis the most basic rights, making the Alawites masters of the sea, the Shia in Iraq kings over the oil and the trade routes, the Yezidi Kurds sheikhs of the mountains, while the Druze became masters of the mountains bordering Israel."

The redrawing of these borders by ISIS is presented as both an act of self-defence in the face of hostile forces, and the potential springboard for future expansion:

> It was both religiously correct and rational to redraw the borders of the provinces and to carefully study every development that takes place in the region. We are thus preserving the Sunni backbone, strengthening its resources and centres, and then regiments can be deployed in order to radically restructure the regions which will be subject to the rule of the Islamic State.

The idea that a "Sunni backbone" is located approximately in the areas where ISIS is attempting to build its state makes some sense in an Iraqi context (provided one accepts particular sectarian narratives), but is illogical in Syria, where Sunnis were the majority everywhere with the exception of the coastal regions around Latakia and the southern province of Suweida.

While it is always possible to read too much into a single document (the authenticity of which it is extremely difficult to prove), the ideas expressed in the *Principles of Administration* do chime with much that ISIS has done in practice. If it is genuine, it provides striking confirmation of the argument that ISIS's success is based largely on alignment of interests between the small number of effective jihadi fighters who lead the organisation, former Ba'athist security and army officers and some of the political and military leaders in Western Iraq, in the context of the social destruction wreaked by war and counter-revolution.

ISIS's ability to succeed as a state also partially rests on the failures of other, smaller competitors. As James Fromson and Steven Simon note:

> The same governance void that paved the way for ISIS's military conquests also led to conditions of insecurity across most of Sunni Syria and Iraq. The result was the rise, particularly in Syria, of banditry and small-time gangsterism as various militias competed for power. ISIS has replaced this with industrial-scale gangsterism, but by largely monopolising the use of

force, it has also temporarily eliminated the sources of internecine conflict responsible for many residents' complaints.[19]

Such analyses certainly oversimplify the complex situation in the liberated areas in Syria, and it would be wrong to think of all of ISIS's competitors as merely "bandits". However, the point about how ISIS's military success has allowed them to take another step along the continuum from protection racket to recognised state, remains valid.[20] One of the advantages of "industrial-scale gangsterism" is that it allows the practitioners to cannibalise existing state institutions. ISIS monopolises enough force in the territories under its control to assert control over these institutions, both as a means to extract resources from its subjects and to provide them basic services, whereas smaller, less successful groups could only plunder or paralyse them. Testimonies from residents and purported ISIS government documents published online point to a consistent pattern of ISIS taking over, rather than dismantling, government institutions. The group has forced teachers, doctors and nurses to return to work under new management under the threat of being declared an unbeliever or losing their homes.[21] A detailed investigation by the *Financial Times* shows how large parts of the oil and gas industry in Syria is essentially shared between ISIS and central government control, with oil workers from regime-held areas being appointed to work under ISIS management by the state oil companies. The main reason for this lies in ISIS's success in seizing control of gas fields which are the main supply of fuel for Syria's electricity grid, leaving the government to conclude that pragmatic accommodation with its rival was a better option than allowing the lights to go out in Damascus.[22]

Underpinning the state-building project lies a formidable military and security apparatus, led at least in part by former Ba'athists.[23] Brutal and arbitrary punishments, combined with an efficient system of informers are the means by which the caliphate ensures compliance with its orders. ISIS appears to have a highly-militarised state apparatus, with the upper reaches of ISIS's institutions firmly under military control.[24] Courts and media institutions are organised

---

19: Fromson and Simon, 2015, p40.
20: "War makes states", Charles Tilly once pointed out in an essay that compared the process of state formation to organised crime—Tilly, 1985.
21: See Al-Tamimi, 2015a.
22: Solomon and Mhidi, 2015a.
23: Atwan, 2015; Fromson and Simon, 2015.
24: See Al-Tamimi, 2015a. The list of ISIS senior figures compiled by Charles Lister in 2014 includes the following ministerial roles alongside more conventional posts: War

centrally, closely following the shape of the Ba'athist state.[25] Former Ba'athist officers have very likely provided crucial battlefield experience in conventional combat, as well as familiarity with some captured weaponry. It is possible they have also inspired or advised on the creation of ISIS's efforts to organise paramilitary forces for children, whose name, "The Cubs of the Caliphate" (*ashbal al-khilafa*) echoes that of the "Saddam's Cubs" (*ashbal saddam*) force set up by the Iraqi government in the 1990s.[26]

Despite this, there are still formidable obstacles in the way of ISIS consolidating as a state. Many of these obstacles are military. If the worldview encapsulated in *The Principles* is accurate, ISIS's leaders are making an ideological virtue out of the fact that they are surrounded by enemies. They also display a rare talent for making them. Until now, ISIS's commanders have been successful in managing battles on multiple fronts, and (despite claims by the Pentagon to the contrary) appear to have lost relatively little significant ground as a result of the US-led bombing campaign against them since June 2014.[27] However, this situation may not last, and beyond having roused too many enemies at once, there are other potential military difficulties on the horizon. ISIS is well-stocked with advanced military hardware, thanks to having captured armaments, vehicles and tanks from the Iraqi and Syrian armies. But bullets are in relatively short supply, and spare parts for their vehicles will become increasingly scarce as the wear and tear takes its toll.[28] Both of these things are critical to ISIS's ability to take their enemies by surprise in unexpected military offensives.

There are questions too, about how successfully ISIS can generate the revenue it needs to function as a state and prosecute its wars. Wildly fluctuating estimates of the group's wealth have circulated in the media, and ISIS itself claimed to have set a budget of $2 billion with a $250 million surplus for 2015.[29] The *Financial Times* estimated ISIS's crude oil production to be running at around 34-40,000 barrels per day, earning the group an average of $1.5 million a day.[30] Other sources have suggested lower levels of earnings from oil: Aymenn al-Tamimi published documents said to be "financial accounts" for December 2014-January 2015 from ISIS's

Minister, Minister of General Security, Minister of Foreign Fighters and Suicide Bombers, Minister for Weapons and Minister for Explosives—Lister, 2014.

25: Al-Tamimi, 2015b; see Caris and Reynolds, 2014, on the ISIS court system in Syria.

26: Davis, 2005, pp232-233.

27: Gilsenan, 2015; Mak, 2015.

28: Fromson and Simon, 2015; Solomon and Mhidi, 2015b.

29: *Al-Araby al-Jadeed*, 2015.

30: Solomon and Mhidi, 2015a.

Euphrates province (spanning Deir Ezzor province in Syria and western districts of Anbar province in Iraq) in October 2015. According to the accounts, daily revenues from oil and gas in this province amounted to $66,400.[31] The largest source of revenue listed in the document was not oil, however, but "confiscations" of property and goods, accounting for 44 percent of the province's income. It would not be surprising if ISIS's income is largely internal and essentially based on plunder. A key question for the future of the state-building project will be if ISIS can transform a warlord economy into a war economy, or if it will start to falter once the loot begins to dry up.

Islamophobia, counter-terrorism and the transnational jihad

The parochialism of the worldview expressed in *The Principles* seems at odds with ISIS's grand claims to the universal loyalties of Muslims (even though its definition of who qualifies as a Muslim is very narrow), and contrasts with the group's success in winning thousands of foreign recruits. In order to understand how these two, apparently contradictory aspects of ISIS's success are linked, we need to analyse the relationship between three processes: the consolidation of transnational networks of jihadi fighters over several generations since the 1980s, the transformation of Muslims into all-purpose scapegoats by a new generation of right-wing populists and fascists (aided and abetted by more traditional conservatives), and the erection of a battery of racist and repressive laws restricting the rights of migrants and lately focused on "counter-terrorism". In countries such as Britain and France, these processes can mesh with long histories of colonialism in the Middle East and active imperialist roles in the region today to potentially produce a self-reinforcing dynamic between the racists who target Muslims in the name of "counter-terrorism" or "defending Western values" and jihadi supporters or sympathisers who carry out attacks on behalf of ISIS.

"We are at war", intoned French president François Hollande in response to the attacks on concert-goers and diners in Paris on 13 November. The fact that the young men who murdered 130 people at the Bataclan and elsewhere were actually almost all French or Belgian citizens prompted sarcastic responses from the stars of the French intellectual right. Éric Zemmour asked whether instead of bombing Raqqa, Hollande should attack Molenbeek, an area of Brussels visited by the attackers.[32] While he may have been joking (as the BBC felt obliged to point out), there are

---

31: Al-Tamimi, 2015c.
32: Morel, 2015; Schofield, 2015.

many in France who take this kind of racist bile more seriously. As Adam Shatz points out, French imperial ambition to integrate its captured colonial territories into the body of the state has flipped over into a rhetoric claiming that whole districts of Paris and Strasbourg are now "lost territories of the Republic".[33]

French imperial expansion in the 19th and early 20th century projected the vision of an indivisible France onto North Africa, Indochina and Africa, driven by a self-proclaimed "civilising mission". The fake universalism of the kind of Republicanism which was constructed in the process masked the creation of settler-colonial societies in places such as Algeria, where a racist order separating colonist from colonised, and non-Muslim from Muslim was only overthrown through a long and bloody struggle for liberation. It is telling that before November 2015, the biggest single episode of mass murder on the streets of Paris was the killing of up to 200 Algerian protesters on 17 October 1961 on the orders of police chief Maurice Papon. The magnitude of this particular crime went unacknowledged by the state for 50 years.[34]

It is also telling that the last declaration of a state of emergency was in 2005, in response to the revolt which shook the suburbs where descendants of France's colonial empire have been trapped in poverty for decades. Branded as perpetual "immigrants" (now labelled "third" or "fourth generation"), they are presented with the impossible challenge of assimilation into a society which simultaneously demands they renounce key aspects of their culture in order to be accepted, and still punishes them for the things they cannot change, such as their surnames and the area where they grew up, by discriminating against them when they apply for a job or attempt to find housing.[35]

The young men who killed the *Charlie Hebdo* journalists and shoppers in a kosher supermarket in January 2015, and those who massacred 130 people in November, were almost all French or Belgian. The only exception was the suicide bomber at the Stade de France who seems to have been carrying a Syrian passport, although that does not mean that he actually was Syrian.[36] The *Charlie Hebdo* killers grew up in poverty in northeastern Paris and attempted to fly to Iraq to join the fight against the US occupation. They eked out a living in hand to mouth jobs between stints in a squalid prison system, where 70 percent of the inmates are Muslims compared to an overall Muslim population of around eight percent.[37]

33: Shatz, 2015.
34: Willsher, 2011.
35: See Delphy, 2015.
36: Reuters, 2015; Chrisafis, 2015.
37: Chrisafis, 2015; Moore, 2008; Alexander, Harriet, 2015.

We should be wary of reproducing a left-wing version of a "conveyor belt" theory which suggests that distressed youth from the banlieues will automatically end up killing their fellow citizens. In the case of the *Charlie Hebdo* group that process took over a decade, while in the meantime the grip of the racist right on French politics intensified and (not coincidentally) the French state shifted to a more directly interventionist role in the Middle East. As Jim Wolfreys has outlined in an earlier issue of this journal, France has been in the grip of an "Islamophobic spiral" for many years, thanks to the efforts of the far-right "to rehabilitate racism by focusing on culture rather than race", with the complicity of the mainstream parties and in the absence of consistent opposition to Islamophobia from the left.[38] The French left's uncritical adoption of the imposition of the Republican creed of laïcitié (secularism) from above by the state has played a key part in weakening attempts to mobilise against racism.[39]

Nevertheless it is important to see Hollande's war cry, not as the traumatised reaction to terrorist attacks, but a product of the interplay of deeply-rooted processes: the specific legacy of France's colonial past, the racist logic of competition between fascists and politicians across the political spectrum who have constructed Muslims as all-purpose "others" and an increasingly interventionist foreign policy in the Middle East. A final crucial element is the failure of the French left to build effective opposition on any of these fronts, partly as a result of the dominance of traditions of anti-clericalism which lend a veneer of radicalism to the imperial and racist strategies of the state.

Elements of this picture are present in many European countries, including Britain. We have our own populist right, which, while far behind the surge of votes for the Front National in France, has profoundly reshaped electoral politics in recent years. For decades, successive governments have compulsively tightened restrictions on migration and demonised refugees. The Tory government's new Prevent counter-terrorism strategy makes it a legal duty for teachers, lecturers and other public sector workers to report on their pupils, patients, clients and co-workers if they suspect them of being "radicalised".[40] The British state has its own toxic history of colonialism and its own stake in the destruction of Iraq and Syria.

38: Wolfreys, 2015.

39: Birchall, 2015.

40: See Asquith, 2015 for a statement by National Union of Students leaders on opposing Prevent.

Conclusion: The alternative from below

The final element in the analysis is the question of how to prepare for the popular uprisings of the future, and what role the analysis of ISIS in particular and the analysis of Islamism more generally can play in this process. In the depths of a brutal counter-revolution which has wreaked havoc across the region, this may seem an academic exercise. Yet, there are plenty of reasons not to write off the potential for future explosions of popular protest. As we have discussed in detail in this article, the revolution and counter-revolution in Syria took place in a context which was already shaped by the catastrophe unfolding in Iraq.

In Egypt, by comparison, although a vicious counter-revolution led by the military and aided by the Gulf states has restored dictatorship, has not experienced the kinds of social destruction we have witnessed in Syria, and some parts of the popular movement have proved surprisingly resilient. Despite killing thousands and jailing tens of thousands, Abdel-Fattah el-Sisi's regime has not been able completely to quell all forms of popular protest. Workers strikes and protests continue, although some of the key leaders of the independent unions have been co-opted by the counter-revolution.[41]

The narrative of the "war on terror" and fear of ISIS has been a powerful ideological weapon in Sisi's hands, however. And much of the repression of the Muslim Brotherhood, the largest opposition force, has been justified by the regime and its apologists as necessary in order to stop "Islamist terrorism". Egypt has its own ISIS affiliate, which declared that Sinai was a province of the Islamic State, although it is notable that until now this group has been more interested in fighting the Egyptian army in Sinai, than embarking on the kind of sectarian massacres that characterise ISIS elsewhere.[42]

There are two reasons why it is important to reject lines of argument that either capitulate to the narrative of the military regime in presenting the Muslim Brotherhood activists as terrorists, or see the Brotherhood as a counter-revolutionary force distinct from, but comparable to the military.[43] The first is that failing to see the contrasts between Islamist organisations such as the Brotherhood, which have a mass popular base and often play a reformist role, and ISIS, makes it more difficult to understand either. The second reason is that characterising the Brotherhood as counter-revolutionary makes it more difficult to organise effective resistance to the regime, as it cuts off the revolutionary forces that have survived the crackdown, from the large

---

41: See Alexander and Bassiouny, 2014, for more on this issue.
42: See Attallah and Afify, 2015.
43: For a survey of this debate, see Alexander, Anne, 2015b.

numbers of people who support or look to the Brotherhood as the main organisation still defying the military.

The question of whether there can be at some point a revival of the popular movements which erupted across the region in 2011 is also important outside the Middle East. The best answer to those who want to justify bombing on "humanitarian" grounds, is to argue that far from needing Western warplanes and tanks to deal with dictators or warlords, ordinary people across the region have weapons of their own: mass strikes and protests. Although the revolutionary promise of 2011 was not ultimately fulfilled, it provides the most concrete demonstration of their power to remake the Middle East from below we have ever seen.

References

Al-Araby al-Jadeed, 2015, "Islamic State Group Sets Out First Budget, Worth $2bn" (4 January), http://tinyurl.com/z295wel

Alexander, Anne, and Mostafa Bassiouny, 2014, *Bread, Freedom, Social Justice: Workers and the Egyptian Revolution* (Zed).

Alexander, Anne, 2015a, "ISIS and Counter-revolution: Towards a Marxist Analysis", *International Socialism* 145 (winter), http://isj.org.uk/isis-and-counter-revolution-towards-a-marxist-analysis

Alexander, Anne, 2015b, "Reformism, Islamism and Revolution", *Socialist Review* (October), http://socialistreview.org.uk/406/reformism-islamism-revolution

Alexander, Harriet, 2015, "What is Going Wrong in France's Prisons?", *Telegraph* (17 January), www.telegraph.co.uk/news/worldnews/europe/france/11352268/What-is-going-wrong-in-Frances-prisons.html

Al-Tamimi, Aymenn Jawad, 2015a, "Archive of Islamic State Administrative Documents" (27 January), www.aymennjawad.org/2015/01/archive-of-islamic-state-administrative-documents

Al-Tamimi, Aymenn Jawad, 2015b, "Principles in the Administration of the Islamic State —full text and translation" (7 December), www.aymennjawad.org/18215/principles-in-the-administration-of-the-islamic

Al-Tamimi, Aymenn, 2015c, "The Archivist: Unseen Islamic State Financial Accounts for Deir az-Zor Province" (5 October), www.aymennjawad.org/17916/the-archivist-unseen-islamic-state-financial

Amnesty International, 2011, "Syria Death Toll Rises as City is Placed under Siege" (9 May), www.amnesty.org/en/latest/news/2011/05/syria-death-toll-rises-city-placed-under-siege

Asharq Al-Awsat, 2011, "Syrian Army Colonel Defects forms Free Syrian Army" (1 August), http://english.aawsat.com/2011/08/article55245595/syrian-army-colonel-defects-forms-free-syrian-army

Asquith, Shelly, 2015, "Why I won't be working with Prevent (and how you can avoid it, too)" (13 August), www.nusconnect.org.uk/articles/why-i-won-t-be-working-with-prevent-and-how-you-can-avoid-it-too

Attallah, Lina, and Heba Afify, 2015, "Sinai: States of Fear", *Mada Masr* (28 February), http://www.madamasr.com/news/politics/sinai-states-fear

Atwan, Abdel-Bari, 2015, *Islamic State: The Digital Caliphate* (Saqi).

Bakri, Nada, 2011, "As Syria Hits City, UN says Toll Climbs", *New York Times* (8 November), www.nytimes.com/2011/11/09/world/middleeast/syria-lays-siege-to-a-city-homs-that-puts-up-a-fight.html?_r=0

Benn, Hilary, 2015, "Full Text of Hilary Benn's Extraordinary Speech in Favour of Syria Airstrikes", *Spectator* (2 December), blogs.new.spectator.co.uk/2015/12/full-text-of-hilary-benns-extraordinary-speech-in-favour-of-syria-airstrikes

Birchall, Ian, 2015, "The Wrong Kind of Secularism", *Jacobin* (19 November), www.jacobinmag.com/2015/11/charlie-hebdo-france-secular-paris-attacks-lacite

Bush, George H W, 1990, "Address Before a Joint Session of Congress" (11 September), http://millercenter.org/president/bush/speeches/speech-3425

Caris, Charles C, and Samuel Reynolds, 2014, ISIS governance in Syria, Institute for the Study of War (July), www.understandingwar.org/sites/default/files/ISIS_Governance.pdf

Charron, Guillaume, 2014, "Syria: Forsaken IDPs Adrift Inside a Fragmenting State" (21 October), www.internal-displacement.org/middle-east-and-north-africa/syria/2014/syria-forsaken-idps-adrift-inside-a-fragmenting-state

Chrisafis, Angelique, 2015, "Charlie Hebdo Attackers: Born, Raised and Radicalised in Paris", *Guardian* (12 January), www.theguardian.com/world/2015/jan/12/-sp-charlie-hebdo-attackers-kids-france-radicalised-paris

Davis, Eric, 2005, *Memories of State: Politics, History and Collective Identity in Modern Iraq* (Blackwell).

Delphy, Christine, 2015, *Separate and Dominate: Feminism and Racism after the War on Terror* (Verso).

Forced Migration Review, 2007, "Iraq's Displacement Crisis" (June), www.fmreview.org/iraq

Fromson, James and Steven Simon, 2015, "ISIS: The Dubious Paradise of Apocalypse Now", *Survival: Global Politics and Strategy*, volume 7, number 3, http://tinyurl.com/z2276p9

Gilsinan, Kathy, 2015, "How ISIS Territory has Changed Since the US Bombing Campaign Began", *Atlantic* (11 September), www.theatlantic.com/international/archive/2015/09/isis-territory-map-us-campaign/404776

Holliday, Joseph, 2013, "The Assad Regime: From Counterinsurgency to Civil War, Institute for the Study of War" (March), www.understandingwar.org/report/assad-regime

International Crisis Group, 2004, "Northern Uganda: Understanding and Solving the Conflict" (14 April), www.crisisgroup.org/~/media/Files/africa/horn-of-africa/uganda/Northern%20Uganda%20Understanding%20and%20Solving%20the%20Conflict.pdf

International Crisis Group, 2014, "Rigged Cars and Barrel Bombs: Aleppo and the State of the Civil War" (9 September), www.crisisgroup.org/en/publication-type/media-releases/2014/mena/rigged-cars-and-barrel-bombs-aleppo-and-the-state-of-the-syrian-war.aspx

Lister, Charles, 2014, "Islamic State Senior Leadership: Who's Who", Brookings Institute (November), www.brookings.edu/~/media/Research/Files/Reports/2014/11/profiling-islamic-state-lister/en_whos_who.pdf?la=en

Mak, Tim, 2015, "Exclusive: Pentagon Map Hides ISIS Gains", *Daily Beast* (22 April), www.thedailybeast.com/articles/2015/04/22/the-pentagon-s-isis-map-is-so-wrong.html

Malik, Shiv, 2015, "The Isis Papers: Behind 'Death Cult' Image Lies a Methodical Bureaucracy", *Guardian* (7 December), www.theguardian.com/world/2015/dec/07/isis-papers-guardian-syria-iraq-bureaucracy

Marsh, Katherine, 2011, "Syrian Forces Fire on Protesters as Tanks Roll into Banias", *Guardian* (7 May), www.theguardian.com/world/2011/may/07/syrian-forces-fire-on-protesters

Moore, Molly, 2008, "In France, Prisons Filled With Muslims", *Washington Post* (29 April),

www.washingtonpost.com/wp-dyn/content/article/2008/04/28/AR2008042802560.
html

Morel, Thomas, 2015, "'Bombarder Molenbeek': la blague d'Eric Zemmour n'a pas fait rire grand monde", *Metronews* (18 November), http://tinyurl.com/hv26hq2

Naisse, Ghayath, 2015, "The "Islamic State" and the Counter-revolution", *International Socialism Journal 148* (autumn), http://isj.org.uk/the-islamic-state-and-the-counter-revolution

Reuters, 2015, "Dead Killers, Hunted Suspects after Paris Attacks" (16 November), http://tinyurl.com/j5zrems

Schofield, Hugh, 2015, "Paris Attacks: Fury Over Claims by Philosopher Onfray", BBC News (25 November), www.bbc.co.uk/news/world-europe-34904939

Shatz, Adam, 2015, "Magical Thinking about ISIS", *London Review of Books* (3 December), www.lrb.co.uk/v37/n23/adam-shatz/magical-thinking-about-isis

Shawcross, William, 1979, *Sideshow: Kissinger, Nixon and the Destruction of Cambodia* (Simon and Schuster).

Solomon, Erika, and Ahmed Mhidi, 2015a, "ISIS inc: Syria's 'Mafia-style' Gas Deals with Jihadis", *Financial Times* (15 October), www.ft.com/cms/s/0/92f4e036-6b69-11e5-aca9-d87542bf8673.html#axzz3uIEAXneJ

Solomon, Erika, and Ahmed Mhidi, 2015b, "ISIS: The Munitions Trail", *Financial Times* (30 November), www.ft.com/cms/s/2/baad34e4-973c-11e5-9228-87e603d47bdc.html#axzz3uIEAXneJ

Tilly, Charles, 1985, "War Making and State Making as Organized Crime", in Peter Evans, Dietrich Rueschemeyer, and Theda Skocpol (eds), *Bringing the State Back In* (Cambridge University Press).

Willsher, Kim, 2011, "France Remembers Algerian Massacre 50 years on", *Guardian* (17 October), www.theguardian.com/world/2011/oct/17/france-remembers-algerian-massacre

Wolfreys, Jim, 2015, "After the Paris Attacks: An Islamophobic Spiral", *International Socialism 145* (winter), http://isj.org.uk/after-the-paris-attacks

A house divided: Jeremy Corbyn and the Labour Party

Mark L Thomas

Something remarkable happened over the summer of 2015. Immediately after Ed Miliband resigned following Labour's defeat in the general election, the grip exercised by Blairism over the Labour Party had seemed set to continue grimly on. The field competing for the Labour leadership was confined to various shades of uninspiring Blairites, with the supposedly "left" candidate, Andy Burnham, rushing to distance himself from the unions. Even after Jeremy Corbyn threw his hat in the ring, most (including Corbyn himself) assumed he would be soundly beaten.

But then, suddenly and unexpectedly, the grip of Blairism seemed to snap. Corbyn's dramatic victory in the contest for Labour leader has broken apart the dominance exercised by an ideology that didn't simply accept neoliberalism at home and imperialism abroad but had at the centre of its political appeal the claim that *only* such a programme could command the support of the majority of the working class at the polls.

Now an open socialist has been elected as Labour leader, standing on a programme that included: opposition to austerity, "public ownership of railways and in the energy sector", "no more illegal wars", an end to the Trident nuclear weapon programme, an end to privatisation in health, an end to scapegoating of migrants and the abolition of student fees and the restoration of grants.[1]

1:   Go to www.jeremyforlabour.com/jeremy_corbyn_launches_standing_to_deliver

One crucial effect of Labour's long march to the right in the 1980s, reaching its apogee in Tony Blair, was that it enabled the construction of a very narrow political consensus at the top of British society. This centred around a combination of the notion that globalisation required the market to have ever greater sway at home and an insistence on the pivotal role of Britain's long-term alliance with US imperialism abroad. Both were underpinned by an appeal to the "national interest" and accompanied by an insistence that class was irrelevant to British society. Such a consensus between the dominant parties at Westminster also reinforced its acceptance across a huge swathe of "opinion formers" in the media, much of intellectual life, across the plethora of think tanks and research bodies that surround parliamentary parties and business. It helped create a "common sense" worldview that could then be projected as the settled view of the whole of society with any challenges to it marginalised and presented as extreme, outdated and utopian.

It was a myth that it did so. Survey after survey, including the government's authoritative annual British Social Attitudes survey, showed that "Old Labour" ideas about equality, class and curbing the excesses of the market through state intervention, including nationalisation, still retained wide appeal.[2] But in the absence of widespread working class militancy, such views often remained latent, hidden beneath the neoliberal mainstream consensus. This helped reinforce a sense of marginalisation among the left in British society, a belief that the left were an isolated minority unable to command widespread appeal for their views. Such views received their most concentrated form in the Labour Party, with its overwhelming orientation on the ballot box and broad electoral appeal, rather than forms of extra-parliamentary struggle and understanding of the significance of mobilising even a militant minority.

The rise of Blairism, its widespread if reluctant acceptance among large numbers of Labour members and supporters, was *a product of defeat*. The successive electoral defeats Labour suffered at the ballot box at the hands of Margaret Thatcher in 1983 and 1987, and then John Major in 1992, pushed Labour to the right, first under Neil Kinnock, then John Smith and finally Tony Blair. These electoral setbacks were ultimately a reflection of a series of major defeats inflicted on the working class in a number of key industrial confrontations of which the 1984-5 miners' strike was only the most significant.

As workers lost confidence in their own collective power, Labour's ability to rebuild its electoral appeal faltered. The conclusions drawn, not just

---

2:   See Thomas, 2013.

Timetable of key events in the Labour leadership campaign

7 May	General election
8 May	Labour loses and Ed Miliband resigns as Labour leader
10-14 May	Liz Kendall, Andy Burnham, Yvette Cooper, Mary Creagh and Chuka Ummuna announce they are standing. Ummuna withdraws after 3 days
3 June	Jeremy Corbyn announces he will stand for Labour leader
12 June	Creagh withdraws, leaving Kendall as the sole hard Blairite candidate
15 June	Corbyn just squeezes onto the ballot with 36 nominations out of 232 Labour MPs
5 July	Unite executive endorses Corbyn
15 July	*New Statesman* reports that "private polling" puts Corbyn up to 15 percent ahead
22 July	A YouGov poll in the *Times* puts Corbyn ahead in both first preferences and the final run off
29 July	Unison recommends a vote for Corbyn, not Cooper as expected
12 September	Corbyn elected as Labour leader with nearly 60 percent of the vote

by the leadership but by wide numbers who had initially been influenced by Bennism and the left, was to lower their expectations and conclude that the working class had accepted Thatcher's appeal to individualistic ideas.

Among a minority this led to open acceptance of the ideas of Blairism, but probably among the greater number it led to a sort of self-denying ordinance among whole layers of working class activists in the unions and in Labour's local parties that their left wing ideas were shared by a minority at best and that electoral victory could only be gained by denying those ideas and appealing to the "centre-ground".

Two developments seem to have now converged to break the hold of such views over the Labour Party: a new generation has emerged unscarred by the defeats of the 1980s. Anyone aged under 30, for example, wasn't even born when Labour lost the 1983 election; anyone under 18 wasn't alive when Blair won in 1997. Instead all they have known is the failure of Blair and New Labour, not the limitations of "Old Labour". Secondly, the self-denying ordinance of an older generation of activists, many returning to Labour after drifting away, has broken. Instead they feel the need for a Labour leadership that challenges rather than capitulates to Tory ideas and neoliberal austerity.

The result is a surge of confidence on the left, a sense that socialism is back as a political current capable of shaping the debate in British society. The suffocating pro-market mainstream consensus has dramatically fractured. But what are the prospects for a Corbyn-led Labour Party—can he survive the fury of the Labour right with its base in the Parliamentary Labour Party (PLP)? How can the desire for a real opposition to austerity, war and racism, so effectively mobilised by Corbyn, be translated into a real shift in the balance of class forces? Can this be done within the framework of the Labour Party as so much of the left now hope?

Why Corbyn won

How do we explain Corbyn's victory, something no one saw coming? It is all the more remarkable if we compare his vote in 2015 to the vote of Diane Abbott, the hard left's standard-bearer in the 2010 Labour leadership election. Abbott, like Corbyn, had little base in the PLP and only got on the ballot paper after other MPs "lent" her their nominations to "broaden the debate" and to show that there was a space for the left in the Labour Party, though a subordinate one. But there the similarities end.

	Abbott, 2010	Corbyn, 2015
Members	9,314	121,751
Registered Supporters	—	88,449
Affiliated	25,938	41,217

Even the apparently more favourable contrast between the vote in the affiliated category for Corbyn and Abbott is misleading. Following the Collins Review in 2014, the Labour Party made significant changes to the way the leadership is elected. As well as introducing the new category of "registered supporter" where non-party members could receive a vote for £3, members of trade unions affiliated to the Labour Party now have actively to "opt in" and agree to support "Labour's aims and values" rather than being automatically entitled to vote as they were in the past.

This resulted in a huge drop in the numbers both entitled to vote and actually voting. In 2010 some 2.7 million ballot papers were distributed to affiliated supporters (overwhelmingly composed of trade unionists) and 211,234 voted. In 2015, 148,182 were balloted and 71,546 voted in this category. So Corbyn won 57.68 percent of those who voted in the affiliated category, while Abbott won just 4.09 percent. In fact, in the light of Abbott's performance, no wonder the small group of left Labour MPs hesitated before even deciding to put up a candidate.[3]

What had changed between 2010 and 2015? Certainly not the organisational strength of the left within the Labour Party. The Socialist Campaign Group of MPs, traditionally the grouping of the Labour hard left in parliament, had only nine members after the May 2015 elections—and two of those seem to have nominated Andy Burnham rather than Corbyn for the leadership! Nor was there any obvious sign of increased Labour left activity or growth among the wider party membership in the run up to the leadership elections. So what had happened since 2010?

The sharpening of an anti-austerity mood and the resilience of social democratic ideas

There was a feeling among wide layers of people on the left and in the working class movement that the welfare state, and the NHS in particular, the jewel in the crown of post-war social democracy, was facing an existential crisis. And Labour seemed increasingly unable and unwilling to defend it. This mood fed into the wave of post-election protests across England and Wales that culminated in the huge People's Assembly demonstration against austerity in central London on 20 June, six weeks after the election. Effectively Corbyn's campaign for Labour leader became a rebellion against the Parliamentary Labour Party, overriding any immediate electoral considerations especially as the next general election is not due till 2020.

The protests mark a desire for an effective opposition to the Tories and austerity. The failure of the existing parliamentary party to offer such a challenge was powerfully symbolised during the leadership campaign by Labour's decision to abstain on the government's Welfare Reform Bill, which included £12 billion of further benefit cuts. Corbyn rebelled and voted against the bill; all three other leadership contenders abstained.

The impact of Syriza

The shift in the international, and especially European, political climate also fed into the upheaval inside the Labour Party. In 2010 the acceptance by social democratic governments and oppositions in Portugal, Italy, the Spanish state and Greece, as well as across northern Europe and

---

3:    Wintour and Watt, 2015.

Scandinavia, that austerity was the only credible response to the banking crisis and Great Recession of 2008-9, served to reinforce the arguments by the Labour leadership that no other policy was possible.

By 2015, the picture looked significantly different, with major cracks in the austerity consensus appearing. Above all, the excitement surrounding the election in January 2015 of the radical left party Syriza, on a clear anti-austerity programme, altered the horizons of what seemed possible. And Syriza did not seem isolated—the dramatic rise from nowhere of Podemos in the Spanish state, the surge in support for Sinn Féin largely thanks to its opposition to austerity and for the socialist left in the Republic of Ireland (in a country where the left has long being marginalised) and the successes of the Red Green Alliance in Denmark all amplified this mood that "social liberalism" did not simply have to be accepted, however sullenly. If the left could reject austerity in a string of countries across Europe and as a result win an enthusiastic and large following, why not in Britain?

The success of the Scottish National Party

The results of the general election also reinforced a sense for many that Britain was not immune to such developments and that anti-austerity politics and a more radical stance in general could deliver electorally—indeed that not adopting such an approach increasingly carried an electoral price for Labour. The SNP's devastating victory in Scotland increased its seats in Westminster from six to 56, while Labour went from having 41 to a single MP (in a country where Labour had won the majority of MPs at *every* election since 1964). This seemed for any serious observer to be connected with the SNP's at least verbal opposition to austerity and Trident nuclear weapons and the mass movement unleashed by the referendum on Scottish independence last September. By contrast Labour had not only campaigned in the referendum for the Unionist status quo but did so on the same platforms as the Tories.

The loss of authority of the Labour right

Labour is above all an electoral party. Its central objective is to win enough votes to form a government allowing it to implement its policies and improve the lives of the majority. The leadership of the party ultimately derives its authority from being able to deliver electoral success. Blair's dominance of the Labour Party rested on the three successive general election victories in 1997, 2001 and 2005. Blair in fact presided over the loss of nearly 4 million votes between the first and final of those victories, with the largest haemorrhage of votes coming even before the invasion of Iraq. But he was able to win each time because the Tories were so widely despised—the legacy of their 18 years in office after 1979.

As a result, large numbers of Labour supporters were willing to put up with Blair's pro-market policies as the necessary price of appealing to the "centre ground" ie the supposed right wing majority in British society. Even the union leaders, often angry and bitter at Blair's treatment of them and occasionally willing to fire shots across his bows (defeating him, for example, over the use of the Private Finance Initiative to fund public services or over NHS foundation hospitals at Labour conferences in 2002 and 2003), in practice accepted his leadership as necessary, blunting their challenge to him. Labour supporters who couldn't stomach Blair simply left, rather than launch any serious campaign to challenge or replace him. Blair was only removed after a large number of once loyal MPs finally grasped that he had become an electoral liability in the wake of the Iraq debacle, but even then only to engage in a "coronation" of Gordon Brown, the other key architect of New Labour.[4]

The picture after May 2015 was very different. The Labour right had now presided over two successive election defeats. Gordon Brown bailed out the banks (and bankers) and lost another 950,000 votes in 2010. Labour's vote of 8.606 million was only a shade higher than its performance at the disastrous 1983 election under Michael Foot, widely held up inside the party as "proof" that Labour cannot win votes if it moves left. And this time the Tories had finally convinced just enough people that they were no longer the "nasty party" of old and crept back into office, though only thanks to a coalition deal with the Liberal Democrats (the Tory vote in 2010 was still nearly 3.5 million less than John Major had received in 1992).

Ed Miliband, a former minister under Brown, did represent a small first crack in the New Labour hegemony. Miliband tried to position himself as representing a break from both New Labour's uncritical endorsement of US imperialism (apologising for Iraq) and the market (attacking some companies as "predators"). Miliband was also willing to give occasional expression to class feeling, so for example, he attacked the Tories for ignoring a cost of living crisis and promised a temporary cap on energy price rises. But his constant concessions to Blairite demands that he prove Labour's "fiscal credibility" by accepting austerity increasingly drowned out such limited breaks from the past and Labour was left offering little real challenge to the Tories'

4: Blair's support for the Israeli attack on Lebanon in 2006 proved the straw that broke the camel's back even for many MPs who had loyally voted for the wars in Afghanistan and Iraq—see Harman, 2006.

insistence on austerity and rolling back the welfare state still further.

The result was another defeat. All the retreats, concessions, sacrifices of radical policies had only resulted in the return of the Tories with a free hand to deepen their onslaught. The authority of the Labour right—resting on the claim that it alone, unlike the "self-indulgent" left, understood how to win elections and "deliver results"—was further undermined.

One figure who embodied this draining of credibility is John McTernan. McTernan, a combative former adviser to Tony Blair, was the person who described those Labour MPs who nominated Corbyn without actually supporting his leadership bid as "morons" who "need their heads felt" for allowing someone supposedly unelectable onto the ballot paper.[5] Yet what of McTernan's own track record for "electability"? His most recent post was as chief of staff to Jim Murphy, the hard Blairite Scottish Labour leader. As John Prescott tweeted, "Who the heck is John McTernan? He advised in Scotland and we lost... He has no authority".[6]

In these circumstances, a section of the PLP felt they had to allow some expression of this left mood, hence, a surprising gaggle of MPs "lending" nominations to Corbyn to "broaden the debate" and keep a layer of the left in Labour instead of letting them drift out to the SNP or Greens, confident, of course, that Corbyn would be comfortably defeated and his ideas exposed as weak and without wide appeal.[7] However, in politics as in war, if the pressure has reached a certain point, sometimes a breach in the enemy's defences is all that is required for insurgent forces to pour through and inflict a sudden, stunning defeat.

The result leaves a paradox. The dramatic revival of left reformism

---

5:   Go to www.youtube.com/watch?v=z-WrOHCsaUA.

6:   The *Scotsman*, 2015. Prescott himself, a great bellwether inside Labour, exemplifies the rise and fall of Blairite hegemony inside the Labour Party. A former working class trade union militant in the shipping industry, by the early 1980s he was a key figure in the parliamentary "soft left", an influential layer which broke from Tony Benn and moved to the right under Neil Kinnock's leadership. Prescott went on to play a key role in persuading Labour to accept, first, John Smith's "One Member, One Vote" reforms in 1993 that sought to erode union influence over the selection of parliamentary candidates, and then, Blair's replacement of the old pro-nationalisation Clause 4 of the party's constitution in favour of an explicitly pro-market statement. Prescott was Blair's deputy for the entire period of premiership and loyally backed the Iraq invasion. He is now to be found attacking Blair, including over Iraq, and even offering some defence of Corbyn.

7:   One of the MPs who nominated Corbyn was Frank Field, firmly on the right of the party. Field defended his decision by arguing that it was necessary to openly take on "deficit-deniers" like Corbyn who wanted to move the party away from supporting austerity, a position he called an "emotional spasm"—Williamson and Murphy, 2015.

as a major pole of attraction, has elsewhere largely taken the form of parties breaking through to the left of the main established parliamentary social democratic parties, such as Syriza or Die Linke in Germany, or entirely new forces like Podemos. Yet in Britain this process has occurred within a party born over a century ago, in part a reflection of the fact that alternatives to Labour from the left such as Respect in the mid-2000s, have been unable decisively to break through, however promising they might be.

One consequence, however, is that Labour is likely to be a bitter battleground between the new, enthusiastic—if largely unorganised—Labour left, and the old, the forces of the Labour right, concentrated in a parliamentary party shaped by decades of right wing dominance.

From backbench activist to unexpected leader

Corbyn's own personal position and qualities also contributed to his success, with his very marginalisation inside the Labour Party over the last 30 years being transformed into his biggest asset as someone uncompromised by the party's Faustian deal with neoliberalism. He is an unassuming but dedicated figure who has demonstrably put principle over career and who seems free of any temptation towards self-aggrandisement.

Corbyn initially developed a career in the labour movement through two of its traditional channels, the unions and local government. He worked successively for the National Union of Tailors and Garment Makers, the Amalgamated Union of Engineering Workers and the National Union of Public Employees (all now either defunct or merged into other unions). In 1974, aged just 24, he was elected as a Labour councillor in Haringey, North London.[8]

Corbyn strongly identified with the Labour left, helping to organise Tony Benn's bid to become deputy leader in 1981. Benn lost by a whisker, winning 49.4 percent to Denis Healey's 50.4 percent. This was the high-water mark of Labour's swing to the left after the defeat of the 1974-9 Labour government. After this narrow defeat Benn's backers in the left trade union bureaucracy retreated from any further challenge for the leadership of the party.

Corbyn was first elected to parliament for Islington North in the general election which followed in 1983. Labour's humiliation in that election was the signal for a further sharp shift to the right inside the Labour Party under its new leader, Neil Kinnock who replaced Michael Foot.[9]

8:    Wheeler, 2015.
9:    Cliff and Gluckstein, 1988, pp345-355.

Labour's moving right show saw a swathe of former Bennites abandon the left and make peace with the Labour right. Some like David Blunkett, a key figure in the 1980s municipal left as leader of Sheffield council (famously dubbed the "Socialist Republic of South Yorkshire"), ended up as front rank figures in Blair's government. Blunkett attacked teachers and championed the market in schools as education secretary, later pursuing authoritarian policies and demonising refugees as home secretary.

Corbyn went against the stream, however, remaining loyal both to the ideas of Bennism and to Benn personally, the figurehead of the Labour left until his death in 2014.[10] This left Corbyn, a serial rebel against the Labour whip, marginalised inside the Parliamentary Labour Party with the path to the front bench and ministerial office effectively closed.

Instead Corbyn immersed himself in a succession of extra-parliamentary causes and movements. For decades he has been a familiar figure on any picket line or in any progressive campaign, however small, in Islington. But overall his main focus seems to have been anti-imperialism and international solidarity, from the fight to end the racist apartheid system in South Africa to Latin America solidarity campaigns, opposition to British repression in Northern Ireland, campaigns for Palestinian freedom, nuclear disarmament and opposition to the Iraq war including participation in the leadership of the Stop the War Coalition. At times he seems to have been effectively a full-time activist who made the occasional speech in parliament![11] Corbyn's orientation on extra-parliamentary campaigns and movements has also encouraged, in a context shaped until very recently by the weakness of the Labour left, a willingness to work with the socialist left outside Labour, including the revolutionary left.

But Corbyn is not, of course, a revolutionary. He is committed to change through parliamentary means, the classic hallmark of reformism. The comments he made in a TV interview with Andrew Marr shortly after his election as Labour leader probably reflect the position he has always held: "I am not in favour of violence on the streets or insurrection. I believe in doing things through persuasive democratic means. That is what

10: The *Guardian* noted that Corbyn for many years would visit Benn's home in Holland Park on Sundays to take part in political discussions with Marxist academics Ralph Miliband and Robin Blackburn, Tariq Ali, former Labour Party general secretary Jim Mortimer and others—Boffey, 2015.

11: I first came across Corbyn in 1991, when he was the speaker at a meeting against the first Iraq war I had helped organise at Charing Cross Hospital where I then worked. I remember feeling embarrassed at the modest size of the meeting, but Corbyn was exemplary and helped give confidence to everyone who was there.

we have a democratic political structure for. People have spent their lives fighting for democracy".[12]

In other words, extra-parliamentary movements, however important they are to Corbyn, are not seen as a potential alternative source of power to parliament but as part of the necessary means of democratic persuasion.[13]

The strategy of the Labour right

The Labour right is at its weakest for three decades. The hard Blairite candidate, Liz Kendall, was humiliated with just 4.5 percent of the vote for Labour leader, while the two "softer" Blairites (both former ministers and close allies of Gordon Brown), Andy Burnham and Yvette Cooper, managed less than two fifths of the vote between them.

But the Labour right's concentration inside the parliamentary party gives them a continued base from which to launch counter-attacks on Corbyn and the left. The PLP is effectively autonomous from the wide Labour Party membership. But this is not simply because of its current right wing make-up. It has long roots inside the Labour Party and reflects the very nature of Labour as a reformist party committed to a parliamentary approach above all. As one observer noted in the 1960s: "The term 'The Labour Party' is properly applied only to the mass organisation of the party *outside* Parliament; it supports in Parliament a distinct and separate organisation, 'The Parliamentary Labour Party'".[14]

Labour's very first electoral breakthrough in 1906, when 29 Labour MPs were returned, immediately provoked a power struggle over who was sovereign inside the party: the MPs or the party conference? The first

12: Wintour, 2015a.

13: John McDonnell, who together with Corbyn was the key figure in the Labour left in parliament after Benn stepped down in 2001, and is now Corbyn's key ally as shadow chancellor in the largely hostile shadow cabinet, had a different set of experiences in the 1980s to Corbyn. He too worked initially for trade unions (as a researcher for the National Union of Mineworkers and then the TUC in the late 1970s and early 1980s), before standing as a councillor. But McDonnell did not enter parliament until 1997. Instead he was a central participant in the battles of the municipal left and the fight over rate-capping between left-led Labour councils and the Thatcher government in the mid-1980s.

McDonnell was elected to the old Greater London Council (GLC) in 1981, when Labour retook control from the Tories. Under Ken Livingstone's left Labour leadership McDonnell became the GLC chair of finance, overseeing a budget of £3 billion, and was appointed deputy leader. As this conflict came to a head in the wake of the defeat of the miners' strike in 1985, he argued for a policy of continued defiance to Thatcher and the law, and clashed with Ken Livingstone, who favoured retreat. McDonnell lost and was removed from the deputy leadership post. The GLC was abolished by Thatcher the following year.

14: McKenzie, 1963, quoted in Cliff and Gluckstein, 1988, p39.

act of those 29 MPs was to create the PLP. And as Cliff and Gluckstein note, "from the moment of its birth the PLP asserted its right to ignore the membership".[15]

The 1907 Labour Conference passed a resolution that declared that "the time and method of giving effect to [Conference decisions] are left to the Party in the House [of Commons] in conjunction with the National Executive". As Cliff and Gluckstein comment, "This gave the PLP all it wanted".[16] And even Keir Hardie could write in the same year that "rigidly laying down the lines which the party must follow...is the road to ruin. If the party in the House of Commons is to succeed it must be free to select its own course...only those on the spot, whose finger is on the pulse of Parliament, can decide... No conference meeting at Hull or Belfast or Derby or Newcastle can undertake this task".[17]

This reflects the logic of reformism. If parliament is key to social change and its claim to represent the will of the people is supreme, then dominance of the MPs is inevitable whatever the formal democratic niceties inside the Labour Party.

The independence of the PLP is the "holiest of holies" inside the Labour Party. Hence the bitter fight over the issue of mandatory reselection of MPs in the early 1980s, one of the issues that prompted the split away of a section of the right to form the Social Democratic Party (SDP), hence the moves by John Smith to weaken the influence of the unions over the selection of parliamentary candidates, hence too the bitter conflict over the role of Unite in the selection of Labour's parliamentary candidate in Falkirk in 2013. This saw the police called in over claims—which essentially turned out to be baseless—of corrupt manipulation by Unite to get its favoured candidate chosen and resulted in the establishment of the Collins Review which further sought to curb union influence (even if this backfired rather spectacularly).

This explains the continued confidence of the Labour right to seek to undermine the democratic decision of the membership to elect Corbyn. However, the size of his mandate makes a direct immediate attempt to overthrow him probably too risky in the short term. So Peter Mandelson has instead invoked a "long haul" to oust Corbyn who, though a "loser", must be proved such at the polls: "the public will decide Labour's future and it would be wrong to try and force this issue from within before the

---

15: Cliff and Gluckstein, 1988, p40.
16: Cliff and Gluckstein, 1988, p40.
17: Quoted in Cliff and Gluckstein, 1988, p41.

public have moved to a clear verdict".[18]

But this does not imply passive waiting. Instead the right's strategy centres on trying to force a series of retreats on Corbyn from the programme he was elected on and to fight a proxy battle targeting some of his key allies to weaken his authority. Luke Akehurst, the current secretary of Labour First, a self-described "moderate" (ie right wing) Labour group, has provided a candid outline of this approach in articles published on the Labour List website and elsewhere.[19] He suggests that there won't be a right wing split from Labour: "Labour will stick together. There won't be an SDP-type breakaway (unless there are sectarian attempts to deselect MPs)." Given the failure of the SDP-Liberal Alliance to break through in the 1980s despite polling over 7 million votes and the parlous current state of the Lib Dems, a split is hardly an appetising prospect.[20] Akehurst also shares Mandelson's rejection of any immediate call to remove Corbyn: "The vast majority of the PLP realises it has to accept the huge democratic mandate Corbyn just got." Any attempt to trigger a new leadership election (which would require just 20 percent of Labour MPs to initiate) would be "a pointless and indeed self-destructive exercise".[21]

Instead, under the watchword of "party unity" the approach is to demand "concessions and compromises" between Corbyn and the non-Corbynite majority in the PLP. Such concessions are, of course, mainly to be extracted from Corbyn. For Akehurst the major concession made by the Labour right is that some of them agreed to serve in the shadow cabinet at all! But, he notes, this was done in a way that secured a series of concessions from Corbyn. These included:

> Clarification that Labour will campaign for a Yes vote in the EU referendum;
> Clarification that he won't be seeking to take the UK out of NATO;
> Acceptance that he can't force MPs to vote against Trident renewal next

---

18: Quoted in Hughes, 2015. This was less than two weeks after Corbyn had been elected as leader.

19: Akehurst is a former national chair of Labour Students, chief whip for Hackney Labour councillors and a Labour NEC member. He describes himself as a "supporter of Europe, NATO/nuclear deterrence, Israel".

20: Though there clearly has been some discussion of this option. A piece in the *Financial Times* suggested as much, though it was written before Corbyn won with a huge mandate. "It also remains possible that anti-Corbynite Labour MPs (the majority of them) could try to remove him within a year or two. In extreme circumstances, there are more than enough wealthy centre-left donors who dislike the Tories, to say nothing of millions of voters in a country in which there is not a Tory majority in the popular vote, to organise the formation of a new, mainstream alternative party"—Martin, 2015.

21: Akehurst, 2015.

year; Disavowal of proposals to bring back mandatory reselection of MPs; Appointment of moderates to all the key positions in the Shadow Foreign Affairs and Shadow Defence teams, including Maria Eagle, a multilateralist, as shadow defence secretary; Reappointment of the top team in the Whips' office—Rosie Winterton, Alan Campbell and Mark Tami, who are trusted and respected by MPs.[22]

Akehurst adds: "It's notable that almost all of these concessions have related to foreign and defence policy where the disagreements are profound ones where the two sides simply have different moral principles"; on domestic policy Corbyn will have a freer hand. And "longer-term, Corbyn's leadership will sink or swim inside the party on whether it works electorally".[23]

The aim of the Labour right appears to be relentlessly to pressurise Corbyn, to blame him if Labour stumbles at the polls and prepare directly to challenge him if the mood of the party shifts against him.

"Beware your friends": Corbyn and the union bureaucracy

"My advice to Jeremy is, beware your friends—of those who are fearful of not taking things too far in the confrontation with the powers that be"—Yanis Varoufakis, former Greek finance minister.[24]

If the Parliamentary Labour Party is dominated by the Labour right, unreconciled to Corbyn's victory and biding their time to remove him, can Corbyn at least look to allies among the unions to act as a counterweight?

Corbyn certainly had the backing of key unions, with the two biggest, Unite and even more surprisingly, Unison, endorsing him. This provided Corbyn with significant early credibility in his campaign for Labour leader and helped establish his position as a serious contender. The CWU, ASLEF, TSSA and the bakers' union BFAWU also backed Corbyn, as did symbolically two unions which disaffiliated from the party in the early 2000s under Blair, the RMT and the FBU. Mark Serwotka, the head of the PCS civil servants' union which has never been affiliated to Labour, also personally backed Corbyn and appeared alongside him at his campaign rallies.[25] Such union support for Corbyn was not universal. The shop workers' union USDAW, long an ally of the Labour right, endorsed Burnham, and the GMB, the third biggest affiliate after Unite and Unison, decided not to back any candidate.

22: Akehurst, 2015.
23: Akehurst, 2015.
24: Varoufakis, 2015.
25: Though Labour refused Serwortka's application to vote as a registered supporter, see Mason, 2015.

The unions remain a significant force inside the Labour Party even after the Collins reforms, the latest of a long series of measures to curtail their formal influence. The unions retain 50 percent of the vote at Labour's conference and 12 of the 33 places on the party's National Executive Committee. And especially after corporate donors and wealthy individuals abandoned Labour after it lost office in 2010, the unions remain the party's biggest financial backers.[26]

What will be the relationship between Corbyn, the Labour Party and the unions? The danger is that they will be cautious and wavering "friends" who at points pressure him to retreat from the bold programme he was elected as leader on. Already we have seen some signs of this. So it was widely reported that Len McCluskey, Unite's general secretary, urged Corbyn not to appoint John McDonnell as the shadow chancellor. Unite together with the GMB effectively stymied moves at the Labour conference shortly after Corbyn was elected to shift Labour policy to opposition not support for Trident renewal.

The overall role that the union bureaucracy plays inside the Labour Party has been obscured by the long dominance of Blairism, with the union leaders frequently to the left of the Labour leadership and indeed sometimes openly clashing with it. Yet this masks the overall conservative role of the union leaders in the party, which is not reducible to the influence of individual right wing union leaders, but is rather a product of the social function that the union full-time machine performs.

It is often argued that Labour was created by the unions—this is true in as far as it goes, but is too limited. The Labour Party was rather the creation of the *trade union bureaucracy*, the full-time union apparatus, to pursue its interests in parliament, not least as an alternative to the risks of collective struggle from below.[27] The trade union bureaucracy is a distinct social layer with separate interests from the rank and file membership of the unions. Pete Goodwin, a former contributor to this journal, gave a good outline of this role in an analysis of Labour in the early 1980s:

> These full-time union officials are by no means mere passive instruments of their membership. They occupy a distinct social position. All are, by definition, taken away from the shop floor. All have higher status than their

---

26: Pickard, 2015a. Between May 2010 and December 2014 the unions gave Labour over £48 million, with Unite alone stumping up over £18 million pounds, according to the electoral commission.

27: See Cliff and Gluckstein, 1988, especially chapter two, "Out of the Bowels of the TUC".

members and most have higher income too. All are professional negotiators, or as the radical American sociologist C Wright Mills once put it, "managers of discontent". All have a stake in existing society, but a stake that depends on their articulating the grievances and maintaining the organisation of their members.[28]

In industrial struggles the consequences are clear. Even the most right wing union leaders have, on occasion, to support strikes, for fear of losing control of their membership altogether. But even the most left wing union leaders are worried about workers' struggles going "too far" and putting at risk the organisation their status depends upon:

> The role of the full-time union officials on their home ground is therefore, ultimately, conservative. It is the same within their creation, the Labour Party. Throughout the history of their party the union leaders have generally sustained its "responsible" parliamentary leadership, both in opposition, and, even more, in office.[29]

Historically the union bureaucracy has repeatedly been willing to use its weight inside the Labour Party to discipline the left if it saw this as a threat to its interests or to Labour's electoral prospects. So the union vote was used to drive the Communist Party out of Labour in the 1920s, to shut down the left wing Socialist League in the 1930s, to defeat Aneurin Bevan and his supporters in the 1950s and to launch the witch-hunt against *Militant* in the 1980s. But just as the union bureaucracy has set limits to the leftward moves inside the party, it has also at times clashed with the party's parliamentary leadership where it moves too far to the right:

> There have been times when union officialdom as a whole has fallen out with Labour's parliamentary leadership: when [Ramsay] MacDonald pushed cuts in unemployment benefit too far in 1931; when [Hugh] Gaitskell tried to weaken the link with the unions in 1959; over [Harold] Wilson's proposed trade union legislation in 1969; and because of the "Winter of Discontent" in 1978-79. At these times the union leaders have shifted leftward, used left rhetoric and left wing currents within the party to pull the parliamentary leadership into line.

28: Goodwin, 1983.
29: Goodwin, 1983, p27.

But as Goodwin also notes, such left swings by sections, at least, of the union bureaucracy have invariably been followed by moves to stop things going "too far" by "reverting to their normal conservative posture and using their block votes at conference to vote the left down".[30]

Owen Jones, close to the Unite leadership, has given expression to the kind of thinking that the union leaders may approach the Corbyn leadership with:

> "Socialism is the language of priorities", as Nye Bevan put it. Yes, we can look at polls and say, look, the vast majority support public ownership of rail. But while most certainly do agree with that, it will be eclipsed by other priorities. The focus must surely be on bread-and-butter concerns, like jobs, health, education, public services, housing, and so on…
>
> Concerns about immigration cannot be addressed by sticking our fingers in our ears, or only emphasising the benefits of immigration… Huge amounts of efforts have to [be] expended into winning over working class voters plumping for UKIP… UKIP voters must be love-bombed, not treated as closet racists, but as people who feel abandoned by the political elite and who have burning concerns on issues ranging from housing to jobs…
>
> A Corbyn-led government has to pick its battles, because it already has enough of them. Take NATO: the merits of membership are so far from the mainstream of political debate, it would be pointless and self-defeating to pick a fight over it. Instead, Labour should suggest a more constructive role for Britain within the Alliance…
>
> Labour needs a strategy for local government cuts. Refusing to implement them is not going to work—the Tories will simply sweep in and enforce their own. Instead, there needs to be a national strategy agreed by Labour councils to protest cuts and emphasise they are imposed by the Westminster government.[31]

This is the logic of electoralism and a continuing half-acceptance of the Blairite argument that the majority of the population is simply too conservative to accept a radical message and therefore the left should avoid challenging those ideas too hard. It is more than likely that even those

---

30: Goodwin, 1983, p28.
31: Jones, Owen, 2015.

union leaders that backed Corbyn share such a view.

The danger is that the cautious approach of the union leaders, even those who backed Corbyn, can play into the hands of the Labour right. Any retreat by Corbyn from his programme risks demobilising his supporters and strengthens the hand of the parliamentary party to contain Corbyn. And ultimately the union bureaucracy shares with the parliamentary party a desire to be electorally successful; after all their goal is a Labour government that can promote their interests—and if Corbyn is seen as unable to deliver at the polls, they may at some point abandon him.

Unstable compound: Corbyn and Labour

The Labour Party is now a battleground marked if not by full-scale civil war then by repeated skirmishes between the right, ensconced inside the parliamentary party, and Corbyn.

In this the hypocrisy of the Labour right knows no bounds. After decades of relentlessly lecturing the left about the need to shut up in the name of party unity and because "divided parties lose elections", open public defiance of Corbyn has been an almost daily event. This reaches far into the shadow cabinet itself. So when Corbyn told the TUC a few days after he was elected as leader that he supported scrapping the cap on welfare benefits introduced by the Tories, the shadow work and pensions secretary Owen Smith immediately appeared on *Newsnight* to contradict this, insisting Labour was only opposed to the government plan to reduce the cap even further from £26,000 to £23,000, "because I don't think the country would support us saying we were in favour of unfettered spending".[32]

Many of the most flagrant attacks on Corbyn have been over foreign policy, especially over Corbyn's opposition to Trident. In response to Corbyn, a longstanding CND member, telling a radio interviewer that he would never authorise the use of nuclear weapons, Maria Eagle, the shadow defence secretary, publicly criticised him and was backed up behind the scenes by a string of shadow cabinet members. Paul Kenny, the general secretary of the GMB, even suggested that Corbyn might have to consider resigning over the question.[33] And Eagle loudly proclaimed that abolishing Trident was not Labour's policy at Westminster, playing straight into the SNP's hands.[34]

Then, after a rather sinister intervention by the current head of the British military, General Sir Nicholas Houghton, who told a TV interview

---

32: Go to www.bbc.co.uk/news/uk-wales-politics-34267755
33: Watt, Wintour and Mason, 2015.
34: Wintour, 2015c.

that he would be "worried" if Corbyn was elected as prime minister because of his opposition to nuclear weapons, Eagle responded by saying she understood Houghton's concerns. And when the Scottish Labour Party conference voted to support scrapping Trident, Kevan Jones, shadow defence minister, turned to the *Daily Telegraph* to pen an article saying this would not affect Labour's policy at Westminster.[35]

The revolt against Corbyn even provoked Simon Danczuk, the publicity seeking Labour MP for Rochdale (and who seems to be on friendly terms with UKIP leader Nigel Farage), to feel able to declare that he was willing to stand as a "stalking horse" candidate against Corbyn if Labour does badly at next May's elections in local government, the Welsh Assembly and the Scottish Parliament.[36]

Labour MPs have also lined up to attack the launch of Momentum, a project to organise pro-Corbyn supporters, issuing dark warnings about the establishment of "parties within parties" and the supposed threat of the left moving to "purge" MPs on the Labour right. Yet for years organisations such as Progress and Labour First have operated inside the Labour Party to promote the views of the right, organise their supporters and, in the case of Progress, seek to influence the selection of parliamentary candidates. It has been the right, not the left, which has to date sought to exclude people from the party, including targeting Corbyn's appointments to his advisory team. Left winger Andrew Fischer, Corbyn's head of policy, was suspended from the party after a number of MPs made much play of an old tweet of Fischer's that called for a vote for a Class War candidate several months before the general election (where Fischer by all accounts campaigned for the Labour candidate). Yet Frank Field told the *New Statesman* that any MPs who were deselected by Corbyn supporters should provoke an immediate by-election and stand as "independent Labour" and "a whole pile of us will go down there to campaign for them. They can't expel 60 of us. Momentum ought to know that they're not the only pair of wide eyes in the business. We're not powerless".[37] No MPs called for Field to be disciplined.

Corbyn and McDonnell face a choice. Do they seek boldly to defend their programme and mobilise their supporters to impose the democratic will of the membership on the parliamentary party, through shifting policy at next year's party conference, moving to challenge for parliamentary

35: Jones, Kevan, 2015.
36: "Corbyn faces leadership challenge from Labour MP if May elections disappoint"—*Observer*, 2015.
37: Eaton, 2015a.

selections, de-selecting disloyal MPs, etc? This is the road to open civil war in the Labour Party. Or do they seek to reach some accommodation with at least the softer elements of the Labour right? But the price that would be demanded would inevitably be at least some retreats from the programme Corbyn stood on in the leadership campaign.

Over the first couple of months of Corbyn's leadership the signs point, to an attempt to do both. So Corbyn and McDonnell have pushed forward where some degree of wider consensus exists for example over opposing austerity and rail renationalisation, but Corbyn's initial talk of renationalising the energy companies seems to have been dropped in favour of "community owned power stations",[38] and the policy of abolishing student tuition fees has been put out to a policy review.[39] Corbyn is sticking to his principles, and mandate, over Trident but is likely to concede a "free vote" over the issue if it is put before parliament. There have also been no calls for Labour councils to refuse to implement the cuts and set illegal budgets.

Meanwhile, the establishment of Momentum does suggest that there will be an attempt to organise the new forces on the left inside Labour with the aim of strengthening Corbyn's position in the future. Momentum was launched in early October with a number of newly elected pro-Corbyn Labour MPs, such as Clive Lewis, Richard Burgon and Kate Osamor, acting as its initial directors. These MPs are all outside the shadow cabinet and formally independent of Corbyn. But as part of Momentum's coordinated media launch supportive statements endorsing Momentum appeared from both John McDonnell and Corbyn himself, giving it an "official" imprint (something reinforced by Osamor's appointment as one of Corbyn's private parliamentary secretaries).[40]

Describing itself as a grassroots network aiming to create "a mass movement for change, for real progressive change in every town and city", Momentum seems to be looking in two directions. One (unnamed) spokesman told the *Guardian* when it was launched that the aim was to link up "people outside the Labour Party as well as inside. We are associated with the Labour Party, and incredibly supportive of it, but not under its control".[41] This involved an accurate recognition that central to Corbyn's success has been drawing on the mass movements that emerged outside Labour and then swept into the party, propelling Corbyn to the Labour

---

38: Pickard, 2015b
39. Adams, 2015.
40: Wintour, 2015b.
41: Wintour, 2015b.

leadership. And in a number of areas socialists outside the Labour Party have been able to participate in Momentum meetings and productively discuss areas for joint extra-parliamentary mobilisations.

But Momentum does also seek to translate the huge support for Corbyn into a counterweight to the Labour right within the party, aiming to "transform the Labour Party into a more democratic party with the policies and collective will to make that change". This raises the question of whether Momentum will seek primarily to operate on the terrain of the internal structures of the Labour Party, focusing on winning policy resolutions and candidate selection battles and so on, or aim to help build mass movements in collaboration with forces outside Labour.

Immediately coming under attack from the Labour right and sections of the media for associating with the extra-parliamentary left, Momentum issued a "code of ethics" which emphasised its links to Labour, possibly suggesting a retreat from the perspective of looking outwards. But it would be a real mistake for Momentum to become focused on winning a lengthy, bitter internal fight inside the Labour Party rather than seeking to build and mobilise extra-parliamentary struggles.

It is precisely through such struggles that not only can the Tories be effectively challenged in the here and now, but that Corbyn's position inside the Labour Party can be most effectively strengthened. A mass movement re-emerging over opposition to Trident and nuclear weapons, an eruption of housing protests, the rebellion by junior doctors over unsocial hours turning into a wider revolt in the NHS, the huge mood of solidarity around refugees developing into a deep-rooted mass movement—such developments would immeasurably strengthen Corbyn. Corbyn and some of those around him do see some of this and his willingness to identify with refugee solidarity and Stand Up to Racism, for example, is significant. But will an orientation towards extra-parliamentary mobilisation be the focus for Momentum and the new Labour left?

The Labour left also, ultimately, shares with the Labour right a common concern with electability, even as they argue over how best to achieve this. After all, their goal is the election of a Labour government to implement progressive policies. In a situation of mass struggles and widespread radicalisation among the working class, the right is even prepared to use the left's enthusiastic activists and programme to win office—even if later the need to provide "responsible" government that limits any challenge to capitalism may require the disciplining, or even a split with the left (in effect the path trodden by Alexis Tsipras and Syriza over the last few years).

But where a left wing programme seems unable to command

an electoral majority, a much more likely situation if the overall level of struggle and collective resistance in the working class is low, the Labour left can feel pressured to retreat and to abandon at least the most "unpopular" parts of its programme.

Bombing Syria, shooting at Corbyn

The drive by David Cameron for Britain to participate in airstrikes against ISIS in Syria in the wake of the 13 November attacks in Paris served to deepen and accelerate all the conflicts inside Labour.

In response to Corbyn's opposition to airstrikes, the aggressiveness of sections of the Labour right towards him reached new heights as they seized on an opportunity to try to humiliate him. Faced with opposition from inside the shadow cabinet, Corbyn did attempt to mobilise his supporters to put pressure on pro-war Labour MPs, emailing Labour members to put the case against bombing. But confronted with the threat of mass resignations from the shadow cabinet, Corbyn shied away from imposing a whip and allowed a free vote.[42]

Corbyn, in other words, was pulled between confronting the Labour right through mobilising his mass support among the wider party membership and a desire to preserve unity with at least a sizeable section of the Labour right. Corbyn's position was, however, boosted by the rekindling of the anti-war movement, which suddenly saw an influx of a new generation of young activists taking to the streets in protests called by the Stop the War coalition.

While these protests were not on the scale of the huge demonstrations of 2003, they did serve to invoke the spectre of Iraq. And public opinion shifted towards scepticism over British participation in yet another war in the Middle East with Peter Kellner of YouGov noting on 2 December that polls suggested that "in just seven days, five million people have joined the ranks of those opposed to air strikes in Syria".[43]

A majority of Labour MPs did eventually vote against the bombing. Together with Labour's comfortable victory in the Oldham West and Royton by-election, despite wild claims that UKIP would inflict revenge on Corbyn for his anti-war views, this did seem to offer a breathing space to Corbyn. But 66 Labour MPs did openly defy him by voting for bombing, led by Hilary Benn, the shadow foreign secretary, in a much-hyped speech that invoked the traditions of socialist internationalism to justify British militarism.

A hard pro-imperialist bloc opposed to Corbyn has thus begun to

---

42: Eaton, 2015b.

43: Go to https://yougov.co.uk/news/2015/12/02/analysis-sharp-fall-support-air-strikes-syria

crystallise inside the PLP. And many of those, like Andy Burnham, who voted against bombing, were adamantly opposed to any moves to discipline those Labour MPs who did back Cameron. If Corbyn is tempted to believe he can work with such "softer" elements of the Labour right, it is clear that the price they will extract is to shield the most aggressive opponents to Corbyn within the PLP.

The nature of reformism

For a generation the Labour Party has been dominated by a very right wing form of reformism, at best claiming to be able to channel some of the fruits of "the enterprise of the market and rigours of competition" into improved public services (even as these too were ever more subject to the "discipline" of the market).

In fact, many on the left regarded New Labour not as a reformist project at all but just another right wing, pro-capitalist party, like the Tories, and this was coupled with much talk of "the end of social democracy". In terms of ideology this was largely true, but it missed the way the social base of the Labour Party, its ties to the unions and roots in working class life even if eroded, still meant it was a very different type of party to the openly pro-capitalist Conservatives or Liberal Democrats.

Nevertheless, reformism has always been a much richer, broader and more deeply rooted phenomenon than its Blairite manifestation. Reformism involves a *combination of two contradictory poles*. Cliff and Gluckstein offer a succinct statement about the nature of reformism, that it:

> combines acceptance of the basic tenets of the system with elements of protest against it. The key element of ruling class ideology is the concept of the nation uniting all people within it. The key element in struggle against capitalism is class consciousness. Labour tries to combine the two by channelling working class aspirations through the institutions of the national state, such as parliament.[44]

Reformism's rejection of at least some elements of the status quo and its search for change to improve the conditions of the exploited majority in society—the working class—coupled with an acceptance of the overall framework of capitalist society as inevitable, "natural" and permanent gives rise to a desire for change within capitalism, rather than its overthrow. This is the essence of reformism.

44: Cliff and Gluckstein, 1988, p2.

Such an outlook, held still by the majority of the working class in Britain, is not a product of manipulation from the top by the Labour Party or the union leaders, but is rooted in workers' own experience under capitalism most of the time:

> On the one hand, they are brought up in capitalist society and take many of its notions for granted. On the other hand, they have experiences of collective struggles in which they stand together and change the world a little to their own advantage. Some of these experiences are direct ones they have had personally. Others are conveyed from one generation to the next within workplaces, communities and organisations such as trade unions... So the mind of the average worker contains elements that look to the future and the values of collective struggle and organisation, as well as elements that pull back to the past, towards class society and its prejudices.[45]

The contradictory nature of reformism—partial rejection but overall acceptance of the system—means that it can both express class consciousness and blunt and contain it, stopping it developing towards a total rejection of the system—we still need bosses, workers can't run society, radical movements shouldn't go "too far", the state can be used to challenge capital, etc. Such ideas can be mobilised by reformist politicians and trade union leaders to limit and derail mass movements from below that have the potential to turn into much bigger challenges to the system.

The balance between the two poles of reformism, the expression and containment of class consciousness, is not fixed once and for all, but is fluid. If Blairism and new Labour represented a strong emphasis on the element of containment and acceptance of the dynamics of the system with only traces of class feeling, left reformism involves the strengthening of the pole of class expression *without, however, overthrowing the other pole of acceptance of the framework of the system.*

Reformism with reforms?

If a Corbyn-led Labour government did get elected on an anti-austerity platform, could it deliver real gains? Is a revival of "reformism *with* reforms" achievable within the framework of contemporary capitalism?

One immediate question that must be faced is the fate of Syriza. Its transformation, within months, from a beacon of hope in the wake of its general election victory, to the soon to be enforcer of an even more brutal

---

45: Harman, 2007, pp60-63.

austerity than its predecessors, surely poses huge questions for the fate of any left government's prospects. Part of answering this question depends on whether austerity, and more broadly neoliberalism, is seen as reversible without the defeat of capitalism, and therefore in some sense not in the interests of at least major sections of capital. John McDonnell told the Labour Party conference, "Austerity is not an economic necessity, it's a political choice".[46]

This is ambiguous at best. While austerity does involve a bitter struggle over which class in society will bear the burden of the economic crisis, austerity cannot be reduced to a mere subjective ideological preference by the Tories or particularly aggressive sections of capital.[47] Indeed underlying the shift to neoliberalism has been a crisis of profitability across the advanced capitalist system since the mid-1970s. The consequent reorganisation of capital in response, especially the growing significance of production across borders, the increased role of debt, finance and speculation, the intensified pressure on workers' wages, including the "social wage" (welfare and services) and the intensification of work—all hallmarks of neoliberalism—are not an aberration but reflect the logic of the system attempting to restore, with only partial success to date, the profitability of capital.

The historical conditions that produced the 1945 Labour government and the post-war boom no longer exist. Genuine reforms from government are dependent on the health of the system—they cannot be simply selected from a historical menu (do you want a Clement Attlee or a Tony Blair government?) through willpower and ideological inclination.[48]

The question of the restoration of profitability is equally the obstacle facing hopes for a Keynesian-style programme of state-sponsored economic expansion. If this was achievable—expanding demand allowing both wages and profits to be boosted—this would clearly attenuate class tensions over paying for the crisis, giving a reforming left government more room for manoeuvre and space to deliver tangible gains for workers. But British capitalism has a chronically weak level of business investment, crucial for any serious sustainable economic expansion—this either requires further drives to boost profitability, and raising the share of wages threatens this, or the state taking over the investment decisions of major firms. As the Marxist economist Michael Roberts points out, while "Corbynomics" has included a welcome plan to renationalise the railways and talk of returning

---

46: Elliott, 2015.
47: For a discussion of the weaknesses of such accounts of neoliberalism, see Harman, 2008.
48: For an assessment of the 1945 Labour government, including the limits of its achievements, see Ralph Miliband's classic study—Miliband, 2009, pp272-317.

the majority of recently-privatised Royal Mail shares to public ownership, this would still leave "swathes of key British economic operations in the hands of profit-seeking companies":

> What about the rest of transport: deregulated buses in the big cities; and all the British companies that used to be part of the public sector? What about British Petroleum, British Airways; British Telecom; British Gas; British Aerospace; the electricity and water boards; Transco; Rolls Royce, British Steel, let alone British Coal? And there are the major strategic sectors that should be part of what is called in Labour parlance "the commanding heights of the economy": the major pharma and auto companies, now mostly in foreign hands where any profits end up overseas.[49]

Even the hugely popular call by John McDonnell for a real assault on the "tax gap"—the huge amounts of legal tax avoidance and illegal tax evasion practised by big business—will require more than simply a change of government or even the law. Again Roberts makes the obvious point that:

> as long as corporations are private entities beholden to their shareholders, both domestic and foreign, and are not publicly owned, they will seek to maximise their profits. Avoiding and evading tax is a big part of doing that. Indeed, evidence shows that if it were not for government's continually lowering corporate taxes (not raising them as Corbyn plans) and turning a blind eye to abuses, then corporate profitability would be seriously impaired and would thus reduce even the level of investment that is currently taking place.

Without taking control over big firms, even significantly reducing the "tax gap"—and therefore providing scope to increase public spending, ie by ending university tuition fees and providing universal free childcare—is liable to prove elusive.

Any real moves towards what the Labour programme for the 1974 general election—which Labour won—called "a fundamental and irreversible shift in the balance of power and wealth in favour of working people and their families" must be expected to be met with fierce hostility from capital, matched by an ability to mobilise vast undemocratic power, backed by the state. This was of course exactly the fate of the Wilson/Callaghan government in 1974-9 which faced orchestrated capital flight and investment strikes with the connivance of the Bank of England, forcing it into the

---

49: Roberts, 2015.

arms of the IMF in 1976 and the adoption of "monetarist" (ie neoliberal) measures three years before Thatcher was elected.

In such circumstances, and there is little reason to believe the picture facing a Corbyn government would much differ, reforms in the interests of the working class must necessarily involve major class confrontation and the mobilisation from below of workers' collective power to paralyse production. A few socialist ministers would not be able to withstand the huge pressures of capital. But this involves a different political orientation to the belief that via the ballot box a left government can use a democratic mandate to deliver from above.

The criticism of Syriza put forward by the Socialist Workers Party and our co-thinkers in SEK in Greece is not that it failed to organise an insurrection but that it was unable to deliver on its own programme of anti-austerity reforms. A period of capitalist crisis, not just the immediate post-2008 crisis but the longer period of instability lasting decades produced by weak profitability, means that reforms increasingly depend on mass direct confrontation and bitter class battles, that is, the methods that point in the direction of revolutionary action.

Corbyn, left reformism and revolutionaries

"Separate yourselves from Turati [the leading Italian reformist], and then make an alliance with him"—Antonio Gramsci, recalling Lenin's advice to Italian Communists.[50]

How should revolutionary socialists relate to the hundreds of thousands of people enthused by Corbyn's sudden emergence as Labour leader? The victory of a left reformist current at the head of the Labour Party is highly contradictory. On the one hand, it gives such ideas a powerful social weight capable of reshaping the political agenda and offers the promise of a real alternative to the Tories and a fight against austerity, war and racism. But to realise that desire, to develop it and turn it into a real movement capable of shifting the balance of class forces, win real gains for workers and start to transform working class self-confidence, cannot be done without confronting crucial obstacles that will block such developments and act as a brake on the radicalisation expressed in Corbyn's victory. Above all, the pole of left reformism that still accepts working within the overall framework of capitalism and its institutions, most importantly the notion that the existing state can be used as a lever for social transformation in the face of opposition from capital, is a notion that will, at key points, blunt and contain workers' advances.

50: Gramsci, 1978, p380.

Revolutionaries must retain their political and organisational independence from left reformism

Revolutionary Marxists insist that the battle for reforms is most effectively waged via self-activity from below and especially through the mobilisation of working class power at the point of production; that is, through direct confrontation rather than methods that rely on negotiation from above. The key arena is the class struggle outside of parliament.

Such ideas are held by a minority. This minority must assemble in its own organisation so as to be able to develop common theoretical traditions and to discuss and then collectively implement common activity and intervention into the class struggle, in turn allowing the testing of its ideas, the development of leaders and the building of wider roots in the working class. Crucially, it must retain a capacity for autonomous initiatives.

This does not rule out revolutionaries participating in wider radical left initiatives even where these are led by left reformist forces, on the condition that they are able to retain their political and organisational independence. So, for example, the revolutionary socialists grouped around Marx21 in Germany are part of Die Linke. But the weight of the trade union bureaucracy, the deep integration of the Parliamentary Labour Party into the state, a process that has roots going back nearly a century, and the lack of space for an independent revolutionary left to operate in the open, rule this out in regard to the Labour Party.

Revolutionaries take sides with the left reformists when they are in conflict with right reformists

Revolutionaries are not neutral in the battle between right wing reformists, who insist that little challenge can be given to the system, and left reformists who do give expression to class feeling, who articulate a desire for real change and who use some anti-capitalist arguments to challenge the defenders of the system. In doing so they can help give socialist arguments a much wider currency and give confidence not just to the left but to the wider working class movement. When Jeremy Corbyn rejects the case for austerity or puts forward arguments against nuclear weapons, these get a much wider hearing in society. We stand together with Corbyn and his supporters when the Labour right echo the media and denounce such arguments as utopian or incoherent.

Any retreat by Corbyn either in the name of "party unity" or electability from the programme he was elected on as leader risks confusing and demoralising his supporters.

Insistence on the centrality of struggle outside parliament

The key to social change remains through collective struggle from below. Every advance in the struggle creates a greater self-confidence among layers of workers, so weakening the hold of right wing ideas. This in turn is Corbyn's best defence of his position against the Labour right. So, for example, a mass movement emerging over opposition to Trident, or in defence of the NHS, would weaken the Tories, pull public opinion to the left and boost Labour's electoral prospects in turn.

But if the mass of Corbyn's supporters are simply drawn into bitter internal battles over Labour policy and candidate selections, in practice their focus will not be mobilising in workplaces and working class communities but on arguing with the right wing in Constituency Labour Parties, at committee meetings and so on. Paradoxically, this can weaken, not strengthen, Corbyn's position.

A constant search to apply the method of the united front

Revolutionaries have to engage in a persistent effort to work alongside any section of Corbyn's supporters in Labour in common activity and struggle. This can both strengthen the potential for resistance and provide an opportunity to discuss and debate how the desire for real change can be achieved with those enthusiastic about Corbyn.

The election of Corbyn to the Labour leadership offers the scope for united front activities between revolutionaries and reformists around concrete initiatives on an even bigger scale than we have witnessed in the recent past. The appearance by Corbyn at a packed Stand Up to Racism rally in central London in early November in defence of refugees, an initiative the SWP is an important part of, significantly boosts the weight of that campaign and draws in wider forces.

But alongside greater united front possibilities goes the need for greater ideological clarity. There is a contrast between the current situation and the high-point of Stop the War, for example. In 2002-4 the SWP worked with Corbyn as we seek to do today. But then he was part of the marginalised Labour left in a campaign against a war being waged by a Labour prime minister with the result that tens of thousands of people left the Labour Party. The argument that Labour was not the way forward was easy. But even then it was never true that simply being the best activists was automatically enough to pull people towards revolutionary politics, especially in a context where working class power was rarely visible. Patient argument and discussion were required.

Today, where nearly 200,000 people have joined the Labour Party and it is now led by a socialist who stands for challenging neoliberalism and imperialism, the pull towards Labour is very powerful. This places a premium on revolutionaries knowing how to combine working with Corbyn supporters in common struggles with also pursuing a friendly argument about the forms of struggle, politics and organisation that can most effectively lead us forward.

Leon Trotsky, writing in the midst of a sharp swing to the left by social democracy across Europe in the mid-1930s, argued that it was crucial for revolutionaries not to stand aside from reformist workers and denounce the hopes they place in left social democracy as pointless, but instead to identify strongly with their desire to challenge capital and fight for improvements in workers' conditions without, however, giving ground to any notion that social democracy's parliamentary orientation can deliver: "We share the difficulties of the struggle but not the illusions".[51] Trotsky translated this approach into the need for revolutionaries to pursue a dual approach, combining "ideological intransigence"—because we do not share the illusion in left reformism and must warn workers about its limitations—with a "flexible united front policy" because we want to share the difficulties, to unite in struggle and prove in practice how the obstacles workers face can be overcome.[52] Such an approach remains indispensable today.

References

Adams, Richard, 2015, "Jeremy Corbyn Tuition Fee Abolition Pledge Vies with Other Policies", *Guardian* (2 October), www.theguardian.com/politics/2015/oct/02/jeremy-corbyn-promise-scrap-tuition-fees-vies-with-higher-education-policies

Akehurst, Luke, 2015, "What's Going to Happen to a Corbyn-led Labour party", *Labour List* (22 September), http://labourlist.org/2015/09/whats-going-to-happen-to-a-corbyn-led-labour-party

Boffey, Daniel, 2015, "Jeremy Corbyn's World: His Friends, Supporters, Mentors and Influences", *Guardian* (15 August), www.theguardian.com/politics/2015/aug/15/jeremy-corbyn-world-supporters-mentors-influences

Cliff, Tony, and Donny Gluckstein, 1988, *The Labour Party: A Marxist History* (Bookmarks).

Eaton, George, 2015a, "Frank Field calls for Labour MPs to Stand as Independents if Deselected", *New Statesman* (14 October), www.newstatesman.com/politics/uk/2015/10/frank-field-calls-labour-mps-stand-independents-if-deselected

Eaton, George, 2015b, "Labour's Syria Split Shows Jeremy Corbyn Needs to Choose Between Peace and War with his MPs", *New Statesman* (2 December), http://tinyurl.com/z7zxs8m

51: Trotsky, 1934a.
52: Trotsky, 1934b.

Elliott, Larry, 2015, "John McDonnell offers Different Economic Tack without Sounding Scary", *Guardian* (28 September), www.theguardian.com/politics/2015/sep/28/john-mcdonnell-austerity-political-choice-not-economic-necessity

Goodwin, Pete, 1983, *Is there a Future for the Labour Left?* (Socialist Workers Party).

Gramsci, Antonio, 1978, *Selections from the Political Writings 1921-1926* (Lawrence and Wishart).

Harman, Chris, 2006, "The Painful Passing of Tony Blair", *International Socialism* 112 (autumn), http://isj.org.uk/the-painful-passing-of-tony-blair

Harman, Chris, 2007, *Revolution in the 21st Century* (Bookmarks).

Harman, Chris, 2008, "Theorising Neoliberalism", *International Socialism* 117 (winter), http://isj.org.uk/theorising-neoliberalism

Hughes, Laura, 2015, "Lord Mandelson: It is Too Soon to Remove Jeremy Corbyn as Leader", *Telegraph* (25 September), www.telegraph.co.uk/news/politics/11890126/Lord-Mandelson-It-is-too-soon-to-remove-Jeremy-Corbyn-as-leader.html

Jones, Kevan, 2015, "Jeremy Corbyn's Plans to Scrap Trident will 'Kick Thousands of People Out of Work'", *Telegraph* (2 November), www.telegraph.co.uk/news/politics/Jeremy_Corbyn/11971185/Jeremy-Corbyns-plans-to-scrap-Trident-will-kick-thousands-of-people-out-of-work.html

Jones, Owen, 2015, "My Honest Thoughts on the Corbyn Campaign and Overcoming Formidable Obstacles", https://medium.com/@OwenJones84/my-honest-thoughts-on-the-corbyn-campaign-and-overcoming-formidable-obstacles-de81d4449884#.9ijhx0vht

McKenzie, R T, 1963, *British Political Parties* (Heinemann).

Martin, Iain, 2015, "The Opposition is not Cameron's Biggest Problem", *Financial Times* (31 August), www.ft.com/cms/s/0/04ebf19e-4fda-11e5-b029-b9d50a74fd14.html#axzz3s3jZiCMR

Mason, Rowena, 2015, "Labour Bans Trade Union Head from Voting in Leadership Election", *Guardian* (25 August), www.theguardian.com/politics/2015/aug/25/labour-union-leader-vote-jeremy-corbyn-pcs-mark-serwotka

Miliband, Ralph, 2009 [1961], *Parliamentary Socialism: A Study in the Politics of Labour* (Merlin).

Pickard, Jim, 2015a, "General Election: Donation Data Reveal Labour's Reliance on Unions", *Financial Times* (16 April), www.ft.com/cms/s/0/34ed154a-e38c-11e4-b407-00144feab7de.html#axzz3s3jZiCMR

Pickard, Jim, 2015b, "Jeremy Corbyn Drops Plans to Nationalise Energy Groups", *Financial Times* (29 September), www.ft.com/cms/s/0/ed7bf010-66ca-11e5-a57f-21b88f7d973f.html#axzz3s3jZiCMR

Roberts, Michael, 2015, "Corbynomics: Extreme or Moderate?" (11 September), https://thenextrecession.wordpress.com/2015/09/11/corbynomics-extreme-or-moderate

Scotsman, 2015, "John Prescott Slams Tony Blair and Ex-adviser John McTernan" (23 July), www.scotsman.com/news/uk/john-prescott-slams-tony-blair-and-ex-adviser-john-mcternan-1-3838718#ixzz3pCc5iaKh

Thomas, Mark L, 2013, "Unpopular Capitalism! Neoliberalism and Working Class Consciousness", *Socialist Review* (December), http://socialistreview.org.uk/386/unpopular-capitalism-neoliberalism-working-class-consciousness

Trotsky, Leon, 1934a, "Revisionism and Planning: The Revolutionary Struggle against Labor Fakers" (January), www.marxists.org/archive/trotsky/1934/01/planning.htm

Trotsky, Leon, 1934b, "Two Articles On Centrism" (February/March), www.marxists.org/archive/trotsky/1934/02/centrism.htm

Varoufakis, Yanis, 2015, "Left Should Beware of Friends who Fear Confronting the Rich", *Socialist Worker* (15 September), http://tinyurl.com/h94py85

Watt, Nicholas, Patrick Wintour, and Rowena Mason, 2015, "Labour Split on Defence Grows as Maria Eagle Criticises Corbyn over Trident", *Guardian* (30 September), http://tinyurl.com/pa879we

Wheeler, Brian, 2015, "The Jeremy Corbyn Story: Profile of Labour's New Leader", *BBC News* (12 September), www.bbc.co.uk/news/uk-politics-34184265

Williamson, David, and Liam Murphy, 2015, "Birkenhead MP Frank Field Defends Decision to Nominate Jeremy Corbyn as Labour Leadership Candidate", *Liverpool Echo* (23 July), www.liverpoolecho.co.uk/news/birkenhead-mp-frank-field-defends-9712490

Wintour, Patrick, 2015a, "Jeremy Corbyn: We do not Support Violent Protest", *Guardian* (27 September), www.theguardian.com/politics/2015/sep/27/jeremy-corbyn-john-mcdonnell-violent-protest-claims

Wintour, Patrick, 2015b, "Jeremy Corbyn leadership campaign gives rise to new social movement", *Guardian* (8 October), www.theguardian.com/politics/2015/oct/08/jeremy-corbyn-leadership-campaign-new-social-movement-momentum

Wintour, Patrick, 2015c, "Maria Eagle Asserts Authority over Scottish Labour on Trident", *Guardian* (2 November), www.theguardian.com/uk-news/2015/nov/02/trident-maria-eagle-asserts-defence-authority-scottish-labour

Wintour, Patrick, and Nicholas Watt, 2015, "The Corbyn Earthquake: How Labour was Shaken to its Foundations", *Guardian* (25 September), www.theguardian.com/politics/2015/sep/25/jeremy-corbyn-earthquake-labour-party

Radical economics, Marxist economics and Marx's economics

Jane Hardy

The major global crises of the mid-1970s and 2008-9 provoked debates among the ruling class about the best economic policies to manage capitalism. For socialists and activists the question was different, and debates about whether and to what extent capitalism could be reformed to avert crisis and instil a more humane and fair system became even sharper. By the mid-1970s the end of the (not so) long boom of the 1950s and 1960s seemed to sound the death knell of Keynesian economics; in 2008 the shock of the near meltdown of global capitalism led commentators from a broad political spectrum to question the efficacy of neoliberal policies, particularly in relation to deregulated finance. Since 2008 it is hardly surprising that there has been a revival of radical economics and a proliferation of books and articles criticising neoliberal capitalism reflected, for example, in the popularity of the huge tome *Capital in the Twenty-First Century* by Thomas Piketty.[1]

Debates in economics have sharpened further as a group of mainstream, radical and Marxist economists have coalesced around the idea that the Great Recession of 2008-9 has morphed into a long depression.[2] The "new normal" is reflected in the global capitalist economy crawling along at well below the

1:    Piketty, 2014.
2:    Roberts, 2015.

post-war trend with little sign of improvement.[3] This is despite low or zero interest rates and governments "printing money" on a massive scale through quantitative easing.

Criticism of neoclassical market-driven economics is also expressed in an increasing dissatisfaction with the way that the subject is taught in universities.[4] This discontent was born in the world economics association, (formally known as the "post-autistic economics movement"), started by students in Paris in 2000, which quickly spread to other countries.[5] In 2014 students at the University of Manchester formed the "post-crash economics society" to demand the hiring of lecturers with a broader outlook and the teaching of a wider range of ideas.[6] The main complaints of these movements are that economics has become another branch of mathematics, has no links with other social sciences and is disconnected from reality. The nature of economics "research" in universities is that only publications in a narrow range of journals count,[7] and these are dominated by ever more sophisticated mathematical models that are completely detached from the "real world" and exclude and are dismissive of any other perspective.

The position of the post-autistic economics movement was vindicated when the financial crisis broke out. Neoclassical economics provides an ideological justification for the free market in general and more specifically had promoted the deregulation of finance in the 1980s and 1990s. However, ideas like the "efficient market hypothesis", which asserted that financial markets would correct themselves, looked foolish and abstract as the financial sector imploded in 2008.

Varieties of radical economics

Radical economics is a loose collective term for those who are critical of the method and prescriptions of mainstream neoclassical economics. This school of economics dominates teaching in universities, provides the "theory" and justification for neoliberalism and underpins the policies of global financial institutions such as the World Bank and International

---

3: Roberts, 2015.
4: Skidelsky, 2014.
5: See www.paecon.net; they are associated with a journal *The Real World Economics Review*.
6: Inman, 2014.
7: In UK universities, journals in economics (and other subjects) are given a ranking. Publication in high-ranking journals determines the reputation of the department and the career progression and job opportunities for individuals. Academics who are heterodox economists (who depart from mathematical modelling and neoclassical economics) find it much more difficult to get work.

Monetary Fund. For convenience in this article radical economists are divided into three groups.

First, the most high-profile and well-known "radical" economists in the United States, who provide explanations of capitalism, crisis and stagnation for a wider audience, are Paul Krugman, Joseph Stiglitz, and more recently Lawrence Summers.[8] Collectively, these "modern avatars of Keynes" as James Galbraith labels them, see the problem as:

> a shortage of effective aggregate demand. The cure is more spending by government, business, foreigners, and private households. This simple argument is aimed mostly at the deficit hawks and debt hysterics…who confect constraints out of accounting relationships and financial statements and live in awe of the bond markets or in fear of the central bank.[9]

This has been reflected in the recent public joust between Summers and ex-chair of the Federal Reserve Ben Bernanke who have different interpretations of the crisis and therefore propose different solutions.[10] In contrast to Bernanke's emphasis on market-based solutions whereby better government policies should stimulate global capital flows and trade, Summers proposed a "secular stagnation" thesis to account for economic weakness since the 2008 crisis.[11] Summers notes falling private investment, which he attributes to slow population growth and poor predicted returns on investment. The solution he proposes is the traditional Keynesian recipe of encouraging governments to invest in the economy (infrastructure for example) in order to jump-start demand.

Between them Krugman, Stiglitz and Summers have authored numerous books and media articles, vociferously criticising austerity and unbridled markets. However, if you look at their publications before 1990 they come from a background of mainstream economics and eschew the radical aspects of post-Keynesian economics, which will be discussed later.

The second group of radical economists are those who take a more

---

8:   See for example Krugman, 2012; Stiglitz 2010 and 2012.

9:   Galbraith, 2014, p238.

10: Larry Summers is a professor at Harvard, was secretary of the treasury in the Clinton administration in 1999 and a key economic advisor in the Obama administration. Ben Bernanke did two terms as chairman of the Federal Reserve, the central bank of the United States, between 2006 and 2014.

11: The thesis of "secular stagnation" is confirmed by a recent IMF Report (IMF, 2015), which argues that global growth is moderate and uneven with weak investment and lack lustre growth in total factor productivity.

eclectic position on crisis and stagnation. For example, Robert Shiller, winner of the Nobel Prize for economics in 2013 for his book *Irrational Exuberance*, places much more importance on cultural and psychological factors in explaining how markets have become inflated and bubbles have developed in the stock exchange and property market.[12] Shiller sees the interaction of capitalist triumphalism (after the "fall" of communism), the pro-market role of the media and the herd mentality of investors as lying at the heart of the crisis.

James Galbraith (who advised Yanis Varoufakis when he was Greek finance minister) argues that simply focusing on a lack of demand in the economy is too narrow a view and proposes four obstacles to stability and growth; uncertainty in energy markets and their high costs; competition from emerging economies and China in particular; radical labour saving technology and the end of the financial sector as a motor for growth.[13] In the UK Ha-Joon Chang is the leading populist radical economist. He considers himself to be an eclectic economist who dips into a range of economic theory pragmatically, but is broadly a supporter of strong government intervention in the economy.[14]

A third group, post-Keynesian economists, are more rooted in academic than policy circles and are less high-profile than Krugman, Stiglitz and Summers. However, they are important because their ideas provide the underpinnings for progressive social democratic thinking. There are three generations of post-Keynesians. Those from the Cambridge School were contemporaries of John Maynard Keynes. The most well known of them was Joan Robinson but it also included such thinkers as Michal Kalecki and Thomas Balogh.[15] They proposed a much more radical variant of Keynesianism and acknowledged insights from Marx.

The next generation of post-Keynesians broadly comprises academics such as Philip Arestis, Malcolm Sawyer and Jan Toporowski in the United Kingdom, who extended Keynes's theories to include inequality and finance.[16] In the United States Hyman Minsky emphasised the fragility and instability of capitalism.[17] More recently another generation of post-Keynesians have focused on the origins of the 2008 crisis, emphasising the interaction of inequality and financialisation.[18] All these ideas will be

---

12: Shiller, 2015.
13: Galbraith, 2014, p240.
14: Chang, 2011.
15: See Marcuzzo, 2012, for an account of the Cambridge economists.
16: Arestis, 1996; Sawyer, 1989; Toporowski, 2005.
17: Minsky, 1986.
18: For example, Stockhammer, 2015, and Keen, 2013.

explored more fully later in the article.

Therefore growing dissatisfaction with neoclassical economics and the crisis has opened the door for a resurgence of radical economics broadly based on the ideas of Keynes. Many of these ideas appear to be common sense. These economists argue that finance and banking are out of control and need to be reined in, and that austerity is not only an unfair burden on working class people, but that it is preventing the recovery of capitalism. These are not arcane debates, but rather raise fundamental questions about the role of finance and inequality and how far capitalism can be reformed or whether crisis is intrinsic to the system and therefore demands its complete abolition.

Although the focus of this article is to look at the main ideas from radical economics that have emerged since 2008, these ideas have to be set in historical context. There are two contributions that provide seminal accounts of bourgeois economics from a Marxist perspective before 2008. First, Chris Harman's article in this journal "The Crisis in Bourgeois Economics" traces the development of and criticises both neoclassical and Keynesian economics.[19] Second, Geoffrey Pilling's book *The Crisis in Keynesian Economics: A Marxist View* concentrates on the origins of Keynesianism and the role it played in the management of post-war capitalism.[20]

Bourgeois economics before Keynes

Before Keynes the ideas of the neoclassical (or marginalist) school, consolidated in the 1870s and 1880s, were dominant.[21] Economists before them had relied on Adam Smith[22] in the 18th century and David Ricardo[23] in the 19th who were interested in the big questions—what made economies grow and how what was produced should be distributed between the capitalist class and the landowners. They saw an objective measure of value as a precondition for coming to terms with these issues. The neoclassical school broke with the classical economists over what economics should be about. As Harman explains:

What mattered to them was not the creation of wealth and its distribution between classes, but rather showing that the fixing of prices through the

---

19: Harman, 1996.
20: Pilling, 1986.
21: This was associated with Carl Menger and Eugen Boehm-Bawerk (Austrian), William Jevons and Alfred Marshall (English), Léon Walras (French), Vilfredo Pareto (Italian) and John Bates Clark (American).
22: Smith, 2014 [1776].
23: Ricardo, 2004 [1851].

market, without conscious human intervention, automatically led to the most efficient way of running an economy. And so they abandoned the old view of value, with its concentration on the objective necessity of labour for production.[24]

This neoclassical school forms the basis of the microeconomics that dominates the study of the subject in schools and universities. Individuals make a subjective judgement of value in terms of how much satisfaction they get from a good or service (utility). Taking into account the cost of labour and capital, capitalists decide how much to supply at every price. Demand and supply curves are constructed and the point at which they intersect is the equilibrium—the price where the amount that consumers want to buy is exactly the same amount that capitalists are willing to supply. If "consumer choice" or the costs of production change then these curves shift and there is a new equilibrium.

Labour and employment are treated in exactly the same way as apples and oranges on a street market. If workers demand higher wages (than the equilibrium) then fewer of them will be employed and there will be unemployment. However, if they were prepared to accept lower wages then supply and demand would once again coincide and full employment would return. All that is necessary is for Say's law to operate. Say's law states that the wages and profits paid out during production are equal to the total sum required to buy the goods produced, which therefore can always be sold. In effect production is the source of demand and aggregate production necessarily creates an equal quantity of demand. For Say's law to work there should be no "artificial" interference in labour markets—such as minimum wages, welfare benefits or pressure from trade unions.

The logic of neoclassical economics is that the existing economic system is the best in the best of all possible worlds, providing the "optimal" conditions for production and laying down the rules for any situation in which "scarce resources" have to be allocated between "competing ends". For free market advocates such as Friedrich von Hayek, Ludwig von Mises and Milton Friedman[25] this was nothing less than the economic expression of democracy as consumers voted with their money through the price mechanism.[26]

This simple and crude understanding of markets is central to neoliberal thinking under the banner of consumer choice and provides the

24. Harman, 1996, pp7 8.
25: Von Mises, 1998; Von Hayek, 1944; Friedman, 2002.
26: Harman, 1996.

justification for marketisation, privatisation and for so-called "flexible" labour markets. Ideologically, neoclassical economists argue that the market is a disembodied and neutral arbiter of the wishes of consumers and producers; no account is taken of class, inequality and the power of big firms. However, far from being neutral and automatic, markets are organised, regulated and controlled by the state in the broad interests of capital.[27]

Keynes's revolutionary contribution

Keynes's *A General Theory of Employment, Interest, and Money*, published in 1936, was revolutionary in attacking the neoclassical orthodoxy of labour markets, which was used to justify wage cuts in the depression of the 1930s. He challenged Say's law, which underpinned the idea that wage-cutting was the way to restore full employment. Keynes pointed out that people might save money rather than spend or invest it, and if this was the case then firms would be left with goods that they could not sell, reducing output and paying out less in wages and profits. Keynes argued that the level of investment depended on the profits that capitalists believed that they could make. He emphasised the importance of "animal spirits", confidence and gut instincts in guiding the actions of capitalists. If future expected profits were low then investment would not take place. Cutting wages would not restore full employment because if wages were cut workers would have less money to spend. This would lead to a fall in demand in other parts of the economy where wages would fall or workers would lose their jobs. This is the "multiplier effect" working in reverse.[28] This process would lead to a downward spiral in demand which would leave the economy in an "equilibrium" with high unemployment.

Therefore Keynes was a fierce critic of the notion, popular among the ruling classes, that the free market system would ultimately solve all economic problems, including unemployment. He advocated that governments should intervene in money markets to drive down the rate of interest, encourage people to save less and firms to invest more. Governments could also undertake direct investment through running a deficit which would have a (positive) multiplier effect as extra workers would spend their wages and produce demand for the output of other workers.[29]

However, although Keynes's ideas represented a radical break from the dominant economic orthodoxy of the time, he was very far from being

---

27: For a good critique of the idea of the market see Sayer, 1995, and Chang, 2002.
28: Kahn, 1931 (Richard Kahn was one of Keynes's students).
29: Kahn, 1931.

a socialist. Keynes himself was not sympathetic to Marx and was almost completely ignorant of his work. Marxism had become very attractive to students in the early 1930s and Keynes's mission was to restore and rescue capitalism because he was worried that his students would become infected by the "dreaded and ridiculous ideas of Marxism". He told students that Marxism was "complicated hocus pocus, the only value of which was its muddleheadedness".[30] He dismissed Marxist and socialist ideas as "exalting the boorish proletariat above the bourgeoisie and the intelligentsia, who...are the quality in life and surely carry the seeds of all human advancement".[31] Keynes refused to support the Labour Party in the 1930s siding with the Liberals because Labour was "a class party and the class is not my class... The class war will find me on the side of the educated bourgeoisie".[32]

Keynesianism and the post-war boom

Influence on social democratic thinking
Although Keynes was not a socialist, he had more influence on post-war socialists than any other economist. His ideas considerably influenced some sections of the left in Britain in the 1950s and 1960s, particularly in the Labour Party and among writers such as Anthony Crosland and John Strachey (a former Marxist). As Pilling argues:

> It is easy to see what attached radical thought to Keynesianism… A trenchant defender of private property, he none the less held that the 'socialisation of investment' would make capital abundant… While private capital would continue, the claims of rentier capital would be destroyed.[33]

In the Fabian-type world that would follow the implementation of Keynesian policies the grosser inequalities of wealth would be removed by fiscal means (Keynes supported some redistribution through taxation to boost consumption). No reward would be extracted by unproductive capital (the financial sector) and employment would be preserved at a near maximum by the manipulation of state investment. Capital left unregulated might still prove crisis-prone, but given social and economic state policies

---

30: Marcuzzo, 2012, p67.
31: Mulholland, 2012, p208.
32: Moggridge, 1992, p453.
33: Pilling, 1986, p3.

any instabilities could be kept within socially and politically acceptable limits.

So-called Keynesianism dominated all teaching and the main textbooks from the 1950s to the early 1970s. It held that governments could intervene in economies, through taxation and government spending, to create sufficient demand to have full employment. Economists were technicians who tweaked and fine-tuned these macro elements in the economy—ultimately capitalism could be managed. However, as is discussed in the next section—these policies were never practised the way that Keynes advocated.

Was Keynesianism responsible for the "long boom"?

A version of the strong belief that Keynes's ideas were responsible for the long boom is accepted even by some Marxists. As Chris Harman points out:

> David Harvey presents a picture of capitalism expanding on the basis of "a class compromise between capital and labour" in which "the state could focus on full employment, economic growth and the welfare of its citizens", while "fiscal or monetary policies usually dubbed 'Keynesian' were widely deployed to dampen business cycles and to ensure reasonably full employment".[34]

Yet, as Harman argues, the most staggering fact about the period in which Keynesian ideas ruled as the official ideology was that the measures that were championed for keeping crisis at bay were not actually deployed.[35] Rather than bosses signing up to Keynesian policies of raising wages and welfare provision in practise they "[never] failed to fight tooth and claw to limit the degree to which wages kept up with the cost of living or with productivity".[36] It was the high rate of profit in the post-war period that explained why capitalists kept investing on a large scale. In the US, massive levels of military expenditure compared with the pre-war years was responsible for the fiscal stimulus. Further, during the Second World War much capital had been written off, which according to Harman, was equal to one-fifth of the pre-existing accumulated surplus value; in the defeated states of Japan and Germany the figure was much higher.[37] However, arms

---

34: Harman, 2009, p163.
35: Harman, 2009, p163.
36: Harman, 2009, p165.
37: Harman, 2009, p168.

expenditure was not a stimulus in the Keynesian sense. As Harman points out the starting point for examining the impact of waste expenditure on arms by Michael Kidron (who referred to a permanent arms economy), was not an underconsumptionist explanation of crises.[38] Rather, in the long term the arms economy had the effect of reducing the funds available for further accumulation and therefore slowing down the rise in the ratio of investment in technology to the employed labour force (the "organic composition of capital") and therefore slowing down the tendency for the rate of profit to fall (this is discussed more fully in a later section).[39]

The end of the Keynesian consensus and the rise of neoliberalism

In 1976 what had supposedly been the tried and tested way of managing capitalism, by Labour and Conservative governments alike, no longer worked. The emergence of stagflation—that is both rising unemployment and inflation—sounded the death knell of Keynesianism as the dominant ideology espoused by governments of the left and the right. The space was open for economists who saw the market as the solution.

Although the end of Keynesian economics is often associated with Margaret Thatcher, it was James Callaghan, then Labour Prime Minister, that signalled its demise in a much quoted speech from the 1976 Labour Party conference:

> We used to think that you could spend your way out of a recession and increase employment by cutting taxes and boosting government spending. I tell you in all candour that that option no longer exists, and that in so far as it ever did exist, it only worked on each occasion since the war by injecting a bigger dose of inflation into the economy, followed by a higher level of employment as the next step.[40]

The interlinking of monetarism (cutting the money supply to reduce inflation) and more market-driven policies such as privatisation and "flexible" labour markets were then systematically and enthusiastically pursued by Thatcher after 1979. The lineage of these ideas lay in the neo-classical and Austrian schools of economics and the work of Friedrich von Hayek and Ludwig von Mises in particular. Basing their ideas on extreme

---

38: Kidron, 1965.
39: Harman, 2009, pp168-169.
40: Go to www.britishpoliticalspeech.org/speech-archive.htm?speech=174. Also quoted in Harman, 1996, p33 and Pilling, 1986, p7.

individualism they were fierce critics of Keynes and Keynesianism. Milton Friedman made an even more significant attack arguing that anything beyond minimum state intervention distorted market signals. According to him, the market is fundamentally sound and only malfunctions if there are disturbances in the monetary sphere. This heavily influenced Thatcher in adopting monetarism at the end of the 1970s, which helped push interest rates to historically high levels, compounding the lack of competitiveness of British manufacturing and contributing to its contraction.

Radical economics from 1945 to 2008

A number of economists, most notably Joan Robinson from Cambridge University, argued that the Keynesianism that emerged in the post-war period was not the real thing and scathingly termed it "bastard Keynesianism". Her view was that what were passed off as Keynesian techniques were used to keep the capitalist system going after the war and obscured the revolutionary character of the real Keynesianism. She described it as "married to a discredited and ideologically bankrupt neo-classical economics and was thereby transformed into a new form of apologetics".[41]

Similarly the American economist Hyman Minsky said of the *The General Theory* that:

> The work contains the seeds for a deep intellectual revolution in economics and in the economist's view of society. However, these seeds never fulfilled their full fruition. The embryonic scientific revolution was aborted as the ideas were interpreted and analysed by academics and then applied by these same academics as a guide to public policy.[42]

Robinson and Minsky and other post-Keynesians were critical of the idea that appeared in the textbooks of the time that likened the economy to a machine governed by a series of laws, the relationship between which is highly stable, in principle knowable and therefore in principle predictable from previous experience. If one economy-wide flow fails to occur at an appropriate rate (consumer spending for example), the deficiency can be repaired by government intervention and regulation of those flows over which it does have control—the levels of taxation and public spending. There are known, stable relationships between government spending and

41: Pilling, 1986, p12.
42: Minsky quoted in Pilling, 1986.

income (and by extension employment); by appropriate manipulation of such flows the volume of employment may be adjusted in line with policy objectives.

Thomas Balogh called this "hydraulic Keynesianism":[43]

> A new theoretical edifice was erected which could be reconnected to the neoclassical theory of harmony and just shares in the distribution of income. The old optimism about this being the best (and just) world was reasserted. The classical automatism of the market economy, maintaining full employment and ensuring optimal allocation of resources was just replaced by the *deus ex machine* consisting of the treasury and the central bank... The new self-consistent and determinate system was completed by the idea that politicians could choose at their discretion the level of unemployment—from a menu served up by econometricians—and that this level would be an expression of the will of the community and depend on how much inflation they were prepared to tolerate.[44]

These criticisms reflected the views of post-Keynesians, who object to the orthodox textbook interpretation of *The General Theory*. However, Keynes had opened himself up to the textbook interpretation by basing his work on a version of marginalism (neoclassical economics), rather than the value theory of Ricardo and Marx. Joan Robinson argued that Keynesian economics (properly interpreted) belongs to the classical tradition of Adam Smith and Ricardo because of its concern with aggregates such as demand and employment, rather than the narrow neoclassical concerns with individual choice and markets.

Post-Keynesianism has developed as a significant and progressive strand in current bourgeois economics.[45] From the 1970s onwards the tradition of first wave post-Keynesians (who were his contemporaries) was continued and developed by a second wave. Both generations have been much less dismissive of Marx and have drawn on and integrated some of his ideas. Despite internal divisions and different perspectives, they were united

---

43: Thomas Balogh was a Professor at Oxford University, President of the Fabian Society in 1970 and an advisor to Labour governments in 1964 and 1974. See Balogh, 1982, for a critique of conventional economics.

44: Balogh quoted in Pilling, 1986, p13.

45: This tradition has a dedicated publication. The *Journal of Post-Keynesian Economics* and the *Cambridge Journal of Economics* also reflects this school of thought. A useful map of post-Keynesian scholars and their perspective can be found at https://en.wikipedia.org/wiki/Post-Keynesian_economics

by seeing themselves as promoting a radical tradition within economics in relating economic analysis to real economic problems. The ideas which are classified as post-Keynesian have a long history and post-Keynesian economics reflects the classical tradition and Marx as much as it does Keynes and Kalecki.[46]

The main tenets of post-Keynesianism are; first, that the default position of the economy is not one of equilibrium, rather that economies are dynamic and therefore always in a state of flux or disequilibrium. Second, neoclassical economics is dominated by the idea of "rational man" who is predictable and immune from history and socialisation. For post-Keynesians the formation of decisions under uncertainty is a crucial aspect of reality as well as how economic behaviour is influenced by institutions and social structures. Third, they are critical of neoclassical analyses of markets and argue that the law of demand does not even apply at the level of a single market and therefore a macroeconomic economic picture cannot be built upward from microeconomics. Fourth, while neoclassical economists assume that money is neutral, post-Keynesians argue money and debt matter and can lead to changes in employment. Fifth, the role of the failure of demand, with investment demand as the driving force, is seen as a primary source of crisis and stagnation. Therefore the government should intervene during a recession to ensure that there is spending.[47]

Further, Arestis argues that post-Keynesianism has a radical spin because:

> Its point of departure is a distinction between social classes rather than the neoclassical classless and atomistic base. Social relations are thus essential to the analysis and the tradition is broadly Marxist in that it adapts his reproduction scheme to tackle the realisation problems.[48]

But although there is a recognition of class and a commitment to social justice, the major flaw in post-Keynesian thinking is that the state is seen as neutral with the potential to be harnessed and to deliver reforms that are more widely in the interests of working class people. Labour and capital are not intrinsically antagonistic with distinct interests, rather they can be reconciled and work in the interests of the common good.

46: Arestis, 1996, 112.
47: See Keen, 2013 for an extensive discussion of these points.
48: Arestis, 1996, p113.

Radical economics after the 2008 crisis

The crisis of 2008 led to renewed and more vociferous criticisms of the neoclassical economics that underpinned neoliberalism. Economists such as Krugman and Stiglitz were elevated to the role of trenchant critics of the US government's role in causing the crisis and perpetuating the austerity that followed (although it is worth noting that some right wing economists took the view that the crisis was caused by markets not being free enough).

This section outlines the arguments of radical economists, from the post-Keynesian perspective and also from the perspective of those Marxists who reject or sideline the notion of the falling rate of profit. Although it is difficult to draw hard and fast lines between the different elements of their arguments, for convenience I focus on three strands of thinking that have dominated radical economics and importantly influenced progressive thinking and anti-austerity organisations such as the People's Assembly against Austerity. First, there has been a focus on financialisation—not surprising since many have seen the crisis as being caused by the deregulation of finance and the proliferation of financial instruments. Second, the gross and increasingly evident presence of inequality has received much attention both in terms of it being "bad" for capitalism and as the underlying cause of the crisis. Third, both the post-Keynesian school and some Marxists have put forward a synthesis, which sees the crisis as the outcome of the interrelationship between inequality *and* financialisation.

Financialisation

The notion of financialisation as the cause of the crisis has been proposed by post-Keynesians and some Marxist economists and some who do not fall into either camp.

The term financialisation is used to summarise a broad set of changes in the relation between the financial and the real sectors of the economy. Financialisation encompasses diverse phenomena such as shareholder value (discussed later in this section), increasing household debt, increasing income from financial activity, an increase in the mobility of capital, the importance of an array of new financial instruments such as derivatives and securitisation. More generally it refers to the way in which working class people have been increasingly drawn in to the financial sector through mortgages, loans and pensions. In the words of Costas Lapavitsas: "The term reflects the ascendancy of the financial sector. Even more important, it conveys the penetration of the financial system into every nook and cranny of society, including housing, education, health and other areas of life that were previously relatively immune".[49]

These developments have been hailed by some as a new stage of capitalism—"financialised capitalism" or a "finance dominated accumulation regime"—that is qualitatively different from what has gone before.[50]

There is nothing new about these ideas; theoretically they have some continuity with those of Rudolf Hilferding, who saw a new stage of capitalism at the beginning of the 20th century, characterised by complex financial relationships and the domination of industry by finance.[51] Keynes also emphasised the role of "whirlwinds of optimism and pessimism" in terms of the way that capitalists valued firms. He warned that: "The position is serious when enterprise becomes a bubble on a whirlpool of speculation. When the capital development of a country becomes a by-product of the activities of the casino, the job is likely to be ill-done".[52]

Minsky emphasised the instability and fragility of the system and the growth of money-managed capitalism.[53] He argued that financial crises are endemic to capitalism because periods of economic prosperity encourage borrowers and lenders to become progressively more reckless. This excess optimism creates financial bubbles which sooner or later burst. The "Minsky moment" refers to the point where the financial system moves from stability to instability when lending and debt levels have built up to unsustainable levels. At this point over-indebted borrowers start to sell off their assets to meet other repayments, which in turn causes a fall in asset prices and loss of confidence. It can cause financial institutions to "dry up" and become illiquid because they cannot meet the demand for cash and may cause a run on the banks as people seek to withdraw their money. Post-Keynesians have referred to the 2007-8 crisis as a Minsky moment.[54]

Some contemporary accounts of financialisation emphasise the rise of "shareholder value"—ie prioritising share prices and dividends, which was enabled by the growth of big institutional investors in the 1970s and by private equity firms (especially before 2008). In addition, the huge increase in the remuneration of CEOs (chief executive officers) is partly comprised of blocks of shares, which ties their bloated salaries to the performance of the firm. The massive growth in corporate bonds since 2009 also gives bosses the incentive to focus on the short-term performance of their

49: Lapavitsas, 2013a.
50: Stockhammer, 2015; Lapavitsas, 2013b.
51: Hilferding, 1981; see Choonara, 2014.
52: Keynes, 1936, p164 quoted in Wray, 2009, p159.
53: Minsky, 1986.
54: Wray, 2009.

firms. According to this argument firms have become more predatory in "Anglo-Saxon" less regulated capitalist countries such as the United States and Britain. Rather than retaining and reinvesting profits (long-term) under a more benevolent capitalism it results in downsizing and asset stripping of firms (short-term) to maximise the returns to shareholders.

There is also an emphasis on the growth and plethora of new financial instruments such as derivatives and securitisation. Derivatives are financial instruments whose value derives from some underlying asset such as interest rates and exchange rates. From the 1980s and 1990s there has been a huge growth in securitisation—that is when an asset such as a mortgage is turned into something that can be traded on financial markets. It was the securitisation of toxic sub-prime mortgages that were then sliced, diced and sold on that triggered the 2007-8 financial crisis. All of this was made possible by a series of measures to deregulate the financial sector and to liberalise international flows of capital.

The policy prescriptions that flow from this are summarised by James Crotty:

> To force financial markets to play a more limited but more productive and less dangerous role in the economy, we need a combination of aggressive financial regulation coordinated across national markets as well as nationalisation of financial institutions where appropriate... For such a transition to be effective, two difficult tasks must be accomplished. Efficient financial theory must be replaced as the guide to policy making by the more realistic theories associated with Keynes and Minsky, and domination of financial policy making by the Lords of Finance must end.[55]

However, beyond theoretical criticisms about the role of finance, which are dealt with in the next section, Marxist economist Andrew Kliman points to problems with the notion that regulation can prevent financial crisis.[56] First, regulations are always fighting the "last war" and the source of the next crisis is unlikely to be the same as the last one. For example, since the 2008 crisis there has been an explosion in the purchase of corporate bonds. This has been fuelled by demand from Brazil, Russia and China and expansionary monetary policies in the core economies (such as quantitative easing). However, as the former countries are experiencing a slowdown and credit is less expansionary

---

55: Crotty, 2009, p577.
56: Kliman, 2011.

in the latter these assets are now being flagged as a new source of instability.[57]

Second, banks and the financial system have always been adept at getting round regulations—in the 1970s when lending was restricted shadow banking developed as a way of circumventing the system. Shadow banks are non-bank institutions (intermediaries) that provide similar services to traditional investment banks, but do not face the same regulation. For example, they are not required to keep particular ratios between lending and deposits. In this way they traded much more risky assets and transactions. A headline study of shadow banking by the International Monetary Fund defined their key functions as securitisation and collateral intermediation (to reduce the risks of the parties). In the US before the crisis the shadow banking system overtook the regular banking system in supplying loans to various borrowers (business, home and car buyers, students).

But it is important not to see shadow banking as completely separate from mainstream banking. It was common practice for "regular" banks to conduct more risky transactions in ways that did not show up on their balance sheets through Special Purpose Vehicles (SPVs). Preceding the last crisis banks created SPVs specifically with the intention of undertaking risky investments, which then contaminated the whole system. By moving assets off their balance sheets banks could escape reserve and capital requirements, as well as regulation and oversight, and could sell assets to investors who wanted a higher yield than could be earned on traditional investment.

The volume of transactions in shadow banking grew dramatically after 2000, was checked by the 2008 crisis and then continued to grow. In 2007 the value of transactions was estimated to be $50 trillion. This fell to $47 trillion in 2008 and subsequently increased to $67 trillion by 2012. This reflects the continued lack of control of this sector.[58]

Third, some on the left have called for the nationalisation of banks. This may be a political demand that we raise under particular circumstances, but it is not a solution to preventing crises from reoccurring. A state-run bank is still embedded in the global capitalist system. It has to get money in before it can lend it out, and therefore has to provide a rate of return to attract people to deposit with them and therefore it cannot be driven by what would be good for workers or the "public good". That is why, for example, institutions that promise "ethical" investments offer much lower rates of return. There is no escaping from the logic of the system. As Marx put it in the *Grundrisse*, "competition executes the inner laws; makes them compulsory laws toward

57: *Economist*, 2014.
58: Moshinsky and Brunsden, 2012.

the individual capital".[59] However benevolent their intentions, putting different people in control of banks cannot undo the inner laws of capitalism.

Underconsumption and inequality

Arguments focussing on underconsumption and those stressing inequality as a cause of financial crises are different takes on the same underlying argument—that is that a lack of collective spending power (aggregate demand) lies at the heart of explaining the stagnation of economies.

Pilling points out that those Marxists who did continue their work in political economy after the Second World War were influenced by the prevailing Keynesian wisdom.[60] This led to a reading of Marx's *Capital* through the prism of one variant or other of underconsumption. One of the most famous works was *Monopoly Capital* by Paul Baran and Paul Sweezy, which appeared in the mid-1960s.[61] This saw capitalism's problem not as the inability of the system to generate surplus value, but rather its creation of excess surplus. Their argument was that there had been a shift from a competitive to a monopoly economy dominated by giant corporations. By effectively banning price competition, these firms were able to drive up the economic surplus, which could not be absorbed by consumption. The result was economic stagnation.

Piketty's argument contributes more indirectly to underconsumptionist theories. His book provides forensic detail and exhaustive statistical evidence of social inequality over the last two centuries in a variety of countries. His basic thesis is that the central crisis for capitalism is a distributional one as the net rate of return on capital outstrips the growth of net national income. The principal destabilising force in his analysis and the central contradiction of capitalism is that the private return on capital (r), can be significantly higher for long periods of time than the rate of growth of income and output (g). If the rate of return on private capital is greater than the growth of income and output then this implies that wealth accumulated in the past grew more rapidly than output and wages:[62]

This inequality expresses a fundamental logical contradiction. The entrepreneur inevitably tends to become a rentier, more and more dominant

---

59: Marx, 1973, p752, quoted in Kliman, 2011, p196.
60: Pilling, 1986.
61: Baran and Sweezy, 1966.
62: See Kunkel, 2014 and Tengely-Evans, 2014 for critiques of Piketty.

over those that own nothing but their labour. Once constituted, capital reproduces itself faster than output increases. The past devours the future.[63]

The link between inequality and underconsumption is that as inequality grows and income becomes more polarised, people on lower incomes and/or the growing numbers of the poor have less money to spend and therefore overall demand in the economy is reduced. The way that a lack of effective demand is cited as the critical cause of stagnation in the post-Keynesianism view is explicit in the solution proposed by Philip Arestis:

> The major objective is to complete the unfinished Keynesian revolution, to generalise *The General Theory*… The principle of effective demand is the backbone of its analysis as it was in Keynes's *General Theory* (1936). Effective demand in post-Keynesian analysis implies that it is scarcity of demand rather than scarcity of resources that is to be confronted in modern economics.[64]

A synthesis of inequality and financialisation in explaining the crisis

While the previous two schools of thought privilege either financialisation or underconsumption as the root cause of capitalist crisis and stagnation, recent explanations from both post-Keynesians and some Marxists provide a synthesis of these two elements.

From the post-Keynesian perspective there is a link between the financialisation school and the notion that rising inequality should be regarded as the root cause of crisis.[65] This finds its clearest expression in the work of Englebert Stockhammer who argues that the crisis should be understood as a result of the interaction of financialisation with the effects of rising inequality. There are four major ways in which he argues that financialisation and inequality are linked.[66]

First, he argues that rising inequality creates a downward pressure on demand in an economy—especially as poor people spend a higher proportion of their income. Second, he argues that international financial deregulation has allowed countries to run large deficits (or surpluses) on their balance of payments current accounts and on government spending. Simply put, if their goods are less competitive in comparison with those of other countries,

---

63: Piketty, 2014, p571.
64: Arestis, 1996, p115.
65: Stockhammer, 2015.
66: Stockhammer, 2015.

imports will be higher than exports and they will be in deficit. Because it is much easier to borrow in international markets this means that they can carry this "overdraft" (although not indefinitely as we have seen with Greece and Spain for example) and has led to a debt-led model (Greece, Portugal, Spain and Ireland) and an export-led model (Germany). Third, in debt-led economies higher inequality has led to higher household debt as working class families try and keep up with social consumption norms or even to access necessities and maintain their standard of living in the face of stagnating or falling wages. Fourth, rising inequality has increased the propensity to speculate as richer households hold riskier financial assets. The rise of hedge funds and subprime derivatives in particular has been linked to the super-rich.

Some Marxists link inequality and financialisation with a different story. They argue that the rate of profit fell from the start of the post-Second World War boom through the downturns of the 1970s and 1980s. By that time economic policy had become neoliberal and this led to the increased exploitation of workers. US workers (and workers in general) faced stagnating or falling real incomes and their share of total income has fallen. Therefore the increase in exploitation led to a significant rebound in the rate of profit.[67]

Writers from the *Monthly Review* are proponents of underconsumption as an explanation of crisis and have fused financialisation with underconsumptionism in their interpretation of 2007-8 and since.[68] According to them the "new financialised capitalist regime" was unable to sustain economic advance for any length of time and a key element in explaining the whole dynamic is to be found in the falling ratio of wages and salaries as a percentage of national income.

Other Marxists, generally sympathetic to the theory of the falling rate of profit, nevertheless do not think that the current crisis is a crisis of profitability. This is reflected for example in the account of Gérard Duménil and Dominique Lévy who argue that while the crises of the 1890s and 1970s can be explained by the declining rate of profit, the Great Depression and the current crisis came out of a period of rising profitability.

In general these Marxist accounts blame financialisation for the failure of the rate of accumulation to rise in line with the recovery of profits. It is argued that financialisation (another component of neoliberalism) has meant that firms have invested an increasing share of their profits in speculation and financial instruments rather than in productive capital

---

67. See McNally, 2011, Choonara, 2009a, and the debate between David McNally and Joseph Choonara (McNally, 2012; Choonara, 2012).
68: Foster and McChesney, 2012.

assets and that this has been the root cause of weaker growth in the past three decades. However, Andrew Kliman and Shannon Williams demonstrate that there has been no diversion of profit from production to financial markets under neoliberalism.[69] They present data that shows that the share of profit that was productively invested was actually slightly higher during the first two decades of neoliberalism than during the prior three decades:

> Our analysis demonstrates that, in the era of "neoliberalism" and "financialisation", corporate profit has become less important and borrowing has become more important as a source for funds for financial expenditures. Additionally, we find that higher dividend payments do not lead to a statistically significant decline in productive investment, and that corporations' access to and use of borrowed funds accounts for the absence of a tradeoff between paying dividends and investing in production.[70]

These data undercut the financialisation argument that profit is being diverted to the financial sector at the expense of the real goods sector.

Marx's economics

Post-Keynesians and some Marxists have usefully and painstakingly set out the changes that have taken place in capitalism over the past three decades with regard to inequality and financialisation. However, acknowledging these developments is not the same as attributing the *cause* of the crisis of 2007 to these changes. As Joseph Choonara points out, there is a very clear dividing line between those economists who put the falling rate of profit at the centre of their analysis and those that either dispute or sideline it.[71] This section builds an alternative to radical economics (and some Marxist accounts) by reasserting the falling rate of profit in Marx's analysis of the capitalist system. This underpins an understanding of the role of credit and finance in crisis, capital and value and enables a critique of the underconsumption debate.

Marx and the falling rate of profit

The tendency of the rate of profit to fall (TRPF) is one of the most contentious and contested elements of Marx's work. It is rejected or ignored completely by contemporary non-Marxist economists, but even Marxist economists who accept Marx's theory of value and many other aspects of

---

69: Kliman and Williams, 2014, p2.
70: Kliman and Williams, 2014, p2.
71: Choonara, 2009a.

his theory are dismissive of it. These debates have been very well rehearsed elsewhere and therefore the argument is only briefly restated here.[72]

The argument for the falling rate of profit is as follows. Each capitalist tries to increase their own competitiveness through increasing the productivity of workers. The way to do this is to increase the "means of production"—for example investment in machinery, robots and computers. Marx called this change in the relationship between the means of production and the labour power using it the "technical composition of capital". This expansion in the ratio of investment to workforce is reflected in the value of the means of production rising compared with wages—what Marx referred to as an increase in "organic composition of capital", that is the relationship between the means of production and labour power translated into value terms. However, the only source of value and surplus value for the system as a whole is labour. Therefore, if investment grows faster than the labour force, it must also grow more rapidly than the creation of new value, from which profit comes. Therefore there will be downward pressure on the rate of profit.

There are implications for the capitalist class collectively. The reason for the growth of investment is competition between capitalists as they push for greater productivity in order to stay ahead of competitors. But, however much competition may compel the individual capitalist to take part in this process in order to make short-term gains, from the point of view of the capitalist class as a whole it leads to a tendency for the rate of profit to fall.

Alex Callinicos quotes Ben Fine and Lawrence Harris to argue how Marx identifies counter-tendencies to the TRPF (the tendency of the rate of profit to fall) at a high level of abstraction:

> As Marx puts it "the same influences which produce a tendency in the general rate of profit to fall *also* call forth counter-effects" (emphasis added). In the light of this we think that the name "law of the TRPF" is something of a misnomer. The law in its broad definition is in fact "the law of the tendency of the rate of profit to fall and its counteracting influences".[73]

Translated into more concrete terms one of the most important strategies that a capitalist might use to counteract the falling rate of profit is increasing the rate of exploitation—in other words cutting wages or increasing the intensity of work (although there are limits to this).

72: See Harman, 2009; Choonara, 2009b; Carchedi, 2011; Roberts, 2009; Kliman, 2011.
73: Quoted in Callinicos, 2014, pp268-269.

Marx, credit and finance

Theories and research that analyse the significant changes in finance in contemporary capitalism are very valuable. In this context the contributions of Costas Lapavitsas, Gérard Duménil, Dominique Lévy and Jan Toporowski are helpful and important.[74] However, there are two problems with the financialisation account. First finance and credit are viewed as the direct causes of the 2008 crisis and as such seen as providing an alternative explanation of the crisis. Second, and related, finance is seen as an autonomous driver that is external to capitalism rather than an integral part of it. In Marx's scheme finance is not a direct cause of crisis, but it is a key intermediary between falling profitability and economic crisis. Kliman quotes the following passage from Marx:

> If the credit system appears as the principal lever of overproduction and excessive speculation in commerce, this is simply because the reproduction process, which is elastic by nature, is now forced [once the credit system has developed] to its extreme limits; and this is because a great part of the social capital is applied by those who are not its owners, and who therefore proceed quite unlike owners who, when they function themselves, anxiously weigh the limits of their private capital.[75]

This passage points to finance as a driver of overaccumulation—in other words it enables capitalists to grow more rapidly than otherwise. In the process of competition production can be expanded and investment in the means of production accelerated. The reference to "anxiously weigh" refers to the increase in risky investment behaviour when the person making the decisions will not suffer the losses—in that they are not gambling with their own money—what economists refer to as "moral hazard". This is taken to extremes by some city traders who have lost eye-watering amounts of the money of the capitalists who employ them to gamble it on their behalf.

Marx argued that a decline in the rate of profit leads to a crisis indirectly by encouraging speculation and over-production:

> If the rate of profit falls...we have swindling and general promotion of swindling, through desperate attempts in the way of new production methods, new capital investment and new adventures, to secure some kind

---

74: Lapavitsas, 2009; Duménil, and Lévy, 2013; Toporowski, 2010.
75: Marx, 1991, p572, quoted in Kliman, 2011, p19.

of extra profit, which will be independent of the general average [profit determined by the average rate of profit] and superior to it.[76]

When debts finally cannot be repaid a crisis erupts and then that crisis leads to stagnation:

The chain of payment obligations at specific dates is broken in a hundred places, and this is still further intensified by an accompanying breakdown of the credit system, which had developed alongside capital. All of this therefore leads to a violent and acute crisis, sudden forcible devaluations, an actual stagnation and disruption in the reproduction process, and hence to an actual decline in reproduction.[77]

This has a very familiar ring and could easily be a description of the 2007-8 crisis.

Therefore, as Kliman points out, Marx's theory implies that a fall in the rate of profit leads to crisis only indirectly and with a time lag.[78] The fall in profits leads to increased speculation and the increase in debt that cannot be repaid is the immediate cause of the crisis. The implications of this are that the recent crisis is not reducible to finance, rather phenomena specific to the financial sector (excessive leverage, risky mortgage lending and the lack of transparency in balance sheets) were the trigger. Financialisation therefore concentrates on the proximate causes of the crisis rather than the longer-term underlying weaknesses in the capitalist system that enabled the financial sector to trigger an especially deep and long recession with persistent after-effects.

Lack of profitability or lack of demand?
As we have seen the underconsumptionist view is that economic crises, recessions and stagnation are caused by a lack of spending as a result of workers being paid too little to buy what is produced—this may result from a polarisation of income and inequality.[79]

The logic of Keynesian interventionism in stimulating demand is that greater consumption causes greater production of goods, greater employment and growth. But capitalism prospers, not if production rises,

---

76: Marx, 1991, p367, quoted in Kliman, 2011, p21.
77: Marx, 1991, p363, quoted in Kliman, 2011, p21.
78: Kliman, 2011.
79: See Kliman, 2011, for a detailed empirical refutation of the underconsumptionist argument in relation to the 2008 crisis and Carchedi, 2011, for a summary of the theoretical objections.

but if profitability rises. Production only increases if profitability rises *and* if there is demand for the extra output—that is if surplus value can be both produced and realised. For Keynesians, profitability is not the essential determinant of production. They see profitability as a consequence of greater demand-induced production; in the Marxist approach higher production is a consequence of higher profitability. In the Keynesian view the demand for consumer goods sets a rigid limit to investment demand, therefore total demand is held down by the restricted growth of consumption demand. A chronic structural tendency therefore exists for aggregate supply to exceed aggregate demand. This leads to a crisis of overproduction.

Writing in 1958 Raya Dunayevskaya explains how underconsumptionists wrongly invert the order of causation:

> The crisis…is not caused by a shortage of "effective demand". On the contrary, it is the crisis that causes a shortage of "effective demand". A crisis occurs not because there has been a scarcity of markets. As we saw in theory, and as 1929 showed in practice, the market is largest just before the crisis. *From the capitalist point of view*, however, there is occurring an unsatisfactory distribution of "income" between the recipients of wages and those of surplus value or profits. The capitalist decreases his investments and the resulting *stagnation* of production *appears* as overproduction. Of course, there is a contradiction between production and consumption. Of course there is [an] "inability to sell". But the inability to sell manifests itself as such *because of the antecedent decline in the rate of profit which has nothing whatever to do with the inability to sell.*[80]

Marx does not dispute the tendency towards underconsumption, but shows that it is not an insurmountable obstacle to the expansion of production. What actually drives productive investment is profitability—past profits fund investment spending and expectations of future profitability provide the incentive.

The anarchic nature of capitalism means that a tendency to overproduction is intrinsic to the system. Individual capitalists expand production, but without knowing what other capitalists are doing. This leads to a fall (in the case of some goods, a collapse) of prices and profitability and weaker capitals going out of business. Overproduction, therefore, has different causes and is not the same as underconsumption.

80: Dunayevskaya, 2000, pp142-143.

Capital, exploitation and accumulation

A critical difference between radical economists and classical Marxism is in the treatment of capital. For Piketty capital is defined as

> the sum total of nonhuman assets that can be owned and exchanged on some market. Capital includes all forms of real property (including residential real estate) as well as financial and professional capital (plants, infrastructure, machinery, patents and so on) used by firms and government agencies.[81]

In effect, for Piketty, capital and wealth (mainly personal wealth) are the same. The post-Keynesian school is influenced by and sympathetic to Marx, and Malcolm Sawyer defines capital as a "shorthand for the owners of the means of production (and their representatives) under the specific condition of capitalism".[82] This leads him to argue, in contrast to the mainstream economists, that there is an intrinsic conflict between the owners of capital and labour. However, post-Keynesians treat capital as an autonomous force. For Joan Robinson capital is equated with "efficient machinery" and the "application of science to industry",[83] while for Malcolm Sawyer "the pace and form of change are largely determined by capital".[84]

As Callinicos argues, this "abstract[s] labour from its relationship with capital, and thereby transform[s] capital into an external force".[85] This is very different from Marx's definition of capital which sees it as a social relation specific to the capitalist mode of production. It is self-expanding value, which comes from the exertion of labour and is realised on a market. It is measured in labour time (and in its monetary expression).

As Tomáš Tengely-Evans points out, Marx writes in the third volume of *Capital*:

> The relation between capital and wage labour determines the whole character of the mode of production...the capitalist and the wage labourer are, as such, embodiments of and personification of capital and wage labour—specific social characteristics that the social process stamps on individuals, products of these specific social relations of production.[86]

81: Piketty, 2014.
82: Sawyer, 1989, p50.
83: Quoted in Pilling, 1986, p16.
84: Sawyer, 1989, p51.
85: Callinicos, 2014, p211.
86: See Tengely-Evans, 2014, p182.

Capital is value accumulated through the exploitation of workers' labour and then set in motion to expand further exploitation. Therefore Marx's definition of capital provides a link to the production process, as opposed to assuming that wealth acts as capital. Whereas Piketty starts with inequality—Marx starts with exploitation and accumulation.

For Marx, capital only exists within the process of economic exchange. Capital is a flow or circuit through which money and commodities move in order to produce value. This circuit is the primary source of value creation in a capitalist society. Studying this circuit allows us to understand how value is produced and distributed throughout our economy.

Benjamin Kunkel spells out the political implications of understanding capital and value in this way:

> If, on the other hand, capital aka the means of production, owes its value to past labour on a natural world that bears no title deed...then all income by rights belongs, one way or another, to labourers or producers... To argue that value derives from labour is ultimately to consider the successive labours that make up history; conflict and change emerge as the essence of economics as they are of history. To focus instead on the instantaneous balance of one person's wish to sell with another's wish to buy is to abstract a moment of harmony from the ongoing clangour and flux.[87]

The logic of the post-Keynesian view that sees capital as autonomous and as a source of the creation of value, justifies policies that enhance capital and ultimately defends capitalism. The argument that capital is a social relation and that labour is the only source of value leads to the political conclusion that workers should reclaim what is theirs in a process of struggle.

Conclusion
Any theories that trace crises to low productivity, sluggish demand, the anarchy of the market, state intervention, high wages, low wages and so on, suggest that capitalism's crisis tendencies can in principle be substantially lessened or eliminated by fixing the specific problem that is making the system perform poorly. But the tendency for the rate of profit to fall suggests that economic crises are inevitable under capitalism because they are not caused by factors that are external to it—that is, factors that can be eliminated while keeping the system intact. As Marx put it: "the violent

---

87: Kunkel, 2014.

destruction of capital" will not come about "by relations external to it, but rather as a condition of its self-preservation".[88]

Some of these ideas may seem either arcane or difficult or both. But the political implications of these debates are profound. If the long-term cause of the crisis is irreducibly financial then recurrent crises can be prevented by doing away with neoliberalism and "financialised capitalism". It is no longer necessary to "do away with the capitalist system of production—that is, production driven by the aim of ceaselessly expanding value, or abstract wealth".[89] This puts on the agenda, instead of changing the socioeconomic nature of the system itself, the need for financial regulation, fiscal and monetary policies to stimulate the economy and nationalisation of parts of the financial system. Of course, we support these demands as a challenge to capitalism and the state—their success as a result of struggle would increase the confidence and combativeness of workers. But at the same time we need to defend the core ideas of Marx from those that have reinterpreted his ideas to project a view of the world in which capitalism can be reformed. If a persistent fall in the rate of profit is an important (if indirect) cause of crisis and recession then these proposals are not solutions; at best they will delay the next crisis. Any artificial stimulus that produces unsustainable growth threatens to make the next crisis deeper and more protracted. To eliminate crises it is therefore necessary to do away with the capitalist system of production.

References

Arestis, Philip, 1996, "Post-Keynesian Economics: Towards Coherence", *Cambridge Journal of Economics*, volume 20, issue 1.

Balogh, Thomas, 1982, *The Irrelevance of Conventional Economics* (Liveright).

Baran, Paul A, and Sweezy, Paul M, 1966, *Monopoly Capital: An Essay on the American Economic and Social Order* (Monthly Review Press).

Callinicos, Alex, 2014, *Deciphering Capital: Marx's Capital and Its Destiny* (Bookmarks).

Carchedi, Guglielmo, 2011, "Behind and Beyond the Crisis", *International Socialism* 132 (autumn), http://isj.org.uk/behind-and-beyond-the-crisis

Chang, Ha-Joon, 2002, "Breaking the Mould: An Institutionalist Political Economy Alternative to the Neo-Liberal Theory of the Market and the State", *Cambridge Journal of Economics*, volume 26, number 5.

Chang, Ha-Joon, 2011, *23 Things They Don't Tell You About Capitalism* (Penguin).

88: Marx, 1973, pp749-750, quoted in Kliman, 2011, p26.
89: Kliman, 2011.

Choonara, Joseph, 2009a, "Marxist Accounts of the Current Crisis", *International Socialism 123* (summer), http://isj.org.uk/marxist-accounts-of-the-current-crisis

Choonara, Joseph, 2009b, *Unravelling Capitalism: A Guide to Marxist Political Economy* (Bookmarks).

Choonara, Joseph, 2012, "A reply to David McNally", *International Socialism 135* (summer), http://isj.org.uk/a-reply-to-david-mcnally

Choonara, Joseph, 2014, "Financial Times", *International Socialism 142* (spring), http://isj.org.uk/financial-times

Crotty, James, 2009, "Structural Causes of the Global Financial Crisis: A Critical Assessment of the 'New Financial Architecture'", *Cambridge Journal of Economics*, volume 33, number 4.

Duménil, Gérard and Dominique Lévy, 2013, *The Crisis of Neoliberalism* (Harvard University Press).

Dunayevskaya, Raya, 2000 [1958], *Marxism and Freedom: From 1776 until Today* (Humanity Books).

Economist, 2014, "It's Back: Once a Cause of the Financial World's Problems, Securitisation is now Part of the Solution" (11 January), www.economist.com/news/leaders/21593457-once-cause-financial-worlds-problems-securitisation-now-part-solution-its

Foster, John Bellamy, and Robert McChesney, 2012, *The Endless Crisis: How Monopoly Finance Produces Stagnation and Upheaval from the USA to China* (Monthly Review Press).

Friedman, Milton, 2002 [1962], *Capitalism and Freedom* (University of Chicago Press).

Galbraith, James, K, 2014, *The End of Normal: The Great Crisis and the Future of Growth* (Simon & Schuster).

Harman, Chris, 1996, "The Crisis of Bourgeois Economics", *International Socialism 71* (summer), www.marxists.org/archive/harman/1996/06/bourgecon.htm

Harman, Chris, 2009, *Zombie Capitalism: Global Crisis and the Relevance of Marx* (Bookmarks).

Hilferding, Rudolf, 1981 [1910], *Finance Capital: A Study of the Latest Phase of Capitalist Development*, (Routledge), www.marxists.org/archive/hilferding/1910/finkap

Inman, Phillip, 2014, "Economics Students Call for a Shakeup of the way their Subject is Taught", *Guardian* (4 May), www.theguardian.com/education/2014/may/04/economics-students-overhaul-subject-teaching

International Monetary Fund, 2015, World Economic Outlook: Uneven Growth, Short and Long-Term Factors (April), www.imf.org/external/pubs/ft/weo/2015/01/pdf/text.pdf

Kahn, Richard, F, 1931, "The Relation of Home Investment to Unemployment", *The Economic Journal*, volume 41, number 162.

Keen, Steve, 2013, "Predicting the 'Global Financial Crisis': Post-Keynesian Macroeconomics", *Economic Record*, volume 89, issue 285.

Keynes, John Maynard, 1936, *A General Theory of Employment, Interest, and Money*, http://cas.umkc.edu/economics/people/facultypages/kregel/courses/econ645/winter2011/generaltheory.pdf

Kidron, Michael, 1965, "International Capitalism", *International Socialism 20* (first series, spring), www.marxists.org/archive/kidron/works/1965/xx/intercap.htm

Kliman, Andrew , 2011, *The Failure of Capitalist Production* (Pluto).

Kliman, Andrew and Shannon D Williams, 2014, "Why 'Financialisation' hasn't Depressed US Productive Investment", *Cambridge Journal of Economics*, published online 6 September.

Krugman, Paul, 2012, *End this Depression Now* (W W Norton and Company).

Kunkel, Benjamin, 2014, "Paupers and Richlings", *London Review of Books*, www.lrb.co.uk/v36/n13/benjamin-kunkel-paupers-and-richlings

Lapavitsas, Costas, 2009, "Financialised Capitalism: Crisis and Financial Expropriation", *Historical Materialism*, volume 17, issue 2.

Lapavitsas, Costas, 2013a, "Finance's Hold on our Everyday Life Must be Broken", *Guardian* (1 January), www.theguardian.com/commentisfree/2014/jan/01/finance-hold-everyday-life-broken-capitalism

Lapavitsas, Costas, 2013b, *Profit Without Producing: How Finance Exploits Us All* (Verso).

Marcuzzo, Maria Cristina, 2012, *Fighting Market Failure: Collected Essays in the Cambridge Tradition of Economics* (Routledge).

Marx, Karl, 1973, *Grundrisse: Foundations of the Critique of Political Economy* (Penguin).

Marx, Karl, 1991, *Capital*, Volume 3 (Penguin).

McNally, David, 2011, *Global Slump: The Economics and Politics and Resistance* (PM Press).

McNally, David, 2012, "Explaining the Crisis or Heresy Hunting? A Response to Joseph Choonara", *International Socialism* 134 (spring), http://isj.org.uk/explaining-the-crisis-or-heresy-hunting-a-response-to-joseph-choonara

Minsky, Hyman P, 1986, *Can "It" Happen Again: Essays on Instability and Finance* (Yale University Press).

Moggridge, Donald E, 1992, *Maynard Keynes: An Economist's Biography* (Routledge).

Moshinsky, Ben, and Jim Brunsden, 2012, "Shadow Banking Grows to $67 Trillion Industry, Regulators Say" *Bloomberg* (19 December), www.bloomberg.com/news/articles/2012-11-18/shadow-banking-grows-to-67-trillion-industry-regulators-say

Mulholland, Marc, 2012, *Bourgeois Liberty and the Politics of Fear: From Absolutism to Neo-Conservatism* (Oxford University Press).

Piketty, Thomas, 2014, *Capital in the Twenty-First Century* (Harvard University Press).

Pilling, Geoffrey, 1986, *The Crisis of Keynesian Economics: A Marxist View* (Croom Helm), www.marxists.org/archive/pilling/works/keynes/

Ricardo, David, 2004 [1817], *The Principles of Political Economy and Taxation* (Dover Publications).

Roberts, Michael, 2009, *The Great Depression* (Lightning Source UK Ltd).

Roberts, Michael, 2015, "The Global Crawl Continues", *International Socialism* 147 (summer), http://isj.org.uk/the-global-crawl-continues

Sawyer, Malcolm C, 1989, *The Challenge of Radical Political Economy: An Introduction to the Alternatives to Neo-Classical Economics* (Harvester Wheatsheaf).

Sayer, Andrew, 1995, *Radical Political Economy: A Critique* (Blackwell).

Shiller, Robert, J, 2015, *Irrational Exuberance* (Princeton University Press).

Skidelsky, Robert, 2014, "Economics Faces Long Needed Upheaval as Students Demand Right to Dissent", *Guardian* (18 June), www.theguardian.com/business/2014/jun/18/economics-upheaval-students-disssent-capitalist-thomas-piketty

Smith, Adam, 2014 [1776], *The Wealth of Nations* (Shine Classics).

Stiglitz, E Joseph, 2010, *Freefall: America, Free Markets, and the Sinking of the World Economy* (W W Norton and Company).

Stiglitz, E Joseph, 2012, *The Price of Inequality: How Today's Divided Society Endangers Our Future* (W W Norton and Company).

Stockhammer, Engelbert, 2015, "Rising Inequality as a Cause of the Present Crisis", *Cambridge Journal of Economics*, volume 39, issue 3.

Tengely-Evans, Tomáš, 2014, "Piketty and Marx", *International Socialism* 143 (summer), http://isj.org.uk/piketty-and-marx

Toporowski, Jan, 2005, *Theories of Financial Disturbance: An Examination of Critical Theories of Finance from Adam Smith to the Present Day* (Edward Elgar).

Toporowski, Jan, 2010, "Institutional Investors, the Equity Market and Forced Indebtedness", in Sebastian Dullien, Eckhard Hein, Achim Truger, and Till van Treeck (eds), 2010, *The World Economy in Crisis: The Return of Keynesianism* (Metropolis).

Wray, L Randall, 2009, "The Rise and Fall of Money Manager Capitalism: A Minskian Approach", *Cambridge Journal of Economics*, volume 33, number 4.

Von Hayek, Friedrich, 2005 [1944], *The Road to Serfdom* (Routledge Classics).

Von Mises, Ludwig, 1998, *Human Action: A Treatise on Economics* (Ludwig Von Mises Institute).

Striking debates

Paul McGarr

Significant discussion has taken place in recent issues of *International Socialism*, echoing wider debates in the movement, around the persistently low level of industrial struggle in Britain.[1] This is part of a wider phenomenon internationally, but the debate in this journal, reflecting the arena of activity of most contributors, has naturally focused on Britain. Answering the question at the heart of these discussions is, as Alex Callinicos has noted: "the most important single task facing revolutionary Marxists today".[2]

This article is an attempt to contribute to that discussion, and reflect on some arguments raised by previous contributors. The problem is clear. The level of industrial struggle in Britain is, and has remained for an unprecedented period, at a historically low level. Simon Joyce summed up the problem: "In every year since 1991 the number of strikes has been lower than the number of strikes in any year prior to 1991".[3]

Why does this matter? Marxism sees the self-activity of the working class as key to social change. That does not mean a one-sided, exclusive focus on strikes and industrial struggle. Socialists must engage with every arena of resistance: street protests and demonstrations; community, student,

---

1: Davidson, 2013; Callinicos, 2014a; Callinicos, 2014b; Hardy and Choonara, 2013; Sherry, 2013; O'Brien, 2014; Darlington, 2014; Joyce, 2015; Lyddon, 2015a and b; Upchurch 2015.
2: Callinicos, 2014a, p123.
3: Joyce, 2015, p120.

pensioners and unemployed organisations; movements against racism and women's oppression; the fight for LGBT liberation; movements for national liberation and against imperialism and many, many more. No movement of resistance or struggle by working class people or the oppressed should be alien to socialists.

Protests and movements outside the workplace can play a crucial role in winning battles. But in many social or political battles victory can depend on whether such movements tap the potential power of workers in the workplace. What workers do at work, the arena that defines us as working class and where our power is potentially at its greatest, is central to any serious Marxist analysis of social change. When workers strike and organise at work we begin to feel our power and sense our collective strength. Rosa Luxemburg's well known saying retains its truth; "where the chains of capitalism are forged, there must the chains be broken".[4]

What is more, when workers strike they are most open to having their ideas transformed. This happens in small ways in even the smallest strike—as workers more keenly become aware of their collective interest; or begin to challenge ideas that may have divided them on lines of gender, race or nationality. It is so much more true when workers strike on a significant scale. Ideas can be transformed on a mass scale, sometimes very rapidly, as struggle leads to a clash between that active reality and pre-existing consciousness and opens the potential for consciousness to shift sharply. There is no path to a socialist society that does not centrally involve workers organising and striking and, through that, transforming themselves and their ideas, and creating the self-organisation to challenge for power.

Explaining the historically unprecedented low level of strikes is therefore crucial, not simply to understanding why this has happened—but also to understanding how the situation may change.

The centrality of politics

There is a problem with the arguments put forward by some contributors to this debate. Many have identified important issues. Some, however, have tended to focus on individual workplaces, industries and unions, or, at best, relate that to structural changes in the composition of the working class, or changes in the legal frameworks within which industrial struggle takes place.

Such a discussion deals with important issues, and many points made are valid and part of any rounded analysis. But it ignores a fundamental issue. I quote Joyce because he expresses this most clearly: "This article,"

4:   Luxemburg, 1918.

he writes, "is not intended as an overall assessment of the present balance of class forces, nor of the current state of political and class consciousness within the working class: it is specifically an analysis of why there are so few strikes".[5] That is precisely the problem. You cannot explain why there are so few strikes without locating that discussion in the context of the very things, the balance of class forces and the state of political and class consciousness within the working class, that Joyce explicitly rejects engaging with.

Marxism is not the political analogue of Newtonian reductionist science. Understanding the molecular processes in the workplace, and the changing structural frameworks within which unions and activists operate, is a necessary part of any serious analysis. But it is not sufficient. You cannot reduce the dynamics of class struggle to the additive aggregate of the molecular processes in individual workplaces, nor to the relation between the union bureaucracy and the rank and file, or the interrelation of the trade union movement and the legal framework within which industrial relations takes place. The question of the prevailing ideas among large swathes of workers—the political and class consciousness, and confidence, of the class or significant sections of it—is crucial. Such class-wide trends, which are conditioned by wider political and social developments, cannot simply be set aside.

Of course we are not dealing with a one-way process. What happens in individual workplaces or unions taken as a whole shapes the balance of class forces and class confidence. But you cannot reject the other side: the way wider political dynamics in society, and class consciousness and confidence impacts on everything in the class struggle.

The 1972 and 1974 victories by miners and dockers over a Tory government had a transformative effect on society. In the smallest working class community and in every workplace millions of people—whether or not they were fully conscious of it at the time—sensed and believed that things once seen as impossible were now achievable. The impact of a decisive victory by our class is like a change in the season. Suddenly spring is in the air. It changes the thoughts and feelings in millions of workers and leads to new possibilities.

More recently, I remember clearly the abrupt transformation in France in the winter of 1995 when I was sent by *Socialist Worker* to report on events there. The early 1990s in France were utterly miserable. Workers' confidence was pitifully low and union organisation weak even compared with post-Thatcher Britain. Strikes were rare and were usually defeated.

5:    Joyce, 2015, p120.

Politics was dominated by demoralisation fueled by a decade of betrayals by the Socialist Party government, and the then seemingly inexorable rise of the Nazi National Front.

When a confident Tory government announced plans to attack welfare, a call by union leaders led to a decent demonstration—but there was no indication it would go beyond ritual protest. Then rail workers (encouraged by some union leaders) stayed out and, first in Rouen and then Paris, moved to pull other workers out. In Paris they dared what no one had even thought possible for years—to march around the postal depots ringing Paris and get those workers out.

Within days millions of workers were striking, and the atmosphere was transformed. Repeated giant demonstrations every few days, reaching into every town, created a momentum, drawing in new layers, forging a new mood of possibility. It was a mood where collective mass struggle was on the agenda but also one which drew in wider issues in society. Racism and other rotten ideas were challenged.

I vividly remember the impact on wider consciousness of striking workers in Paris opening metro stations at night to allow the homeless to sleep in some warmth, or of hundreds of workers from every sector (rail-workers, teachers, postal workers, health workers, the unemployed and many more) cramming into rank and file strike organising meetings in one tiny area of the east of Paris. Such things no one had even thought possible a few weeks earlier. Now millions believed they were and acted on that belief. A slogan painted on the wall near where I was staying summed up the mood—"Encore de grèves! Plus de rêves!" ("Still more strikes! Yet more dreams!)

Though a much greater victory could have been achieved, the struggle nevertheless decisively pushed the government back and changed the mood among millions. For the next few years France was a different country, and for some years became a byword for workers' confidence, militancy and struggle.[6]

The opposite is also true. Political developments and influences, and decisive defeats for our class can affect ideas and shape the possibilities, or lack of them, among millions of workers. In the mid to late 1970s the relationship between the trade union bureaucracy and the Labour government, and the politics dominating a key layer of shop stewards (linked to the then influential Communist Party), played a decisive role in shaping the struggle—the shift to what in this journal became known as the "downturn" following

---

6:   For a detailed analysis, see Harman, 1996.

the industrial and political upturn of the early 1970s.[7] The most obvious and important example, in relation to current debates in Britain, is the miners' defeat in the year-long 1984-5 strike, followed by defeats for other key sections of workers in the print industry, along with seafarers and dockers.

These changed the mood within the working class, and for everybody else—from trade union leaders to workers in the smallest workplace and town. If the big battalions had been smashed what hope was there for others successfully to fight? Perhaps the left in Britain has been guilty, if anything, of underestimating the seriousness of these defeats and their long lasting impact—in many ways they still hang like a black cloud over the minds of everyone who wants to fight. Of course many workers today do not remember the defeats personally—they are too young. But the impact has deeply affected the whole class, and young workers are not immune from that class-wide impact.

Structural change

Some have argued that the key reason for the low level of strikes is rooted in changes in the structure of the working class over recent decades. In the pages of this journal this has been most clearly articulated by Neil Davidson—but his arguments reflect much wider currents. Jane Hardy and Joseph Choonara have dealt with many of Neil's arguments.[8] Here I wish to add a few observations.

There has been a significant change in the composition of the working class in Britain—with a shift from manufacturing towards the public sector and service industries over the last quarter of a century. A similar picture has been seen in some other European countries (Belgium, France, Italy and parts of Eastern Europe included). However, even with the relative decline in manufacturing, Britain is still the 11th largest manufacturing country in the world, with 100,000 workers in aerospace, 600,000 in the chemical industry, 850,000 in electronics and 2 million in construction.[9] Britain will soon produce more cars than any year on record, topping the previous historical high of 1972.[10] Automobile production is the biggest export earner for the British economy in terms of value. There are still some 143,000 workers in Britain directly employed in motor vehicle manufacture, with

7:    See Cliff, 1979, for the original analysis.
8:    Davidson, 2013, and Hardy and Choonara, 2013. The growth of the world working class is a main theme of Harman, 2002.
9:    UK Manufacturing Statistics from www.themanufacturer.com
10:   Sharman, 2015, which estimates that by 2017 Britain's car production will be at an all time high, and may even reach that record during the course of 2015.

over 500,000 more employed in industries directly dependent on that production. Numbers of workers in the car industry have declined compared with a quarter of a century ago—but that is due to an enormous increase in productivity. Furthermore, it means that the potential power of the workers producing these cars is greater than ever.

Moreover, "service" industries, which have grown massively as a proportion of the working class in recent years, include enormous centres of potential class organisation. A Unison survey suggests there are around 1 million workers in around 5,000 call centres in the UK, with most employed in centres of between 300 and 700 workers.[11] There is no doubting the potential to organise, fight and strike. The issue is how to actualise that potential.

Look at the UK food retail industry dominated by four giant chains (Tesco, Asda, Sainsbury's and Morrisons) with almost all the rest in the hands of five other firms (The Co-op, Waitrose, Aldi, Lidl and Iceland). These employ huge numbers of workers in giant stores and in huge regional distribution centres usually with several hundred and sometimes over 1,000 workers on one site—and these concentrations give these workers enormous potential power. In some cases they are already formally organised (with the GMB representing 117,000 Asda workers and Usdaw more than 100,000 Tesco workers). The issue, again, is not one of the structure of the working class or its potential for collective struggle but why such organisation is not made effective.

One area that has grown in Britain (and internationally) is the public sector—teachers, health workers, council workers and so on. Most of these workers have always been an important part of the working class. What has changed is the degree of "proletarianisation" they have experienced as the autonomy they once possessed has been replaced by similar levels of managerial discipline endured by workers in other sectors. This has moved these workers further along the road from being part of the class "in itself" towards being part of a class "for itself". This is indicated by the fact that these workers are often relatively well organised, with high levels of union organisation, and account for the bulk of strikes we have seen.

Some have argued there has been a decisive shift from traditional forms of work to a new paradigm where temporary, part-time and zero-hours jobs dominate. Some have sought to elevate such talk to a more erudite level with notions of a new class, the "precariat". There has been a growth in the number of part-time and zero-hours contracts in Britain.

11:   Go to www.unison.org.uk/at-work/energy/key-issues/call-centres/the-facts

But, first, the numbers are often exaggerated—the vast majority of workers have full-time and more secure jobs. Secondly, the issue is how these workers can be organised. Precariousness does not automatically mean workers cannot be organised, as the example of previous generations of precarious and initially unorganised workers, for example dockers in Britain in the late 19th century, demonstrates.

The real issue here is the same as we began with—the state of organisation, confidence and consciousness within the working class and why there is so little fightback and so few strikes. Capitalism constantly changes and with it the nature of jobs and work. As long as capitalism exists that will be true. But this has little explanatory power as to the patterns of industrial struggle. The key issue is whether workers are, or can be, organised and that brings us to the crucial issues of collective and union organisation.

Unions, the bureaucracy and rank and file

Union membership does not tell you everything. There have been major workers' struggles when unions have been relatively weak. But union membership does give some feeling for the state of class organisation, certainly in an established capitalist democracy such as Britain.

Trade union membership has declined in Britain compared with its peak of around 13 million in 1979. About a quarter of workers are in a union, but that masks a difference between the public sector, with an average density of 55 percent, and the private sector at 14 percent. These percentages in turn mask pockets with high and low densities in both.[12]

There are still around 6.5 million trade union members in Britain. This is higher than almost any year before the Second World War (only briefly in 1919-20 did numbers move slightly ahead of today's total). The number of trade unionists in Britain today is almost the same as that in 1919, perhaps the year Britain came closest to a revolutionary workers' movement. Trade union membership today is higher than during the 1925 Red Friday victory of the unions over the government or the 1926 General Strike, and higher than during the Great Unrest of 1910-14, or during the first shop stewards movements of the First World War. Those historical examples should underline that, despite its size, the trade union movement in Britain is one that still has the potential for mass struggle, and struggle that can have a transformative effect on society.

Furthermore, government figures suggest there are also still around

---

12: Go to www.gov.uk/government/uploads/system/uploads/attachment_data/file/313768/bis-14-p77-trade-union-membership-statistical-bulletin-2013.pdf

150,000 workplace reps in Britain. A real decline from the 300,000 in 1979 yes, but a figure that nonetheless demonstrates a remarkable resilience in the face of low levels of struggle, and declining union membership in general.[13]

A key issue in these discussions is the relation between rank and file union members, their workplace reps and the union bureaucracy. This journal has long been associated with a distinctive analysis which sees the divide between the union bureaucracy and rank and file membership as primary. The social role of mediating between workers and bosses played by the bureaucracy means union leaders will vacillate—sometimes responding to pressure from below by leading struggles, at the very least to retain their membership and also to ensure bosses and governments take them seriously. But they will always seek to contain such struggles inside the limits set by negotiating within the framework of existing social relations—and shy away from decisive struggles. This applies to all union leaders, even the most left wing fighters are ultimately caught by their social position into shying away when the stakes are highest. All historical experience confirms this analysis—with the 1926 General Strike in Britain being perhaps the sharpest example.

None of this means we can ignore or bypass union officials and leaders. They have real influence over the workers they represent. At any time short of a revolutionary situation the experience of most workers is of accepting the limits set by capitalism while seeking to ameliorate the conditions of existence under capitalism. This creates "reformist" consciousness among the majority of workers, and underpins the hold of union leaders over many workers, as the social role of union leaders expresses that consciousness most clearly—as can reformist political organisation too. In the context of Britain the relationship between sections of the union bureaucracy and the Labour Party has played a particularly critical role.

The picture is far more complex than a simple dichotomy of bureaucracy and rank and file. There are many qualifications needed to this big picture, but anyone who loses sight of the fundamental divide will lose their bearings on the stormy seas of the class struggle. As Duncas Hallas argued, in 1980 "it is always possible to say of *any* generalisation—things are more complicated than that. Yes. Yes of course they are, but it is useful to look at the complications *only* if you have first grasped the big thing, the central issue".[14] That central issue is the need for an orientation on the rank and file "rooted in the recognition that the bureaucracy, as a social layer is, at bottom, conservative and that this is true notwithstanding the fact that,

---

13: Darlington, 2010.
14: Hallas, 1980.

at times, sections of the bureaucracy can be *formally* more left than most of the working class".[15]

Having grasped the big picture, further discussion is, of course, needed. The core of the union bureaucracy are full time officials—usually unelected—and the national full time leadership (usually the elected general secretary and national officers) of unions. There are also all sorts of mediating layers between that and the rank and file—ie workers actually doing the job. There are what are sometimes called "lay officials or officers" in most unions, neither fully part of the bureaucracy, nor rank and file workers. For example, my own union, the National Union of Teachers, has local officers, elected annually, still employed in their school but released on facility time under agreements. Some are on facility time five days a week, though many are on less and go into work some days. Such people make up the bulk of the national executive, and play a predominant role in the internal life of the union, setting the strategic direction of the union and participating in decisions to call, or not, national action.

They are not part of the trade union bureaucracy. They are much closer to the rank and file and subject to more immediate pressures from the rank and file than any full time official or national leader. But neither are they part of the rank and file. They do not, like school reps, go into work each day doing the same job on the same terms as those they represent. They are also not a homogenous bloc, but are cut across by real political divisions. Some are closely tied to, and share the political ideas of, the bureaucracy. They act as a transmission belt for the bureaucracy, into the rank and file, shaping what happens or does not happen. Others are very conservative, opposing those sections of the bureaucracy and national leadership who are more serious about building the union around a campaigning, fighting and organising agenda. This conservative grouping want a narrow, service provision model of trade unionism centred on quasi-legal services and casework, rejecting much engagement in wider political questions in society.

Similar patterns can be seen in other unions. In Unison the national bureaucracy called off the pay dispute in local government, cancelling planned strikes in October 2014. This provoked a revolt, not only by sections of rank and file workers but crucially by sections of this "middling layer"—including elements previously loyal to the national bureaucracy and Unison leader Dave Prentis. The North West region (around Manchester) of lay officers—a group previously loyal to Prentis—played a key role in this. The revolt forced only the second special conference in the union's

---

15: Hallas, 1980.

history and a 2-1 vote to reinstate action—though it was not strong enough to ensure the action was restored in reality.

None of this should be collapsed into seeing this layer within the unions as being the same as the rank and file. There are those within it (including members of the SWP) who are serious about a rank and file approach, but we are a long way from anything approaching a rank and file movement with any capacity to act independently of the bureaucracy. Those serious about a rank and file approach should use every opportunity to take initiatives which point in that direction. This can shape the future—but we should not pretend that future is already here.

The most famous British rank and file movement, the First World War Clyde Workers Committee, defined itself by the slogan:

> We will support the officials just so long as they rightly represent the workers, but we will act independently immediately they misrepresent them. Being composed of delegates from every shop and untrammelled by obsolete rule or law, we claim to represent the true feeling of the workers. We can act immediately according to the merits of the case and the desire of the rank and file.[16]

By that measure—what Mark O'Brien has called rank and file "moments" certainly exist today in many struggles,[17] but have nothing near the capacity to take serious and sustained independent action on a significant scale. The divisions and currents within unions, and within that mediating layer of lay officers, are largely political ones—with alignments not determined by differing social positions, but by political affiliations. All the various formations within unions today are what are usually labelled broad lefts (with a focus on winning union elections) rather than rank and file organisations.

With and against

Chris Harman spoke of the need to be "with and against the bureaucracy". Even at times of great waves of rank and file struggle this is the case—as the Clyde Workers Committee slogan makes clear, and more recently as Dave Lyddon usefully reminded us in relation to the struggles during the upturn of the early 1970s.[18] But for socialists the present situation—where rank and file workers have very little capacity or, "confidence" to act, and certainly

---

16: Cited in Cliff and Gluckstein, 1986, p64.
17: O'Brien, 2014.
18: Lyddon, 2015a.

to strike, independently of the bureaucracy—makes this understanding particularly critical.

There is always an interplay between official and unofficial action, there can be no crude counterposition of "pure" rank and file activity and fighting for official calls for action. The more rank and file activity the more the pressure for official calls, which help mobilise greater layers of rank and file workers.

Harman did not mean you move from supporting to opposing the bureaucracy in temporal succession, switching from cheerleading to denouncing union leaders. Rather, there is a constant and simultaneous process of working alongside and with the bureaucracy while at the same time having a tension and opposition to it. Getting this balance right is a difficult art, and one of the biggest challenges facing socialist activists in the unions today. But it is crucial in seeking to extend the influence of socialists over workers who look to the bureaucracy, especially its more left elements. It is all too easy to fall into either tailing left sections of the bureaucracy, or simply denouncing them.

In seeking to practise this art we need to understand that the key is not to take abstract left stances, but to do two things simultaneously. One is to articulate the voice of and seek to organise the minority who want to fight, and are clear about the limitations of the bureaucracy, including its left wing. The second is simultaneously to relate to those (greater numbers) of workers still influenced by the bureaucracy, and seek to work with, influence and win them—this necessarily involves relating to the bureaucracy and especially the left bureaucracy in a serious way.

There is no short cut, either in ideas of looking towards breakaway or "pop-up" unions—which leave most workers under the influence of the existing bureaucracy—nor in simply denouncing the bureaucracy and appealing over them directly to the workers they influence. A serious approach, grounded in the spirit of what Leon Trotsky outlined in his writings on the united front tactic, is the only route.

The fact that in the current period workers in general do not have the capacity to initiate action on a significant scale independent of the bureaucracy, yet generally respond magnificently to any official call, makes the question of leadership particularly important. Would it not have made a difference if union leaders had built on the strikes in November 2011 by rejecting the government's "heads of agreement" on pensions and pressed on for more action? Of course it would!

If the left-led unions had together fought the retreat it would have made a real difference. Imagine if the PCS, NUT, FBU, UCU and others had called for more strikes—it would have created the possibility of a different outcome. In the event only the PCS's Mark Serwotka moved swiftly to denounce the retreat while others hesitated—and allowed the right to set the agenda. That is why it is right socialists stand for election to official positions, seeking to win seats on national union executives and the like, because it can make a difference in securing official calls for action which can play a critical role in mobilising workers in a way that, given the prevailing class consciousness, would be otherwise unlikely to happen. Of course, any socialist in such a position always risks accommodating to the bureaucracy, which is why he or she must be absolutely accountable to networks and currents based in and oriented on the rank and file.

Social movement trade unionism

Many of the more left wing union leaders articulate ideas today about the model of trade unionism needed. The Unite leadership (headed by Len McCluskey) has pushed the idea of community membership and organising, opening up the union to the unemployed, pensioners, students and others. This is a serious initiative and has made possible some excellent work and played a crucial role in the fight against the bedroom tax for example.[19] Unite has also played a key role in important political initiatives such as the People's Assembly against Austerity, and has led some significant strikes.

In other unions, most notably the civil servants' PCS and especially the teachers' NUT, a slightly different emphasis has been pushed by their left leaderships, one often referred to as social movement trade unionism. This model has roots in trade union movements a decade or so ago in developing industrial countries such as Brazil, South Africa, South Korea and the Philippines. But in the British trade union movement today explicit comparisons are often drawn with recent models from the United States—in particular teachers in Wisconsin and Chicago. Wisconsin teachers' union leader Bob Peterson clearly articulates a model of a "three legged stool"—organising in the workplace, pressuring politicians and reaching out to the wider community.[20] Essentially the same model is echoed by the Chicago teachers union, whose victory in a 2012 battle has given authority to the approach.

For socialists, our vision of trade unionism has never been a narrow sectional one, but precisely one of taking up political questions and reaching out from workplaces to engage with wider sections of the "community"

19: For a detailed account of McCluskey and Unite, see Sherry 2013.

20: Pamphlet by Bob Peterson printed by left activists in the NUT and given out to delegates at 2015 NUT conference.

(I prefer the local working class). But some criticisms of the way the idea of social movement unionism is used in current debates in Britain are necessary. Building union organisation cannot be separated from struggle. At all times we are for organising and building the best union organisation possible. But such molecular work will not, by simple addition, lead to fundamental change in the level of union membership, rep density and the like.

Ralph Darlington rightly argues: "The strong historical association between high levels of nation-wide strike activity and periods of rapid union growth and powerful shop stewardships' movements in Britain, notably between 1910-20, 1935-43 and 1968-74, underlines the manner in which unions have in the past been built through conflict and struggle".[21]

There are very significant differences between the situations in the US cited as the inspiration for this model and Britain. In Wisconsin the work done in organising at the base and in reaching out to the wider "community" is fantastic. But that has been forced on the unions by a terrible defeat that removed all bargaining rights at state level. In the US in general, local action, or state or city wide action, is the highest level at which most action can be organised. That is not true in Britain where unions have (as amply demonstrated in recent years) the capacity to call effective national action. These differences are often glided over in discussions here. And in too many discussions in Britain it is almost forgotten that at the heart of the Chicago victory was a determined all-out strike!

The tendency of some left union leaders here to emphasise local action spills too easily into downplaying the question of national action and the responsibility of national leaderships in calling, or not calling, it.

Marxism is not a calculus of probability

Here I would take issue with another of Joyce's formulations. He writes, "While it is important for Marxists to retain an appreciation of the possibilities inherent in any historical situation, the most important service we can provide for the labour movement is not to highlight what might happen but to develop an understanding of what is most likely to happen".[22]

At all times we need a sober assessment of what is "most likely" to happen and to be careful not to exaggerate. Joyce is absolutely right that there is a danger in always seeing the next struggle as heralding the big breakthrough, and there have been those on the left who have fallen into this trap. But Joyce's correct attempt to guard against that risks a slide

21: Darlington, 2010.
22: Joyce, 2015, p141.

towards being commentators rather than active subjects seeking to affect the course of events.

A recent example is the attempted victimisation of PCS union rep Candy Udwin at the National Gallery. The most likely result was that Candy would stay sacked. She wasn't because action and leadership based around pushing for an all-out strike, reaching out for solidarity and applying political pressure—with strikes at the centre of this trinity—scored a victory. But it was a victory that was unexpected against the general background of 2015, which is what we want to change precisely through creating unexpected facts which begin to change that background.

We are above all fighters and revolutionaries seeking to change the course of events. I strongly agree with O'Brien's argument that we must have what he calls the "actuality of the strike", the potential it could happen, at the centre of our thinking. Without this, as O'Brien argues, the danger is that fighting for action becomes something you discount in advance or reduce to propaganda and replace with an excessively narrow focus elsewhere—on, for example, health and safety, or individual casework.[23]

The year 2011

The pages of this journal have seen debates around the strikes over pensions in Britain in 2011. Some observations on that struggle are relevant. First, it is important to recognise what led up to the public sector strike of 30 November 2011—the largest one-day strike in Britain since 1926. Until late 2010 there was a general sense across the working class of little resistance to the austerity measures being pushed by the government. The left argued for resistance, but it was an uphill struggle—given the prevailing ideas of large sections of workers, partly convinced by the argument that the money wasn't there, that we needed to cut the deficit (in other words precisely by factors weighing on "the state of political and class consciousness within the working class").

What began to change that was not workplace organisation but the sudden eruption of student protests in November 2010 at Millbank. That had a dramatic affect on the ideas of a layer of workers. Suddenly the idea that resistance was possible became easier to put. The next stage in the revolt was the 26 March trade union demonstration against austerity—the largest ever official trade union demonstration in British history, with over half a million marching—and the UCU higher education strike of March 2011.

23: O'Brien, 2015.

The strike (and Sean Vernell is right about this[24]) would not have happened without the determined effort of a layer of socialists within the union. When PCS general secretary Mark Serwotka argued, "imagine what a difference it would make if we didn't only march together but took strike action together," he captured the mood of a significant section of the class which now felt that resistance and strikes were possible in a way that they had not been even a few weeks earlier.

The wider political mood also mattered. The Tunisian and Egyptian Revolutions of late 2010 and early 2011 fed into the feeling among at least a layer of key activists that there were new possibilities—as anyone who was active in the movement at the time will recall, there was much talk of "if they can topple Mubarak, we can fight Cameron" or "we should turn Trafalgar Square into Tahrir Square". It is not true that millions of workers in Britain thought like that, but such sentiments, meshed with the student revolt and the union demonstration, certainly changed the mood among a significant layer of activists and reps who played a crucial role in the events of that year.

Without the student protest, the UCU action, and especially the March demonstration, I am not sure that the June strike of the NUT and PCS, UCU and ATL, would have happened. As anyone involved, as I was, in one of the key unions will know, it took an enormous amount of arguing, from rank and file activists, lay officers and sections of the left bureaucracy within some unions to make that strike happen. Lyddon on this point is right to argue that pressure from the government and its attack on pensions, coupled with the response to the previous Labour government's similar attack in 2005, was part of the reason why almost the entire union bureaucracy backed the 30 November pensions strike.[25] But I think he comes too close to arguing there was some inevitability about the union leaders calling action in November. I dispute that and insist that the impact of the June strike was a key, though not the only, factor in ensuring the November strike happened.

Lyddon, in my opinion, also comes perilously close to excusing the retreat led by some union leaders in the wake of November 2011, suggesting that, once the government put up its "heads of agreement" on pensions, union leaders were just doing what they usually do. What union leaders did—whether usual or otherwise—was a disastrous sell-out, which threw away the chance of a victory that could have transformed the situation in Britain and instead led the movement to an unnecessary and serious defeat.

24: Vernell, 2013.
25: Lyddon, 2015a.

Lyddon, along with O'Brien and Sean Vernell have been among those debating the characterisation of the 2011 strikes in this journal, and whether or not they should be labelled as bureaucratic mass strikes. Of far greater importance is that we heed the warning from Harman:

> Most living struggles escape any watertight compartmentalisation. Trade union bureaucrats may initiate action from above, with the clear intention of keeping it under their own control and ending it on their own terms. But this does not mean they are always able to impose their own will on the mass of workers who respond to their call. Once workers move into action they begin to discover their own capacity to fight and to control things—and there is always at least the beginnings of a threat to the trade union bureaucracy in this. Indeed, this is one powerful reason why trade union leaders call off struggles just as the employers begin to fear the power displayed by the working class movement.[26]

Harman's point, which O'Brien clearly acknowledges, is borne out by real examples. The Danish mass strike of Easter 1985 was entirely initiated and controlled initially by the union bureaucracy. Yet within days it had escaped such control and the country was paralysed with incredible examples of rank and file initiative in town after town going far beyond anything the union leaders had envisaged.[27] Similarly, as referred to earlier, the mass strikes of France 1995 were initiated by union leaders—but unleashed a rank and file dynamic that for a while completely escaped such bureaucratic limits.

In any real struggle socialists could, using a calculus of probabilities approach, say it is unlikely the strike called by union leaders will go beyond the limits they set. This would be wrong. Without getting carried away, the duty of socialists is to work to maximise rank and file activity and initiatives which point beyond those limits. O'Brien gives excellent examples of attempts to do that in Liverpool in 2011, and this was not isolated. In East London local activists organised not just pickets but gatherings on the day of the strike bringing different groups of strikers together and knitting together local networks. Hundreds of people marched all the way through the City of London to join the main central London demonstration. Similar stories could be told across Britain. On this occasion such initiatives were not successful in creating a dynamic able to overcome the retreats sounded by the union leaders, but it was nonetheless the right thing to try.

26: Harman, 1996.
27: Clark, 1985.

The road since 2011

The retreat at the end of 2011 threw away the chance for further large-scale strikes which could have broken the government's assault on public sector pensions. We should be wary of counterfactual history—the "what if?" approach—rather than seeking to understand and explain what did happen. But this much can, I think, be ventured: the developing strike movement around pensions held within it the potential to transform the balance of class forces and open up a new period of struggle. The retreat meant that this potentiality never had the chance to be realised, and our class suffered a defeat.

What of the pattern of struggle since? The overall picture of few strikes remains. Official figures are that there were 303,000 strike days involving 152 strikes in the 12 months to July 2015.[28] But this not the total picture. The situation over the past four years has been complicated and contradictory.

Despite the retreat on pensions it is not true that this left the big unions in the public sector broken. There have been continued attacks since—on pay, privatisation, and jobs across the public sector. These have hit hard—and cost jobs, worsened services and made life harder for many workers. It also remains the case that workers on a national scale do not have the confidence to take action without a lead from above. But workers' organisation in the areas at the heart of the 2011 strikes remains essentially intact. It has not been decisively weakened despite the retreats, and in some areas, such as schools, has grown with more members and significantly more reps.

In many cases activists in the big public sector unions in the course of 2013 and 2014 have again and again been able to press for a lead to be given and action called. Workers have repeatedly responded magnificently when such a lead has come and large-scale action has been called. In 2013, teachers—this time in both the major unions the NUT and NASUWT—staged highly effective strikes in joint action on pay, pensions and conditions which completely closed schools in a series of rolling regional walkouts. The action ensured employers backed off from a new assault on teachers' conditions. More could have been won but, in a familiar pattern, the strikes were not built on. NASUWT leaders retreated, and NUT leaders hesitated then retreated too.

In 2014 another huge opportunity for a victory that could have shifted the balance of class forces was thrown away by union leaders. In July that year around 1.5 million council workers, school workers and civil servants struck over pay—giving another glimpse of the potential for a movement that could win a real victory and have a class-wide impact.

28: ONS, 2015.

Once more the strike was not built on and union leaders retreated.

The same frustrating pattern was evident in the autumn of 2014 when half a million health workers responded magnificently to pay strikes—with the Royal College of Midwives for the first time joining such action. The strikes struck a chord with millions and were popular, symbolising the defence of the NHS against the drive to privatise it—and should have been the signal for more action. Again that did not happen.

Time and time again we see the pattern of workers, activists and lay officers pressing for a fight in the face of assaults. That results in union leaders calling ballots and those delivering resounding votes for action, and when a day of strikes is called workers respond brilliantly. Yet union leaders then duck building for more action to try to win a decisive victory and sound the retreat. That leaves many activists and workers bitter and frustrated. At times they have been able to mount opposition to the retreats, but not enough to force union leaders to put the action back on, or to deliver action despite them. This is a deeply frustrating situation. But it is important to recognise the full picture and not miss the potential seen in the one-day public sector strikes.

There have been other tests of leadership too for those at the top of the unions—and too often they have missed the chance to mobilise a fight which could have won significant victories. One was the surrender by Unite leaders in 2013 faced with bosses' blackmail at the Grangemouth refinery in Scotland—when a serious campaign and action could have won. More recently, in the autumn of 2015, we saw the dismal response by union leaders to the massacre of jobs in the steel industry—when a determined campaign of protest, demonstrations and action linked to a political fight for nationalisation could have transformed the situation.

There are other important nuances to the general background of a low level of actual strikes. Trade union density in the private sector is comparatively low. But where unions are present in the private sector they can often have a level of organisation that would be the envy of most public sector trade unionists. As Richard Morgan argues elsewhere in this issue, in some sectors of the economy, especially those where profits are good, workers with good organisation have been able to win some impressive victories—often without strikes, but rather via the threat of strikes. In fact, over the last couple of years there have been a number of important pay strikes in private industry—such as at Tyneside Safety Glass and EDF—that have won at least some gains. These strikes have helped ensure private sector pay has outstripped inflation.

Construction is another area where there have been encouraging signs and it has not all been quiet since the BESNA electricians' victory back in 2010, which gave a glimpse of a new level of organisation among electricians. There has been a ripple of disputes on key sites, involving electricians but also others from crane drivers to scaffolders. The most recent examples are the "pay the rate" disputes concentrated on Merseyside and Teeside where a better level of workers' organisation than has been seen in many years is, with some success, calling protests and actions—usually without waiting on official processes.

Among some small but visible and powerful sections of workers there has been an almost constant round of moves towards action, retreats, and then further action—the most obvious example being the series of disputes on the London underground—and the power shown when tube and rail workers have struck and paralysed the capital, as in the summer of 2015.

The frustration here too though is that, while strikes have won some gains, too often that power has not then been harnessed to press home the advantage and win decisive victories. A glaring example has been that of London bus workers who have had a live ballot for strikes at the same time as tube workers, who have been on strike, yet union leaders have repeatedly passed up the chance to call joint action which would quickly win victories for both groups.

While one-day strikes in the public sector account for the most visible strikes recently, as Lyddon shows, a significant proportion of strikes last longer than one day—in both public and private sectors.[29] Here too the picture is complicated and contradictory. There have been defeats after long battles and lots of strike action—such as the Doncaster Care workers, and fights which have seen union reps victimised, and attacks driven through—such as at London Metropolitan University and Bromley council.

There have also been significant victories or partial victories where workers have gone for hard-hitting or all-out strikes and tapped wider networks of solidarity. We should avoid seeing these as harbingers of a new summer of struggle—but they indicate a new potential at least. This year we have seen the victories by the Glasgow homelessness caseworkers and the Dundee hospital porters, and partial victories at DSG defence contractors and at Lambeth College. We have also seen the successful defence of union rep Candy Udwin at London's National Gallery through an all-out strike, and the successful defence, through unofficial walkouts by support staff and lecturers, of Unison rep Sandy Nichol at the School of Oriental and African Studies in London. The recent Bridgwater postal workers'

29: Lyddon, 2015b.

victory after unofficial walk-outs in defence of a sacked disabled colleague provides another example. These victories have not been on a scale to shift the wider mood in the class, but they contain lessons about how to operate at work and point to key elements in how any such shift may emerge from the battles we will face in the coming period.

The resilience, despite the low strike figures, of workers' organisation, and the pattern of struggle of the past four years suggest that significant battles lie ahead. The issue is whether any of these battles develops into a fight with the scale and outcome to shift the wider mood among large swathes of workers. The latest assault on workers, the new anti-union laws pushed through parliament in the autumn of 2015 is, however draconian, also testament to the fear of those at the top of society that there is a real prospect of resistance as they continue their austerity drive.

Politics matters

To return to earlier discussions, of course Joyce is right that there have been important shifts in the legal and structural frameworks affecting both the number of strikes and the relation between trade union bureaucracies, reps, and rank and file workers. These were largely a consequence of the defeats suffered in the 1980s, and they make the job of those who want to see resistance harder.

The anti-union laws introduced over the last quarter-century have made it much more difficult to organise official strike action. Through their targeting of union funds in the case of a breach of the plethora of anti-union laws they have pushed union bureaucracies into a much greater degree of control over, and policing of, workers' action, and shifted control over action away from workplace reps and into the hands of the bureaucracy. The new anti-union laws are designed to make strikes and resistance even more difficult. Many workers, just as they accept the legitimacy of the law in general, give some legitimacy to the anti-union laws today. It is also true, however, that a successful ballot in conformity with all the anti-union laws can then give workers' action, in their eyes, a greater legitimacy too.

On all this Simon Joyce is essentially correct. The issue is whether such changes are decisive in explaining the low level of strikes. I would argue that they are not, and that more significant is the wider "state of political and class consciousness" and the "confidence" of reps and the workers they represent. There are examples of workers today seizing the initiative and going beyond what union leaders say, even of defying the law—and winning.

There are very few cases of the laws being used when workers have ignored them. The electricians' dispute in 2011-12 saw a high level of unofficial action which repeatedly breached anti-union laws. Yet not a single worker was hauled in front of a court for such defiance. I can vouch from personal experience that when teachers at my school voted this year to walk out if a technician employed by the Capita corporation was sacked the laws meant nothing in the face of a resolute stand, and the company retreated within hours.

When workers move in a determined way the anti-union laws are not decisive, nor is the ability of the bureaucracy to control workers' action. The real issue is that workers in general do not have the confidence to act independently of the bureaucracy or in defiance of the law. Examples show a potential, but none of those cited have been on a scale or of a significance to generalise, and affect the thoughts and actions of a large enough section of the class to make a material difference to the overall "balance of class forces". For that to happen something needs to break the ice formed over the past 25 years in the minds of many workers and activists (ice that has frozen solid in the minds of many union officials, leaders and officers).

There is no single model for how such a shift can take place—only the certainty that at some point we will see a rise in the level of strikes. That is not just wishful thinking. All historical experience points in that direction. We may have had an unprecedentedly long period of a low level of strikes in Britain, but at some point that will change. How that will happen is not predetermined, and what socialists should do to hasten its advent at the present time needs thinking through. It can be that an accretion of smaller victories and struggles builds organisation which prepares the way—as was the case in the lead up to the upsurge in Britain in the 1970s.

But there are plenty of examples of other routes. In a small way the explosion of struggle in 2011 shows how a complex interaction of wider political movements, in Britain and internationally, involving some movement by the union bureaucracy under pressure from employers and government, and initiative and drive by the left, can come together to create significant struggle with the potential to transform the situation.

In the mid-1930s the situation in France was suddenly transformed with the mass strikes of June 1936—which rocked the country and won hugely significant victories for workers. These were not shaped by prior movements or battles in the workplace. Instead a successful political mobilisation against fascism gave new confidence to layers of workers and then the election of a left Popular Front government changed the mood and sparked an explosion of struggle which transformed the whole situation.

Today we face a new onslaught of austerity, against a background of a low level of resistance in the wake of union leaders' pitiful response to the past five years of austerity and their throwing away the chance of real victories in 2011 and 2014. The landslide victory of Jeremy Corbyn in the Labour leadership election signals a possibility of a new political landscape encouraging resistance. Socialists need to seize every opportunity to build union organisation and initiate workplace struggles. Though the general level of struggle remains low, it is not non-existent. Initiative, activity and leadership at the base are crucial.

Two other things are especially important today. One is seeking to build networks, linking up and generalising examples of resistance. That means solidarity is a key question. Taking the argument for solidarity with those who are fighting into as many workplaces as possible is not simply a moral one, it is a key political task, seeking to spread the idea that resistance and struggle are possible. Sending messages of support, taking collections, visiting protests and picket lines are a key part of this strategically important task. Seeking to link up networks in every locality around such solidarity is also key—shaping the contours of local networks that will be crucial in pushing forward any bigger upsurge in struggle.

A second focus has to be bringing wider political issues into the workplace, again not simply from some moral standpoint, but because they can play a key role in shaping ideas and organisation within and in between workplaces, and in mobilising workers who may not be confident to strike unless union leaders call action. To take the most important example. taking the need to organise against racism into unions and workplaces can—as well as being important in itself—pull some workers into greater activity than they would otherwise engage with. A workplace collection in support of refugees, or a few workers from a workplace becoming involved with Stand Up To Racism can help rebuild confidence and organisation in that workplace. Such "political trade unionism" has to be a central thread of any serious socialist approach in the unions today.

A key feature of the struggle today, especially for public sector workers such as in health and education, is how the attacks on the services these workers provide has made the political defence of those services a central issue for struggle. The drive to privatise and marketise services such as education and health means fighting for a different vision of what a health service should be or what education should be—rooted in the "professional" ethos many of these workers hold dear—has become critical in mobilising resistance. Acting to defend not just jobs but what workers believe their jobs should be about has become more important.

In conclusion, arguments about the structural changes in the working class, though important, are often overstated and are of little explanatory power in understanding the current situation. Discussion of the changed legal framework within which unions operate is likewise important—but not decisive. The crucial questions of politics, a recognition of the reality of, and determining significance of, the balance of class forces and the "state of political and class consciousness" among workers are of critical importance in understanding the situation we are in.

Given the analysis outlined here, it follows that key strategic priorities for socialists in the workplaces are: organising at the base; fighting for solidarity networks in every locality; and bringing wider political issues of all kinds into the workplace. This can organise and shape the ideas of a section of workers who can then play a key role in the struggles to come. This depends on socialists in the workplace not being passive commentators simply weighing up the most probable course of events, but seeking to shape events. As Luxemburg said in one of her final speeches in 1918: "Our motto is: In the beginning was the act."

References

Callinicos, Alex, 2014a, "The Left after Grangemouth", *International Socialism* 141 (winter), http://isj.org.uk/the-left-after-grangemouth

Callinicos, Alex, 2014b, "Thunder on the Left", *International Socialism* 143 (summer), http://isj.org.uk/thunder-on-the-left

Clark, Pete, 1985, "The Strike That Shook a Country: Report from Denmark", *Socialist Worker Review* 76 (May), www.marxisme.dk/arkiv/clarkpete/1985/05/easterstrikes.asp

Cliff, Tony, 1979, "The Balance of Class Forces in Recent Years", *International Socialism* 6 (autumn), www.marxists.org/archive/cliff/works/1979/xx/balance1.htm

Cliff, Tony, and Donny Gluckstein, 1986, *Marxism and Trade Union Struggle: The General Strike of 1926* (Bookmarks).

Darlington, Ralph, 2010, "The State of Workplace Union Reps' Organisation In Britain Today", *Capital and Class*, volume 34, number 1.

Darlington, Ralph, 2014, "The Rank and File and the Trade Union Bureaucracy", *International Socialism* 142 (spring), http://isj.org.uk/the-rank-and-file-and-the-trade-union-bureaucracy

Davidson, Neil, 2013, "The Neoliberal Era in Britain: Historical Developments and Current Perspectives", *International Socialism* 139 (summer), http://isj.org.uk/the-neoliberal-era-in-britain-historical-developments-and-current-perspectives

Hallas, Duncan, 1980, "Trade Unionists and Revolution: A Response to Richard Hyman", *International Socialism* 8 (spring), www.marxists.org/archive/hallas/works/1980/xx/turev.html

Hardy, Jane, and Joseph Choonara, 2013, "Neoliberalism and the Working Class: A Reply to Neil Davidson", *International Socialism* 140 (autumn), http://isj.org.uk/neoliberalism-and-the-british-working-class-a-reply-to-neil-davidson

Harman, Chris, 1996, "France's Hot December", *International Socialism* 70 (spring), www.marxists.org/archive/harman/1996/03/france.htm

Harman, Chris, 2002, "The Workers of the World", *International Socialism 96* (autumn), www.marxists.org/archive/harman/2002/xx/workers.htm

Joyce, Simon, 2015, "Why Are There so Few Strikes?", *International Socialism 145* (winter), http://isj.org.uk/why-are-there-so-few-strikes

Lyddon, Dave, 2015a, "Bureaucratic Mass Strikes: A Response to Mark O'Brien", *International Socialism 146* (spring), http://isj.org.uk/bureaucratic-mass-strikes-a-response-to-mark-obrien

Lyddon, Dave, 2015b, "Bureaucratic Mass Strikes: A Rejoinder", *International Socialism 148* (autumn), http://isj.org.uk/bureaucratic-mass-strikes-a-rejoinder

Luxemburg, Rosa, 1918, "Our Programme and the Political Situation" in Howard, Dick (ed), *Selected Political Writings* (Monthly Review Press), www.marxists.org/archive/luxemburg/1918/12/31.htm

O'Brien, Mark, 2014, "The Problem of the One-day Strike: A Response to Sean Vernell", *International Socialism 142* (spring), http://isj.org.uk/the-problem-of-the-one-day-strike-a-response-to-sean-vernell

O'Brien, Mark, 2015, "Revolutionaries in the Unions: The Reality of the Strike", *International Socialism 147* (summer), http://isj.org.uk/revolutionaries-in-the-unions-the-reality-of-the-strike

Office for National Statistics, 2015, "Statistical Bulletin: UK Labour Market" (September), www.ons.gov.uk/ons/dcp171778_414231.pdf

Sharman, Andy, 2015, "UK Car Production Climbs for Fifth Year", *Financial Times* (23 January), www.ft.com/cms/s/0/0c1ff088-a232-11e4-aba2-00144feab7de.html#axzz3shM1fc2W

Sherry, Julie, 2013, "Can Len McCluskey Reclaim Labour?", *International Socialism 140* (autumn), http://isj.org.uk/can-len-mccluskey-reclaim-labour

Upchurch, Martin, 2015, "The End of the 'Safe Space' for Unions? A response to Simon Joyce", *International Socialism 146* (spring), http://isj.org.uk/the-end-of-the-safe-space-for-unions

Vernell, Sean, 2013, "The Working Class, Trade Unions and the Left: The Contours of Resistance", *International Socialism 140* (autumn), http://isj.org.uk/the-working-class-trade-unions-and-the-left-the-contours-of-resistance (online only)

Strikes, ballots and the class struggle: An addition to the strikes debate

Richard Morgan

Simon Joyce has helped galvanise a long overdue discussion in *International Socialism* on the state of workplace class struggle in the UK.[1] Though I partially disagree both with his claim that shop stewards have lost control of the strike weapon and with his point that workers lose on "perishable" issues, that is, "issues that management would win by default if workers did not act immediately",[2] I agree with the tone and emphasis of Simon's article which points to a refreshingly more positive assessment of workplace organisation than is commonplace on the left. In particular he makes four very important points:

- "The current low level of strike action is not straightforward evidence of a lack of combativity".[3]
- The downturn was not only a time of defeat but also "a period of transition from one regime for conducting relations between

---

1: Joyce, 2015. See also Upchurch, 2015, Gluckstein, 2015, O'Brien, 2015, and the related debate between Mark O'Brien and Dave Lyddon (O'Brien, 2014, and Lyddon, 2015). I wish to thank Charlie Kimber and Michael Bradley for suggesting I write this and to the comrade from the shipyards who spoke at Marxism 2015 stating that, contrary to all the pessimism, he had not had a below inflation pay rise for years. He demonstrated that someone else was also winning and that I wasn't living in a parallel reality! The opinions expressed in this article are my own.

2: Joyce, 2015, pp132-133.

3: Joyce, 2015, p140.

unions and employers to another".[4]

- Making simple comparisons between today's workplace struggles and those of the 1968-72 upturn is a fruitless activity; "it is a mistake to measure the present situation using standards derived from a historically unusual period, and will only lead to disorientation".[5]

- He also rescues casework from the appalling condescension of revolutionaries—on which I comment further in Appendix 2.

In this article I will expand on my disagreements but will also argue for a positive explanation for the lack of strike days *in certain circumstances*, which supports the general positive tone of Simon's work. This argument will need to be absorbed into our understanding of the balance of class forces *as a part of* the picture (but not the whole picture) that contradicts the overall pessimistic tone about the workplace of so many writers on the left.[6] I will add some practical examples of organising under neoliberalism to provide a specific counter-argument to the workplace pessimists. Like Simon's article this will be entirely Britain-centric and I apologise to comrades from other countries for this, but given that most of it is drawn from my own experience there is little I can do about that.

The discussion so far on the level of strike action has concentrated solely on the position of our side, on our strengths and our weaknesses. Every article assumes that whether or not there is a strike is up to the working class and the working class alone. So if there aren't strikes, this is solely a sign of weakness on our side. Therefore the debate concentrates on finding that weakness.

But in the class struggle it takes two to tango. For there to be a strike, the employers too must need to fight. As Tony Cliff once said, if everyone knew the result of a strike in advance there wouldn't be any—if the employers knew they were going to lose they would concede, and if the workers knew their action would fail, they'd forget it. One trend that can be observed is that of employers conceding enough for the unions to deliver significant gains without the members ever having to take action. In many cases, the ballot process can be used as a test of strength, allowing employers to retreat when union support looks too strong—and employers do indeed retreat.

4: Joyce, 2015, p137.
5: Joyce, 2015, p142.
6: For example, Davidson, 2013; see also the response—Hardy and Choonara, 2013.

Ballot victories

Let me give some examples. The first is from my own experience. In 2008, at the beginning of the financial crisis, I was lead lay negotiator for the pay claim for the Collective Bargaining Unit (CBU) at the company where I worked. With the retail price index (RPI, the measure of inflation) at 3.2 percent the company withdrew their initial offer of 2.2 percent and sought to impose a wage freeze. To cut a good but long story short, we balloted for industrial action and on an 88 percent turnout received a 92 percent vote for strike action and a 93 percent vote for action short of a strike. The mass meeting held after the ballot voted unanimously to strike one day in week one, two days in week two, three days in week three, etc, until we ended up on indefinite strike. The company caved in and conceded our claim in full (RPI+1.75 percent for four years, with RPI being the highest figure from November to February) without us having to take any of our planned action. The only compromises were that we agreed a) to delay payment for three months till the start of the new financial year (it would be backdated) and b) to keep the deal embargoed. A victory based on the ballot but not on any actual strike days—a "ballot victory".

The second example is from the 2014 pay deal for Jaguar Land Rover (JLR) workers. The company's initial pay offer also included an attack on the pension scheme. It was overwhelmingly rejected. Of approximately 15,000 ballot papers issued some 12,881 voted against the offer and only 454 in favour. JLR returned to the table and a much better offer was negotiated by the unions. The ballot of the revised offer saw workers vote overwhelmingly in favour of the deal. The deal can be summarised as follows:

- All attacks on the pension scheme removed.
- A two-year deal of pay offers above RPI (2.2 percent above RPI in year one).
- *All* skilled employees converted to permanent on 1 January 2015.
- All semi-skilled employees on fixed term contract converted to permanent on 1 January 2015.
- Increases in the rate at which employees progress through their salary band, so that the deal was effectivley worth 8.4 percent of basic salary to a production operator in year one.

This was another victory based on the ballot and not on any actual strike days. This ballot wasn't even an industrial action ballot, just a consultative ballot.

A third example is from a lorry drivers' dispute. In a Socialist Workers Party internal bulletin in 2011 I quoted the example in the East Midlands whereby "a logistics company was forced to increase its annual social hours payments from £1,000 to £2,400. No strike was taken. So this does not appear in our "class struggle" statistics. However, if you were one of those lorry drivers who voted for strike action, you'd be pretty pleased with the resultant extra £1,400 per annum.

Indeed, the late Bob Crow's reputation for militancy was based far more on winning strike ballots than on the actual number of strikes called (though strikes were called). As Ralph Darlington has written of the RMT on the London Underground:

> During the nine years between January 2000 and December 2008 the RMT balloted for industrial action on no less than 50 different occasions, with ballots leading to strike action on [only] 18 of these occasions... Frequently such ballot results have been used as a form of sabre-rattling designed to bolster the union's bargaining leverage, with no action resulting, although sometimes with significant concessions being extracted.[7]

In other words, only 36 percent of successful strike ballots were turned into actual action by the most militant trade union leader of the time. Dave Sherry from Glasgow has quoted his own experience in twice defeating attempted attacks on his members' pension scheme simply by overwhelming ballot results in consultative ballots ("on a 70 percent turnout we got an 80 percent yes for industrial action").[8]

The final example I wish to use is the success of Unite the union in defending pension schemes at Rolls Royce in 2014. Faced with the company proposing further attacks on their pension scheme, Rolls Royce stewards agreed the strategy of balloting all sites on contributing to a strike fund to allow one crucial section in Derby to be balloted for indefinite strike action, their official strike pay to be topped up by their own dispute fund. The specific Derby section delivered a 96 percent vote for strike action on a turnout of over 80 percent. The company backed down and not only withdrew all attacks on the pension scheme but also ended up agreeing to absorb the extra national insurance costs caused by the government's abolition of the State Earnings Related Pension scheme. (Unite at GKN aerospace also recently followed the same strategy on this issue with similar results.)

As Simon has previously written, "Balloting has had an unintended consequence: ballots give legitimacy to a grievance or demand in the

---

7: Darlington, 2009.
8: Personal communication by email.

eyes of employers, union members and others".[9] However, in discussions with comrades—both members of the Socialist Workers Party and non-members—about these "ballot victories", the argument I receive is that these are exceptions rather than the rule. Of course, this is correct; if they weren't exceptions we'd be in an upturn. But to state that they are exceptions is simply to observe them rather than analyse them. So let's analyse them.

The victory in the Rolls Royce pension dispute offers a contrasting example to the public sector pension dispute of 2011. The same issue, but with a very different result. Yet the trade union bureaucracy is the same. The Marxist analysis of the trade union bureaucracy does not differentiate between bureaucracies in the public and private sectors. So how do we explain the very different outcomes?

There are three differences that need to be highlighted. First, the Rolls Royce workers were not fighting the government, while the public sector workers were; secondly, the Rolls Royce workers had an industrial action strategy for their pensions to win. This contrasts with the public sector one-day strikes which were more strike action as protest than strike action as industrial action.[10] And thirdly, the union at Rolls Royce delivered a massive vote on a huge turnout, compared to the 29 percent turnout in Unison's pension ballot.[11] I don't know the specific details of how they delivered that ballot outcome, but it cannot have been done without strong workplace organisation.

By way of example I do know how we delivered our 88 percent return referred to previously. We used the industrial action ballot as an organising tool—going round the offices checking that everyone's address was correctly recorded by the union (at least 10 percent of our members' details were incorrect), getting these details updated, initiating the ballot, going round again and checking that everyone had received a ballot paper, then going round again and checking that everyone had voted. Such activity meant that the workplace was taken *into* the postal ballot.

In the examples above, the union had strong workplace organisation and the ballot ended up proving this to the employers such that the employers retreated. In contrast, our analysis of the public sector disputes has tended to concentrate only on the undisputed failings of the trade union bureaucracy. This is correct in and of itself but is only a *partial* explanation.

There remains an additional explanation, the lack of workplace

---

9:    Joyce, 2015, p138.
10:   See my SWP internal bulletin contribution in 2014 and Lyddon, 2015.
11:   Go to www.bbc.co.uk/news/business-15570669

organisation within the public sector. Undoubtedly there were a small number of public sector workplaces that replicated this process, for example schools in Tower Hamlets and Camden delivered high votes for strike action in June 2010 on exactly the same balloting basis, but I am unaware of them being used as examples to spur other public sector activists to follow suit. By failing to analyse the "ballot victories" in the private sector we are undermining our argument for workers' power and at the same time depriving public sector activists of examples to show the necessity of improving their workplace organisation to better control the bureaucracy in their fight against austerity. If Unison's workplace organisation had been strong enough to deliver a 92 percent vote on an 88 percent turnout, the bureaucracy would have found it much harder to sell out.

When I've discussed this with public sector trade unionists they have pointed to the reality of objective circumstances in the public sector that makes workplace organisation more difficult than organising in just one factory, eg council trade unionists can often be spread across tens of different workplaces in the one city. This is correct. But these are circumstances to be overcome. Consider the British Airlines Stewards and Stewardesses Association branch of Unite. Their workplaces (the planes!) will often be thousands of miles from each other. This does not prevent them from organising. Or bus drivers, who spend the majority of their working day on their own away from their workmates. I'll quote from a trade unionist who was a British Gas engineer in Leamington. His workforce would collect their work cases and then set out individually in their vans. This presented an organisational problem. How to get them together collectively? He did this by organising a breakfast club to which everyone contributed and which in turn provided cheaper coffee and tea before they set off. The majority joined and this provided the opportunity for collective discussion. I'm not suggesting that everyone follows this specific tactic. I'm just pointing out that with imagination the objective difficulties to organisation can be overcome.

Rank and file activists need to formulate specific demands on their trade union bureaucracy to help build that workplace organisation rather than just propagandistic demands for this or that strike action, eg help with printing hard copy newsletters to be desk dropped,[12] running education for specific workplaces on the organising agenda, recruitment days, etc. Do not assume the union will not help, because often it will, and if they won't then pressurise them to do so.

12: Building a network to desk drop hard copy newsletters is a first step to building a shop stewards' committee.

"Perishable" issues

On the "perishable" issues, that is, "issues that management would win by default if workers did not act immediately", my own experience is that our recognition agreement protects the "status quo" so that as long as we spot management introducing something new and shout about it, then the company returns to the previous situation until we have negotiated on the issue. The key element here is *at least* to have enough members in every section who know who their representatives are, such that the union is informed about new management procedures as soon as they are implemented. If a new management procedure has been in place for 12 months before you notice it, then you have little chance of changing it; if it's only been in place for 12 days then you have a good possibility of changing it. This takes us back to the crucial importance of workplace organisation.[13]

Are shop stewards losing control over the strike weapon?

Simon argues that "by the early 1990s the strike weapon had effectively been taken out of the hands of shop stewards. This key development has important implications for the way workplace trade unionism has subsequently developed, and is the main explanation for the stability of the current low level of strikes in the UK".[14] I think this exaggerates the situation. If Simon had written that the strike weapon was no longer *the sole prerogative* of the shop stewards, then I would have agreed. But to suggest that shop stewards have no say is simply not my experience of the last 25 years of private sector workplace activity. In the private sector, particularly in Unite, lay stewards will always be involved in national negotiations and will definitely have a say on whether or not to call a strike ballot. In the Tata steel pensions ballot, for example, the decision to recommend the compromise "was taken at a meeting in London of 100 senior trade union delegates from across the company".[15] In the rejection of the JLR offer mentioned previously, the final decision was taken by 200 shop stewards.[16] This is the norm, not the exception.

I accept that it is often difficult to win the demand for a strike ballot as nearly every union expects stewards to prove that they've exhausted every possible route to a negotiated settlement before seeking to resolve

---

13: My experience may not be the norm so I would very much appreciate contributions from other workplace activists on this point.

14: Joyce, 2015, p120.

15: Go to www.unitetheunion.org/unites-tata-steel-workers-suspend-strike-to-vote-on-new-pension-proposals

16: Go to www.birminghammail.co.uk/news/midlands-news/angry-jaguar-land-rover-shop-8015912

any grievance or claim by industrial action. The crucial point is that the reps tend to agree with this procedure. They take the new "regime for conducting relations between unions and employers" as a given *and have as yet no mass reason to challenge it.*

The consciousness of workplace activists

This raises the question of the consciousness of workplace activists. In many ways this is a subjective question, on which it is difficult to construct quantifiable indicators. However, qualitatively I can offer some examples.

Last year we secured a 16 percent pay rise for tens of call centre workers. From start to finish the claim took just under six months with the pay rise being backdated to an earlier date than the members had hoped to achieve. It involved two apparently contradictory processes—on the one hand stacks of meetings with the employer, days[17] spent researching wage rates and writing papers presenting the case that it was in the employer's interest to grant this pay rise (to reduce the use of much more expensive agency staff by making a permanent job more attractive). On the other hand regular organising meetings with the relevant members needed to be held, involving them with every decision, taking votes at every meeting, and keeping everything off social media. My concern throughout was that the rank and file would lose interest given the time it was taking. But they never showed any sign of wavering and we achieved the desired result. Our leverage in this situation was twofold. On the one hand was the market situation whereby these workers were being underpaid and knew it.[18] The existence of agency staff earning significantly more than the permanent staff was a constant source of discontent which management were aware of. At the same time we had the leverage of a union organising among the staff with a local leadership which had previously shown itself to the employer as being capable and willing to win strike votes should it be required.

But the key point is that the process delivered. No one showed any sign of frustration with the new "regime for conducting relations between unions and employers". Why would they? It delivered.

We have just recruited a wave of new shop stewards of which five are under the age of 28. What else does this younger generation understand about industrial relations other than ballots and so forth? What older activists

---

17: Most of it in my own time. I am on nothing like 100 percent facility time and in general am opposed to 100 percent facility time.

18: I make no apologies for making use of a specific labour market situation. What else was the "do it yourself reformism" of the 1950s and 1960s but precisely local stewards taking advantage of their labour market?

may regard as a restricting and frustrating industrial relations environment, younger shop stewards accept as being the situation they will work within. But their acceptance of this situation is not due to lack of combativity or lack of confidence, because from their point of view it can deliver.

I see no hostility from activists (young or old) to the principle of strike action, as demonstrated by their willingness to give solidarity donations to workers on strike. Our union branch voted unanimously two years ago to add a regular solidarity item to our monthly branch meeting standing orders. So every single month we look for a dispute to support. And whether there are 53, 35 or 8 people attending there is never any opposition to giving solidarity. My impression is that workers in dispute do not find it hard to win solidarity donations from other trade union activists. For example, the PCS strikers at the National Gallery raised over £160,000 in solidarity donations. It would be good to hear from other activists whether this is their experience too, as it gives us an important indication of the mood of trade union activists.

Let me give a further example of the consciousness of activists from the November 2013 Unite sector conferences. Members of the Socialist Workers Party intervened in a session of 500 workplace delegates over the issue of the Grangemouth defeat. My Unite comrade Ray put our argument, which was primarily that the defeat was unnecessary given the fact that Unite was recognised at the other nine Ineos manufacturing sites in the UK where solidarity action was possible; that solidarity from electricians and tanker drivers at Grangemouth itself was possible; and that industrial action could have been used to put political pressure on the Scottish National Party and Labour. What is interesting is the reaction of the delegates to Ray's speech. The reaction verged from polite agreement to enthusiastic endorsement, with a small minority cheering his comments. Ray put our case well in a non-sectarian manner. But, as Marx argued, social being determines consciousness rather than the reverse.[19] So a positive reaction (of varying degrees) from 500 workplace delegates speaks less to Ray's powers of persuasion but more to the fact that the audience was receptive to the argument. And this speaks of their social being. They were (and are) used to the union being able to stand up to the employer, should the union adopt the right tactics for the right occasion. The consensus was that the union had suffered an unnecessary defeat by not having a plan B, and that therefore a winning result was possible. However, if the same situation had occurred in the New Realism years immediately after the defeat

---

19: Marx, 1859.

of the miners, we would have been laughed out of court for making such a contribution. In other words the consciousness of workplace activists over the last 20 years has recovered from the depths of late 1980s and early 1990s and does not support the pessimistic analysis of workplace organisation.

Workplace pessimism on the left

In an SWP internal document in 2013 Neil from Edinburgh wrote that "our class has suffered a series of defeats since the 1970s with only the abolition of the poll tax" as an exception. Neil is not alone in his pessimistic assessment. In a meeting at Marxism 2015 another SWP comrade spoke about how we'd gone through "a 30-year period of defeats".

Think about what those two comrades are saying. Either 25 or 30 years of defeat. I'm going to argue with Neil's position simply because it's mathematically the less pessimistic position. So for 25 years week in, week out, month in, month out, year in, year out, decade in, decade out—defeat, defeat, defeat. I've been a workplace rep for every single one of those 25 years. Indeed for most of those 25 years I've been a senior lay negotiator with whichever private sector employer I was working for. So do I deserve the Lenin award for resilience for keeping going in the workplace during 25 years of defeat? Or do I need to be taken outside and shot for being so utterly useless as a rep that I was incapable of empowering my members over 25 years to win even the tiniest of victories?[20] And while we're at it, shouldn't those same questions be asked to all the existing 200,000[21] lay workplace reps? Indeed, how can a movement of defeat have 200,000 workplace reps? There are 6.4 million trade unionists in the UK, a level that has declined a little but not drastically since 1996.[22] Why would millions of workers pay up to £14 a month to stay in a movement that has only delivered defeat after defeat for the last 25 years?

The "decades of defeat" argument is wrong. It's not wrong because it's nine years of defeat rather than 25 years. It's wrong because we have not gone through a period of permanent defeat ever since the signal workers' qualified victory of 1994. Instead we've been in a period where sometimes we win, sometimes they win and sometimes it's a draw. Given that average real wages have risen for the vast majority of this period,[23] this would

---

20: I'm not bothered about the award but please don't vote to shoot me!

21: According to data at www.gov.uk/government/uploads/system/uploads/attachment_data/file/245570/09-931-reps-in-action-workplaces-gain-from-union-representation.pdf

22: Go to www.gov.uk/government/uploads/system/uploads/attachment_data/file/313768/bis-14-p77-trade-union-membership-statistical-bulletin-2013.pdf

23: A 2014 Office for National Statistics report stated that "since 1975 average earnings for full time employees have more than doubled after taking into account inflation"—www.ons.

suggest that we have won more times than we have lost. Similarly the sharp rise in income inequality which took place from 1974 to 1991 effectively paused in this period; the Gini coefficient—a measure of inequality—was at 0.24 in 1979 and rose to 0.34 in 1991. It has fluctuated around that level since then such that in 2014 the Gini coefficient level was still at 0.34.[24]

What the "decades of defeat" comrades are doing is misconstruing what Simon calls the new "regime for conducting relations between unions and employers" as a permanent situation of defeat. Hopefully I have already given enough evidence to prove otherwise. Though the creation of this new "regime for conducting relations between unions and employers" was the result of a defeat, *it is not itself a defeat*. The older generation may whine about having to go through collective procedures to achieve the 14 percent pay rise achieved earlier, but the younger generation do not. They do not perceive this regime as a defeat because they know of no other and because it is still very possible to achieve worthwhile results under this new industrial relations regime. It is true both that in order to achieve a return to the pre-downturn balance of class forces our side needs a major industrial offensive, and that we haven't had one. But not achieving such a breakthrough is not the same as being defeated. Indeed the current balance of forces is not just the result of the downturn defeat but is also the result of the *resilience* of trade unionism.

Here I want to return to Simon's point about comparisons with the 1974 high point of trade unionism leading to disorientation. In 1974 trade union membership reached 11.75 million. Today it is 6.4 million—an awful decline of 45 percent.[25] If you look at the statistics in this manner then workplace pessimism is justified. That is precisely why ruling class commentators always choose to make the comparison between today's level of trade union membership and that of 1974. Yet the vast majority of that decline took place between 1974 and 1996. For the 12 years from 1996 to 2008 trade union membership stabilised around 6.9 to 7 million until the recession of 2008 caused it to fall by 7 percent to 6.4 million.[26]

It would be better if there were no decline at all, but it is incorrect to describe the last 19 years as an "era of weak and declining trade unionism" as

gov.uk/ons/dcp171776_368928.pdf

24: Go to www.equalitytrust.org.uk/how-has-inequality-changed

25: Simon's article gives good objective explanations for the decline in membership, to which I'd like to add the abolition of the closed shop. If this existed today in all the workplaces covered by trade union agreements we could probably add another 1 million members to our figures.

26: Go to www.gov.uk/government/uploads/system/uploads/attachment_data/file/313768/bis-14-p77-trade-union-membership-statistical-bulletin-2013.pdf

Neil Davidson does in *New Left Review*.[27] And this relates to the consciousness of workplace activists. From my experience (I am unable to find any statistics) the majority of trade union activists have become active since 1996, ie in the last 19 years. Indeed, in my workplace committee I am the only rep who was a trade union activist before 1996. But this hardly makes the others "newbies". So their experience is one of national trade union stability, not at all of decline. For the best activists who adopt the organising agenda (see my appendix 3 below), their own workplace experience will be one of growth, not decline. Basing your industrial perspective on the massive decline prior to 1996 rather than the recent 19-year stability since that date puts you out of touch with the lived experience of most trade union activists.

Conclusion

My conclusion differs very little from that offered by Martin Upchurch.[28] But I would add three things. First, socialists have to strive consciously to use the normal route of industrial relations in an "organising" manner. This means always seeking to increase rank and file involvement by whatever means. For example, I ask every single person that I do casework for if they will help the union in any way. Every union meeting I run, whether a section meeting for a collective grievance or a branch meeting, has a sheet where attendees are asked if they will help distribute union newsletters. If strikes are harder to achieve (and that is not always for negative reasons) then we have to use the situation we are in to build workplace organisation.

Secondly, the "ballot victories" referred to earlier are objective evidence that parts of British capitalism can afford to pay, that parts of UK capitalism are not "in crisis". But should this situation end, then their room for manoeuvre will be reduced. In other words, we would be in a different situation if JLR or Rolls Royce or Tata Steel had been forced by economic circumstances to take their workforces on.

Thirdly, the Tories' attack on the current legal situation for trade unions opens the possibility of a wide layer of those 200,000 trade union activists being politicised as the rights they have got used to come under threat. The Unite the Resistance initiative, which is campaigning against the Trade Union Bill, could be about to find its biggest audience.

An overly pessimistic analysis of the balance of class forces will not help us take the movement forward. This article has been an attempt to address that.

27: Davidson, 2014.
28: Upchurch, 2015.

Appendix 1: Two examples against the workplace pessimists

I want to produce a couple of examples from my own experience to argue against the workplace pessimists, the "neoliberalism has removed the ability of the working class to fight back" brigade.

Example one

I started my "career" as a workplace white collar activist in the IT department of a multinational manufacturing company in 1980. The shop floor was very well organised. The clerical, technical and scientific staff were also well unionised. However, in the 1950s the unions had accepted that so-called "professional" jobs were excluded from collective bargaining and union recognition. Over time the company pursued a strategy of declaring more and more jobs as "professional", such that by the time I joined the company "professional" staff were the single biggest unit of white collar workers and were excluded from trade union recognition.

The IT department was designated as "professional" and was part of the first wave of mass IT workers.[29] None of my colleagues lived in a council house. The majority were homeowners with mortgages. The minority were younger private renters aspiring to become homeowners. It was a new industry with no traditions of trade unionism for the simple fact that it was new. In my department pay rises were awarded on an individual basis dependent upon performance appraisals. So what does a Marxist do in that situation? You could theorise on the way that capitalism is changing the workforce and its culture (all true) and draw conclusions about neoliberalism and the knowledge economy etc. Or you could try and organise. I chose the latter, using the lessons taught to me by the comrades from the International Socialists shop floor factory branch at Woodhead's Coil Springs, part of the automotive industry.

This was not a difficult choice for me. Marxism has always stressed the dynamic nature of capitalism—"the bourgeoisie cannot exist without constantly revolutionising the instruments of production, and thereby the relations of production, and with them the whole relations of society".[30] Therefore new occupations are always being created by capitalism: car workers; air crew; air traffic controllers; film crew; sound engineers; telephone engineers; electricity workers; gas engineers; and so on and so forth. At one time or another all these jobs were new; all of them would have had

---

29: You no longer needed to be a geeky genius to write computer languages (such as COBOL, IMS, JCL and SQL) that were now English-like.

30: Marx and Engels, 1976.

no traditions of trade unionism precisely because they were new occupations. But they all have trade union recognition now, because workers somewhere decided to organise and build rather than theorise about their "newness".

So how to organise? The issue I chose was individual pay, on the understanding that, whatever the situation, capitalism will always try and get away with paying the least it can to any workforce. So each year I received my pay rise and was told to "keep it secret, you're in the top 5 percent". This sounded unlikely to me. I conducted a verbal survey and discovered that, lo and behold, every single person was apparently "in the top 5 percent".

On revealing this at a social gathering,[31] the more experienced colleagues just laughed as if this was obvious but many were very angry. I argued that the company knew what we were all paid so they were the only people to benefit from keeping the pay rises secret. This must have made sense as we agreed to share pay rise information. Within a few years this had the desired effect of pushing up pay rises in a sort of white collar version of the shop floor "do it yourself reformism". Eventually the majority of the department were union members. The company prevented recognition by the simple device of merging my department with another whenever I reached a majority union membership (at least four times) and thus reducing the trade union density for the now enlarged unit. It was also because the membership were unwilling to take action for recognition, though they were willing to take action to defend me. So I never achieved formal trade union recognition, and thus this was only a partial victory. Yet in 1984 we were sufficiently organised to have a lunchtime meeting of over 60 people addressed by Coventry National Union of Mineworkers which voted unanimously to hold a weekly collection for the miners, something we continued until one month after the end of the miners' strike.

Example two

In the late 1990s my colleagues and I were outsourced to an offshoring company. Six months previously a group of similar workers from a different company (call it company B) had been outsourced to the same offshoring company. Each group of workers had union recognition with the same trade union, both groups worked in the same industry doing similar jobs and both groups were outsourced to the same company. Yet their experiences of the outsourcing were very different. The workers in company B found their union organisation ignored, and a majority of the outsourced employees

---

31: Until the office became more confident, most discussions about the union and pay had to start by taking place outside of work itself.

were moved off their original employer's workplace and dispersed around the country such that almost 50 percent of them resigned. By comparison our union organisation grew from strength to strength (see reference to previous victory earlier): not only did we never suffer a single compulsory redundancy, but we never even had a single person put at risk of compulsory redundancy.

Now if the workers of company B had been avid readers of our literature, I'm sure that Neil from Edinburgh's arguments about neoliberalism would have made sense—outsourcing, offshoring, globalisation, weak unions. His workplace pessimism would have completely fitted with their experience. However, to my members it would have made no sense. We consistently got above RPI pay awards, and overtime pay and rates were always without exception strictly enforced. The difference between the two was not *objective* circumstances. The difference between the two experiences was *subjective* organisation. My workplace had rank and file workplace organisation with a socialist leadership. Company B had neither. And this is my argument with the workplace pessimists. They misunderstand subjective weakness as objective structural weakness. In doing so they reduce the scope for human agency and turn an English hill into an unconquerable Everest. Their arguments provide absolutely no help whatsoever to any workplace activist.

Appendix 2: On casework

Individual casework is seen as being a crucial part of the trade union rep's job. According to a government commissioned focus group of workplace reps, "for the vast majority of participants their union work was dominated by individual representation and casework".[32] Another study said that "most [shop stewards, convenors, branch officers and the like] help individual members by representing them in grievance and disciplinary matters or by resolving other personal issues at work",[33] and the 2011 Workplace Employment Relations Study found that "taking both union and non-union representatives together, the most common issues that representatives spent time on were discipline and grievances"; this accounted for, on average, 66 percent of the time spent on union activities.[34]

The left has rarely discussed casework. The usual attitude has been that it's a necessary burden that socialists have to undertake in order to retain creditability, an attitude that I have shared. Yet the previous quotes show that casework takes up the majority of the union time of the majority

32: Department of Trade and Industry, 2007, p59.
33: Department for Business, Enterprise and Regulatory Reform, 2009, p15.
34: Department for Business, Innovation and Skills and others, 2011, p16.

of reps. I think a discussion on this activity is long overdue. This is just a start of the discussion and I hope other workplace activists will contribute and add to it. The following are points from casework that I have learnt from the last few years:

- Activists need to take casework seriously and embrace it as a necessary part of the job. If the individual is supported correctly, then even when the union loses the individual is still supportive of the union.

- Individuals who have been supported can be persuaded to become reps or newsletter distributors for the union, ie to get more active.

- Casework provides a picture of what is going on at work under the surface—an office may appear all calm and peaceful, then an individual case highlights the tensions underneath the surface calm.

- Casework is incredibly time consuming—there is no escape from this fact. But it can be used to create collective issues. So whenever you can see beyond the individual issue to collectivise the situation you are taking a step forward; for example I defended various individuals against sickness absence disciplinaries and this ended up being a collective successful campaign to modify and weaken the sickness absence process, but that campaign would never have started without the individual cases to begin with. Reps should always check whether the individual case is in fact a sign of a collective issue which can be addressed as such.

- Casework throws light on the employers' procedures, so can be used to change these procedures for the better.

- If you and an individual discover a fault in a procedure then try and persuade the individual to help you win the motion to correct it at your next branch meeting.

- Without breaching confidentiality, always let your immediate section know of the sort of issues your casework is covering—this will ensure their support for your time away from work

- Always celebrate every casework victory—our reps always email each other when we win—every step to boost confidence helps.

- Cases can be won by a mild threat to go outside the procedure such as "if the company does not stop this disciplinary then I have the member's permission to write up their situation in a union newsletter and distribute to every member of staff in the building. If you are confident of the correctness of your position then let me get on with it. If not, then I suggest you halt this process ASAP". Activists must not underestimate the power of union newsletters to challenge the employer's hegemony. Management do not like their poor behaviour made public within the company; it is a more useful threat than you imagine. But you have to have the workplace organisation to enable you to carry it out.

Appendix 3: The official organising agenda
The TUC's organising academy was created in 1998 and the TGWU's in 2004. Unite's "organising agenda" is a continuation of the TGWU's[35] and has two main strands to it:

- The 100 Percent Unite campaign to increase membership where recognition exists.
- The spreading of trade union recognition into previously unrecognised areas ("greenfield organising").

The TGWU's organising strategy met a target of 10,000 new members per year, plus recognition wins in the airline Flybe, and in the poultry industry such as in Bernard Matthews. Unite's 100 Percent campaign, launched in 2011, had by 2014 delivered 144,182 new members. And new recognition agreements continue. There is no research that summarises the total of new trade union agreements but Unite claims nine new recognition agreements in the motor supply industry in 2014 alone. The TUC claimed in 2006 that since 2000 "over 1,100 deals have been signed and over 310,000 employees have gained the right to be collectively represented by a trade union".[36]

35: Unite the union was created by a merger of the Transport and General Workers Union (TGWU) and Amicus in 2007.
36: Go to www.tuc.org.uk/union-issues/union-recognition-campaigns-treble-deals-get-tougher-secure

References

Darlington, Ralph, 2009, "RMT Strike Activity on London Underground: Incidence, Dynamics and Causes", paper presented at the 15th International Industrial Relations Association Conference, www.ilera-directory.org/15thworldcongress/files/papers/Track_2/Poster/CS1W_33_DARLINGTON.pdf

Davidson, Neil, 2013, "The Neoliberal Era in Britain: Historical Developments and Current Perspectives", *International Socialism* 139 (summer), http://isj.org.uk/the-neoliberal-era-in-britain-historical-developments-and-current-perspectives

Davidson, Neil, 2014, "A Scottish Watershed", *New Left Review*, II/89, https://newleftreview.org/II/89/neil-davidson-a-scottish-watershed

DBERR, 2009, Reps in Action: How Workplaces can gain from Modern Union Representation" (May), www.gov.uk/government/uploads/system/uploads/attachment_data/file/245570/09-931-reps-in-action-workplaces-gain-from-union-representation.pdf

DBIS and others, 2011, "The 2011 Workplace Employment Relations Study: First Findings", www.gov.uk/government/uploads/system/uploads/attachment_data/file/336651/bis-14-1008-WERS-first-findings-report-fourth-edition-july-2014.pdf

DTI, 2007, "Consultation Document: Workplace Representatives: A Review of their Facilities and Facility Time" (January), http://webarchive.nationalarchives.gov.uk/+/http://www.berr.gov.uk/files/file36336.pdf

Gluckstein, Donny, 2015, "The Question of Confidence: A Reply to Simon Joyce", *International Socialism* 146 (spring), http://isj.org.uk/the-question-of-confidence-a-reply-to-simon-joyce

Hardy, Jane, and Joseph Choonara, 2013, "Neoliberalism and the British Working Class: A Reply to Neil Davidson", *International Socialism* 140 (autumn), http://isj.org.uk/neoliberalism-and-the-british-working-class-a-reply-to-neil-davidson

Joyce, Simon, 2015, "Why are there So Few Strikes?", *International Socialism* 145 (winter), http://isj.org.uk/why-are-there-so-few-strikes

Lyddon, Dave, 2015, "Bureaucratic Mass Strikes: A Response to Mark O'Brien", *International Socialism* 146 (spring), http://isj.org.uk/bureaucratic-mass-strikes-a-response-to-mark-obrien

Marx, Karl, 1859, "A Contribution to the Critique of Political Economy", www.marxists.org/archive/marx/works/1859/critique-pol-economy

Marx, Karl, and Frederick Engels, 1976 [1848], "Manifesto of the Communist Party", in Marx and Engels, *Collected Works* (Progress Publishers), www.marxists.org/archive/marx/works/1848/communist-manifesto

O'Brien, Mark, 2014, "The Problem of the One-Day Strike: A Response to Sean Vernell", *International Socialism* 142 (spring), http://isj.org.uk/the-problem-of-the-one-day-strike-a-response-to-sean-vernell

O'Brien, Mark, 2015, "Revolutionaries in the Unions: The Reality of the Strike", *International Socialism* 147 (summer), http://isj.org.uk/revolutionaries-in-the-unions-the-reality-of-the-strike

Upchurch, Martin, 2015, "The end of the "safe space" for unions? A response to Simon Joyce", *International Socialism* 146 (spring), http://isj.org.uk/the-end-of-the-safe-space-for-unions

Jobs, justice, climate: The struggle continues

Martin Empson

A review of Paul Hampton, **Workers and Trade Unions for Climate Solidarity: Tackling Climate Change in a Neoliberal World** *(Routledge Studies in Climate, Work and Society, 2015), £90*

The complete and utter failure of the world's governments to take meaningful action on climate change was once again apparent at the COP21 talks in Paris in December 2015. In Britain, the Conservative government was barely into its new term before it announced policies that undermined even the minimal commitments its predecessors had made. Their policies favoured fracking and other fossil fuels over renewable energy, airport and road expansion over public transport, and introduced reductions in funding that should have helped insulate homes.

Discussions about how we get a sustainable society—reduce emissions and force action upon unwilling governments—are ever more important. For socialists one key aspect of this debate in recent years has been the question of climate jobs and the role of trade unions.

Paul Hampton is head of research and policy for the Fire Brigades Union. His new book begins by locating the source of the climate crisis with capitalism. While noting that capitalism is a system based on the accumulation of wealth for the sake of accumulation, with inevitable environmental impacts, he also points out that the increased use of machinery to increase relative surplus value in the exploitative relationship between capital and worker also has an environmental aspect. Thus, the "technological revolution", powered by the burning of fossil fuels for energy, is part of what Hampton calls the "subsumption of climate to capital". The importance of fossil fuels lies in their "flexibility, fitting capitalist society's particular relationship to nature" and their centrality to the capitalist economy is the outcome of the development of capitalism, rather than "market forces or pluralistic decision-making". Thus Hampton argues climate change cannot be seen as a result of "market failure", as mainstream economists like Nicolas Stern argue, but as a result of how capitalism works. To avoid runaway climate change a "critique of capitalism...is the logical starting point".

How does this fit in with the role of trade unions—which tend not to be revolutionary anti-capitalist organisations? The first point that Hampton makes is that unions, and by extension, workers have mostly been overlooked in "mainstream social science". Bosses are often discussed as "climate actors", those with the potential to enact changes such as reduction of emissions. But the people they employ are often ignored.

This is a mistake for two reasons. The first is that, as Hampton points out, workers have a vested interest in dealing with climate change because they are not only "likely to be among those most vulnerable to the physical impacts of climate change and to have fewer resources to adapt" but they are "also likely to be the victims of government policies designed to tackle climate change, especially those that shift the costs of mitigation and adaption from capital onto labour" (p39). It is for the latter reason that socialists and environmental activists must argue for a "just transition", so that those who face losing jobs because of action on climate change, such as the closure of a highly polluting factory or the transition from fossil fuel generation to renewable energy, do not lose out.

The second reason is that workers are in an excellent position to help reduce emissions in workplaces. The last decade has seen a growing awareness from the official trade union movement of environmental issues, demonstrated by the number of conferences, policy documents and meetings as well as the support for campaigns such as that for one million climate jobs. But there has also been a significant growth in the number of workplaces where union reps are part of reducing emissions. Often these are "environmental reps" and in some unions, notably Unison, PCS, UCU and Prospect, such reps have formed national networks. The TUC estimates that there are also over 1,000 union green workplace projects in the UK.

While some of this work might concern workplace-based issues such as campaigning for facilities for cyclists, remote working, or even different dress codes in high-temperature weather, it can also lead to attempts to force more responsibility onto the employer. One survey reported that trade unionists from Unison, Prospect, Unite and GMB at the energy company EDF had "negotiated an international agreement on corporate responsibility, which includes commitments to tackle climate change" (p129).

But many reps report that they have difficulty raising environmental issues at work, and almost three-quarters say that they do not have facility time for environmental work. Hampton shows that in many workplaces, even ones that have green workplace projects, management often drag their feet on environmental issues, citing costs or lack of resources. Part of the problem is the lack of legal recognition of the role of environmental reps. This is in part because the last Labour government failed to pass legislation, leaving environmental reps with limited powers. Hampton cites one example of a trade union survey which pointed out "virtually no one outside union circles accepted the validity of the case, even in organisations with successful voluntary arrangements" for statutory rights to time off for environmental training for union reps.

There is also an ambiguity that arises from how environmental questions are framed in the workplace. Plymouth City Council, for instance, signed a Green Workspace Agreement with the three local government unions, "to encourage council staff to work with their managers to reduce carbon, encourage sustainability and save money" (p141). This emphasis on reducing costs as well as carbon can lead to situations where trade unionists might end up policing the behaviour of their colleagues on behalf of management. One example is from the supermarket chain Asda, where GMB reps were "encouraging workers to close walk-in fridge and freezer doors when they are not in use". This might lead to a situation where union environmental reps play a role in disciplining workers for not following procedures, rather than fighting to defend their members.

However, Hampton notes that a 2009 survey showed that a quarter of reps surveyed had taken independent action on environmental issues. This suggests, says Hampton, that environmental reps saw their activity as coming out of the interests of their members and the union, rather than "common interests" with the employer. He continues: "Employment relations on climate issues were not uniformly harmonious, but subject to the pressures of consent and coercion. To write environmental reps off as merely a new form of class collaboration would be to miss some important antagonistic aspects of the activity" (p146). I would add that environmental reps can play an important role in raising wider environmental questions in the workplace, as well as getting workers involved in demonstrations and protests.

The British trade union movement's attitude to climate change can be best understood as a form of "ecological modernism". Hampton argues that this is a framework that is distinct from both Marxist and neoliberal approaches:

> Ecological modernisation utilises familiar metaphors such as "win–win" co-benefits, "low-hanging fruit" and "technological crutches". Three key features of ecological modernisation stand out: (1) an emphasis on state and non-state actors as significant agents for constructing climate alliances; (2) greater sensitivity to the social implications of climate policy; and (3) a wider range of instruments alongside market mechanisms (p20).

The Ecomodernist approach has become more mainstream recently. In April 2015, the Breakthrough Institute published *An Ecomodernist Manifesto* which emphasised the importance of technological solutions to climate change over solutions based on social change. For the authors of the *Manifesto*, technology reduces humanity's dependence on nature, and thus technology (and demographic trends) can de-couple "human well-being from environmental impacts".

As the authors write:

> Accelerated technological progress will require the active, assertive and aggressive participation of private sector entrepreneurs, markets, civil society, and the state. While we reject the planning fallacy of the 1950s, we continue to embrace a strong public role in addressing environmental problems and accelerating technological innovation, including research to develop better technologies, subsidies and other measures to help bring them to market, and regulations to mitigate environmental hazards.[1]

While this can sound positive, in practice it means an over-emphasis on the state and business and a reliance on partnerships between capital and workers to achieve change. Despite talk of the importance of "non-state actors", this rarely means the ability to hold corporations to account.

Ultimately ecological modernisation means looking to a more environmentally friendly capitalism, despite the impossibility of such an aim. This reflects the nature of trade unionism under capitalism, with unions trying to win reforms from the system to benefit their members. However, even such limited ambitions can give opportunities for more radical ideas.

1:   *An Ecomodernist Manifesto*, April 2015, available at www.ecomodernism.org

"Social movement unionism" shows some of the potential to raise more radical demands around climate. This, Hampton suggests, is best shown by the way that the RMT in Britain related to the factory occupation in 2009 by workers at Vestas on the Isle of Wight. This action was against the closure of a plant that manufactured wind turbine blades. The RMT gave unprecedented support to the occupiers, helped the workers outside the occupation organise and helped build a national solidarity campaign. Bob Crow, the then general secretary, even promised a helicopter to deliver food should the company not end its blockade of the occupation. While this wasn't needed, RMT lawyers did represent workers in the courts.

Social movement unionism means relating to wider social movements, campaigns and political questions and is particularly important to environmental questions, as one study argues: "it is difficult to imagine preservation of the earth and a broadening of human rights unless unions join such coalitions as enthusiastic proponents and partners" (quoted on p37). But social movementism on its own does not automatically mean progressive positions. The Canadian Auto Workers union, for instance, was often seen as a model of social movementism, but its leadership ended up supporting car manufacturers' calls to make SUVs in Canada and hostility to hybrid vehicles, because the leadership ended up accommodating to "market pressure".

The limitations of the trade union movement on environmental questions are unfortunately all too apparent. Over the summer of 2015, for instance, the GMB took a position of support for fracking, signing an agreement with oil and gas exploration firms. In the early 2000s the TUC as well as Amicus, the TGWU, GMB and Balpa (which represents airline pilots) jointly called for a third runway at Heathrow with Brendan Barber, then TUC general secretary, speaking alongside BA, Virgin and BAA in support of expansion. In both examples the question of jobs was at the forefront of the unions' arguments. In the case of Heathrow they supported market mechanisms, such as carbon trading, to reduce the impact on the environment.

The problem is that the TUC (and by extension most of the union movement) is limited by the framework imposed upon it by mainstream politics. Hampton uses the example of the union movement's attitude to the building of a new coal-fired power station at Kingsnorth. Resolutely opposed by the environmental movement, the expansion of the Kingsnorth site by E.ON was supported by the TUC and other unions in existing power stations. They acknowledged arguments against the burning of coal by saying Kingsnorth must only go ahead as a viable carbon capture and storage (CCS) demonstration plant, though they did not argue for a "moratorium on new coal-fired power stations until CCS was developed". Eventually, under pressure from protestors, E.ON pulled the plug on plans for Kingsnorth, leading to a "bitter" response from the union movement. Kingsnorth demonstrated how easy it is to drive a wedge between the union and environmental movements.

That said, the union movement has moved on, in places, from simply arguing in defence of jobs or the creation of new jobs irrespective of the environmental impacts. One example of this is the question of climate jobs itself. The one million climate jobs campaign, which originated with the Campaign Against Climate Change's Trade Union Group, now has the support of six national unions and has spawned a number of similar campaigns internationally. In the run-up to the protests at the COP21 meeting, the ITUC helped organise a global union climate conference, in the summer of 2015, which had the question of climate jobs at its heart.

The campaign for climate jobs fits with existing ideas of "just transition" within the union movement, but also has concrete demands that call for the creation of new jobs and new industries leading to the reduction of emissions. Hampton notes that the demand for climate jobs is "perceived as a key mobilising tool, shaping an alliance between trade unionists, environmentalists and other activists to tackle climate concerns alongside other wider issues arising from the economic crisis. Implicitly, it is not aimed at partnership with employers or indeed with existing governments" (p86).

The climate jobs campaign was given renewed momentum by the Vestas dispute, which demonstrated the potential for trade unionists to unite with wider forces over economic and environmental questions. Hampton provides a detailed account of the struggle to save the 600 jobs at Vestas, demonstrating the importance of the role of socialists in raising the question of occupation, of bringing solidarity and building the campaign. He also shows the limitations of the TUC approach which "prioritised partnership" between the workers, employers and government despite the fact that the bosses were particularly belligerent and the Labour government was uninterested in saving the factory through nationalisation.

Labour's failings at the time are summed up well by Joan Ruddock, then minister of state for energy, who told a delegation of Vestas workers: "We live in a market economy, all the advanced economies think the same. The only economy that does not have a market is North Korea... It's not appropriate! The government does not want to be producers of wind turbines, and we did not want to be bankers" (p173).

Hampton makes it clear that dealing with climate change means rejecting strategies that rely on the market. We need "structural change" on a global scale involving:

> A rapid retooling of production and distribution systems... These will only come about as a result of massive, democratic public intervention and widespread global and national regulation of the market-based regime. Transitional reforms could limit the power of capital and point towards more social, planned and democratic forms of climate governance (p204).

This book shows that there is enormous potential within the unions for a movement that has questions of climate and social justice at its core. Socialists have made very important contributions to shaping that and beginning to move the debate away from the dominant ideas of ecological modernism. There is much more work to be done and this useful book contains lots of relevance to trade unionists and environmental campaigners keen that unions play a more prominent role in the climate movement. My only gripe is the high price. I hope a cheaper paperback becomes available soon.

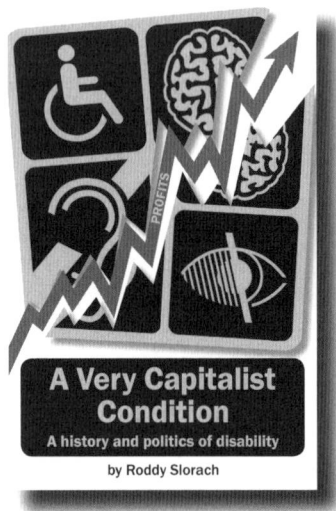

Between Marx and Freud: Erich Fromm revisited

Iain Ferguson

More than three decades after his death, the ideas of Erich Fromm are enjoying something of an intellectual renaissance. Fromm (1900-1980) was a German-Jewish psychoanalyst, writer, public intellectual and activist whose life-long concern was with developing an understanding of the relationship between capitalism and mental health, based on his attempt to integrate the ideas of Karl Marx and Sigmund Freud. Recent years have seen the publication of no less than three new biographies of Fromm,[1] all of which challenge to a greater or lesser degree the very negative view of Fromm that has prevailed on much of the left for several decades, while 2014 saw the publication of two new collections of essays devoted to discussing his ideas.[2] His work has been cited approvingly both by popular psychologists such as Oliver James and also by Marxists such as Kevin B Anderson, Michael Löwy and long-standing Socialist Workers Party member Sabby Sagall, who draws heavily on Fromm's concept of social character in his recent study of genocides.[3]

Fromm's work merits our attention for several reasons. First, unusually for a psychoanalyst, he considered himself to be a Marxist right until the end of his life. While his main interest was in a critical integration

---

1:    Thomson, 2009; Friedman, 2013; Durkin, 2014.
2:    Miri, Lake and Kress, 2014; Braune, 2014.
3:    James, 2008; Anderson, 2007a; Anderson, 2007b; Löwy, 2013; Sagall, 2013.

of the ideas of Marx and Freud, he was clear as to which thinker he saw as the more important. As he wrote in *Beyond the Chains of Illusion: My Encounter with Marx and Freud*:

> My concern in this book…is only with Marx and Freud. By putting their names together the impression might easily arise that I consider them as two men of equal stature and equal historical significance. I want to make it clear at the outset that this is not so. That Marx is a figure of world historical significance with whom Freud cannot even be compared in this respect hardly needs to be said.[4]

Secondly, he held at least some political positions in common with the traditions of this journal. For example, during the 1950s he viewed the Soviet Union as being state capitalist and, immediately following the statement quoted above, went on to "deeply regret the fact that a distorted and degraded 'Marxism' is preached in almost one third of the world". He deplored "the general habit of considering Stalinism…as identical with, or at least a continuation of revolutionary Marxism" and, remarkably, at the height of the Cold War in the late 1950s, he defended Lenin and Leon Trotsky. In a review of *Trotsky's Diary in Exile* in 1958, he wrote: "They were men with an uncompromising sense of truth, penetrating to the very essence of reality, and never taken in by the deceptive surface; of an unquestionable courage and integrity; of deep concern and devotion to man and his future; and with little vanity or lust for power".[5]

Thirdly, he was a key contributor to the socialist humanist movement that emerged in the mid to late-1950s from the wreckage of Stalinism and which has recently attracted renewed interest. His book *Marx's Concept of Man*, published in 1961, contained the first English translation of Marx's *Economic and Philosophical Manuscripts* (and he opposed those who argued that there was a "break" between the young Marx of the manuscripts and the mature Marx). Although by his own admission, he was never primarily an activist, he did play an active role in the social movements of the 1960s—against nuclear weapons, around civil rights and in opposition to the Vietnam war, as well as being a lifelong opponent of Zionism and the Zionist state.

For reasons that will be discussed below, Fromm has been an unfashionable, even forgotten, figure on the political and academic left for several decades even though (or perhaps because) his books such as *The Fear*

4: Fromm, 1962, p11.
5: Cited in Anderson, 2007b.

of Freedom, *The Sane Society* and his bestseller *The Art of Loving* attracted a huge popular readership (the latter having sold in the region of 25 million copies—in Germany second only to the Bible!). The current revival of interest in his work, however, suggests that a re-assessment of his legacy from the perspective of classical Marxism is overdue.

This article is an attempt to contribute to such a reassessment. To do so, I shall first provide a brief biographical overview. Secondly, I shall critically assess three key elements of Fromm's thought: his view of human nature; his concept of social character; and his radical humanism. In my concluding comments, I shall consider some of the reasons for the renewed interest in Fromm's work and the extent to which his ideas are useful for those seeking to build a saner society in the second decade of the 21st century.

Erich Fromm: his life and times

Fromm was born to Orthodox Jewish parents in Frankfurt am Main in 1900. His father was descended from a long line of rabbinical scholars and although Fromm the younger formally renounced Judaism in his late twenties, he was deeply influenced throughout his life by aspects of the Old Testament tradition, particularly the writings of the prophets Isaiah, Amos and Hosea. What attracted him to these figures was their "prophetic messianism", their vision of the "end of days" when nations would "beat their swords into ploughshares and their spears into pruning hooks; nation shall not lift sword against nation; nor shall they learn war any more". He referred to these writings as "an inexhaustible source of vitality".[6]

After initially studying jurisprudence at Frankfurt University, Fromm transferred to Heidelberg where he studied sociology under Alfred Weber, brother of the sociologist Max Weber—though in contrast to his more famous brother, Alfred was described by Fromm as "a humanist, not a nationalist, and a man of outstanding courage and integrity".[7] This was a highly significant period in Fromm's life. It was at Heidelberg that he first systematically studied Marx's writings. It was here also that he met his future wife Frieda Reichmann, a well-known psychoanalyst, with whom he underwent psychoanalysis; together they also developed a life-long interest in Buddhism.

Fromm went on to train as a psychoanalyst in Berlin where he attended seminars for dissident young psychoanalysts organised by the left-leaning analyst Otto Fenichel. The main concern of these seminars was with Marxist-Freudian theoretical integration and with promoting social

---

6:   Durkin, 2014, pp18-19.
7:   Durkin, 2014, p20.

and economic reforms. Fromm's evolution towards Marxism dates from this period and in 1928 he offered a lecture on "The Psychoanalysis of the Petty Bourgeoisie".[8]

In 1929 Fromm was invited by Max Horkheimer, the director of the recently formed Frankfurt Institute for Social Research, to participate in the Institute's research programme. A central concern of the Institute, amongst whose other early members were Herbert Marcuse, Theodore Adorno and Walter Benjamin, was to explain the failure of the German Revolution between 1918 and 1923 and the subsequent rise of National Socialism. Dissatisfied with the mechanistic Marxism of the Second International, which emphasised the role of "objective" economic factors, the Institute looked instead to the writings of Marxists such as Karl Korsch and George Lukács, who highlighted the central role of working class consciousness as a factor in the success or otherwise of the revolution. A key challenge for Korsch and others was to explain why the German working class had apparently failed to develop such a revolutionary consciousness:

> In the fateful months after November 1918, when the organised political power of the bourgeoisie was smashed and outwardly there was nothing else in the way of the transition from capitalism to socialism, the great chance was never seized because the socio-psychological conditions were lacking.[9]

In seeking to understand why these conditions were lacking, Horkheimer and his colleagues looked to the new science of psychoanalysis being developed by Freud and his colleagues. The notion that Freudian concepts of the unconscious, of sexuality as the key driver of human behaviour, or of the Oedipus complex can contribute to an understanding of class consciousness may seem odd, if not downright bizarre, to many contemporary Marxists. This has not always been the case, however. While many Marxists in the early 20th century were hostile to Freud's ideas, not all were. Trotsky and other leading Bolsheviks such as Karl Radek defended, albeit critically, the use of psychoanalysis in Russia; Marxists such as Wilhelm Reich as well as those associated with the Frankfurt Institute emphasised what they saw as the revolutionary kernel in psychoanalysis and its compatibility with Marxism; and Freud's close colleague Sándor Ferenczi was the first ever professor of psychoanalysis in the short-lived communist government in Hungary in 1919.

8:   Friedman, 2014, p26.
9:   Korsch, cited in Sagall, 2013, p7.

The shift in attitude, as Andrew Collier argued in an earlier issue of this journal, came with the rise of Stalinism in Russia and its influence on the communist movement worldwide:

> The great downturn in prospects of cooperation came with Stalin. The suppression of psychoanalysis in Russia was part of the same puritanical programme which led to prison sentences for homosexuals, the prohibition of abortion, the preaching of sexual abstinence to students, the awarding of state prizes to particularly prolific mothers and so on.[10]

Fromm's first task within the Institute was to undertake a comprehensive survey of the attitudes of the German working class (published after his death as *The Working Class in Weimar Germany: A Psychological and Sociological Study*). During this period Fromm also wrote a series of articles that saw him develop his own particular fusion of Marx and Freud at the core of which was what was to become his trademark concept of "social character", which will be considered in more depth below.

The rise of Nazism, however, forced Fromm to flee Germany and in 1934 he settled in the United States. During the 1930s he became increasingly critical of some of Freud's key concepts, above all the central role he gave to biologically-based drives in the formation of personality, and this brought him into conflict with leading figures in the Institute. Writing in 1936 he argued that "the problem within psychology and sociology is the dialectical intertwining of natural and historical factors. Freud has wrongly based psychology totally on natural factors".[11] For these views Fromm was to be fiercely attacked by Horkheimer, Adorno and later Marcuse. He left the Institute in 1939.

In 1941 Fromm published *Escape from Freedom* (published in the UK as *The Fear of Freedom*). Here he argued that while the transition from feudalism to capitalism meant that human beings were now "free" in the sense that they were no longer tied to the land or to a particular master, there was a downside to that freedom, namely unbearable feelings of isolation, powerlessness and anxiety: "Our aim will be to show that the structure of modern society affects man in two ways simultaneously: he becomes more independent, self-reliant and critical and he becomes more isolated, alone and afraid".[12]

People could respond to that dilemma in two main ways: either through "automaton conformism", a form of escapism involving submersion

---

10: Collier, 1980, p51.
11: Cited in Funk, 2000, p94.
12: Fromm, 2013, p104.

of the self into the "mass", the most common response in the so-called "mass societies" of Nazi Germany, Stalin's Russia or US consumerist capitalism; or through courageously facing up to and embracing freedom in a creative way.

The book struck a chord with many and its success turned Fromm into a public intellectual. He was a prolific writer and *Escape from Freedom* was followed by many more publications over the next 40 years including *The Sane Society, Man for Himself* and his most famous book, *The Art of Loving*.

While his popular reputation grew, his political and academic reputation was severely damaged, however, by a debate with Marcuse in the magazine *Dissent* in the mid-1950s.[13] In essence, Marcuse argued that Fromm, in rejecting Freud's biologically-based libido theory as the key force in character formation and emphasising instead the role of social structures, had abandoned the radical kernel of Freud's thought. In place of Freud's instinct theory, Fromm had substituted an "idealistic ethics" of human productivity, love and sanity in a society that was alienated and driven by the market.

Whatever the fairness or otherwise in Marcuse's description of Fromm as a moraliser and "sermonising social worker", there is no doubt that much of his work from the 1950s onwards did indeed verge on the self-help genre. As Friedman (a sympathetic if occasionally critical biographer) comments on Fromm's best-known publication:

> Unlike *Escape from Freedom* or *Man for Himself, The Art of Loving* did not seem to come from the pen of a public intellectual. Earlier, millions of readers had turned to Carnegie for lessons in business success and to Peale for God's assistance in enhancing their social and economic mobility. Now, they embraced Fromm for concrete and upbeat guidelines for bringing love more amply into their lives. Fromm coupled his instructions on how the individual could garner love with the caution that it was extremely difficult to do under marketplace constraints. That warning was easy for readers to overlook amid the optimism of America's post-war economic boom. Fromm gave primacy to an upbeat message of self-enhancement in a "sunny-side up" post-war world and pushed the harsher themes of his social criticism to the periphery.[14]

The fact that, as Friedman notes, Fromm's standards of scholarship sometimes fell short of what would normally be expected within the academy, particularly in respect of historical matters, did not help either.

13: The debate and its context is described in detail in Friedman, 2014, pp191-198.
14: Friedman, 2014, p182.

What is clear is that as Fromm's academic reputation diminished, his popular reputation grew through the 1960s and beyond. His books sold in millions globally (*To Have or to Be*, for example, published in 1976, was translated into 26 languages and sold more than 10 million copies worldwide), he became an adviser to leading American politicians, he was in high demand as a lecturer and he became a leading figure in psychoanalysis in Mexico where he had moved for health reasons in the 1950s. He remained there until the mid-1970s when he moved with his wife to Locarno in Switzerland where he died in 1980.

Fromm's concept of human nature

The notion of a shared, universal human nature is at the heart of Fromm's thought. It is the cornerstone of his "radical humanism" as well as providing the criterion for his assessment of particular societies as "sane" or otherwise. The concept of the "sane society", the title of one of his best-known books, provides a useful starting point for a discussion of his view of human nature. In what sense can whole societies be labelled as sane or not sane? Isn't this an example of Fromm falling into what the philosopher G E Moore called the naturalistic fallacy, inferring what "ought" to exist from what does exist? Or is there some criterion that allows us to make this judgement? Fromm believed that there was. As one recent commentator has argued:

> Fromm's entire concept of critical theory, of ethics and of social and cultural critique is premised on the thesis that there exists, in some sense, normative statements about the nature of human beings that are objectively valid and that must serve as an anchor to any theory of society if it is to be understood as critical in any sense.[15]

What, then, was Fromm's theory of human nature? In *Man for Himself*, he began by dismissing what he saw as two erroneous views. The first is that put forward by conservative thinkers which sees human nature as fixed and unchanging, the idea, for example that people are "basically selfish". That assumption, he argues, is essentially an ideological one since it "served to prove that their ethical systems and social institutions were necessary and unchangeable, being built upon the alleged nature of man".[16] It was a view that reflected their norms and interests but one which was not supported by any evidence.

15: Thompson, 2014, p44.
16: Fromm, 1949, p21.

However, in reacting against that view, Fromm argued, progressive thinkers had sometimes adopted an equally erroneous view of the infinite malleability of human nature, a view usually referred to as "sociological relativism". As he acknowledged, if this was the case and human beings were simply puppets to be shaped in any way whatsoever by the dominant social arrangements, then "no social order could be criticised or judged from the standpoint of man's welfare since there would be no concept of "man". This is not to say that human beings cannot adapt to the most extreme conditions. They can—but there is a price to be paid:

> Man can adapt himself to slavery, but he reacts to it by lowering his intellectual and moral qualities; he can adapt himself to a culture permeated by mutual distrust and hostility, but he reacts to this adaptation by becoming weak and sterile. Man can adapt himself to cultural conditions which demand the repression of sexual strivings, but in achieving this adaptation he develops, as Freud has shown, neurotic symptoms. He can adapt himself to almost any culture pattern, but in so far as these are contradictory to his nature he develops mental and emotional disturbances which force him eventually to change these conditions since he cannot change his nature.[17]

In contrast, then, to these erroneous views, Fromm's own understanding of the nature of human beings, his "philosophical anthropology", drew selectively on the ideas of both Freud and Marx. To deal first with Freud, two aspects of Freud's thought scandalised early 20th century European society more than any others: first, his view that the source of much of our experience and of our actions is unconscious and secondly, his stress on the role of sexuality in the formation of personality and character.[18] Fromm accepted the first proposition but rejected the second. As a practising psychoanalyst until the end of his life, he accepted and worked with Freud's concept of the "unconscious" (while making clear that the term is actually "a mystification… There is no such thing as *the* unconscious; there are only experiences of which we are aware, and others of which we are not aware, that is, *of which we are unconscious*"[19]). He also developed a theory of the "social unconscious" as referring to those areas of repression common to most members of society or of a particular class. However, by the end of the 1930s, he had rejected Freud's instinct theory and in particular its emphasis on

---

17: Fromm, 1949, pp22-23.
18: Collier, 1980; Mitchell, 1974.
19: Fromm, 1962, p93, emphasis in original.

sexuality. First, he argued, Freud's theory was reductionist in seeing human beings' need to relate to others as simply derived from, and an expression of, a biological instinct. Freud, he argued, had got things the wrong way round. Rather, sexuality was one expression of human beings' fundamental need for relatedness. Freud's over-emphasis on sexuality and his "mechanistic materialism" reflected the society and the period in which he had lived. Secondly, while humans were part of the animal world, through evolution they had developed an ability to reason that allowed them both to plan their environment in a way that other animals could not and also to reflect on their own thoughts, feelings and behaviours. Or, as Marx put it in *Capital*:

> A spider conducts operations that resemble those of a weaver, and a bee puts to shame many an architect in the construction of her cells. But what distinguishes the worst architect from the best of bees is this, that the architect raises his structure in imagination before he erects it in reality.[20]

Fromm then, like Freud, argued for a theory of human nature, but it was a human nature rooted not in libido but in what he called "the conditions of existence":

> Powerful as the sex drive and all its derivations are, they are by no means the most powerful forces within man and their frustration is not the cause of mental disturbance. The most powerful forces motivating man's behavior stem from the condition of his existence, the "human situation".[21]

By "human situation", Fromm is referring to a situation where, he argues, having lost his original unity with nature as a result of having developed the power of reason, "man cannot live statically because his inner contradictions drive him to seek for a new equilibrium, for a new harmony instead of the lost harmony with nature".[22] It is clear that Fromm sees these "inner contradictions" as arising from the problem of the meaning of human existence rather than having their origins in social production:

> After he has satisfied his animal needs, he is driven by his human needs... All passions and strivings of man are attempts to find an answer to his existence, or as we may also say, to avoid insanity... All cultures provide for a patterned

---

20: Marx, 1976, p284.
21: Fromm, 1991, p27.
22: Fromm, 1991, p27.

system in which certain solutions are predominant, hence certain strivings and satisfactions. Whether we deal with primitive religions, with theistic or non-theistic religions, they are all attempts to give an answer to man's existential problem.[23]

He then identifies five sets of "needs or passions" that stem from the "existence of man": the need for relatedness, transcendence, rootedness, the need for a sense of identity and the need for a frame of orientation and devotion: reason vs irrationality. Failure on society's part to meet these needs will lead to mental ill health.

What these arguments show is that Fromm's views on human nature had moved a long way from those of Freud. Assessing the strengths and limitations of Freud's mature thought is beyond the scope of this article.[24] However, we should be cautious in assuming that a shift from a biologically-based approach to one emphasising the role of culture and social structures is necessarily closer to a Marxist approach. Freud is concerned with the effects of the conflicts arising from the formation of human individuals with biologically-based drives within social structures, especially, but not only, in the family. This is a materialist position, even if not necessarily Marxist. Fromm, by contrast, despite his disavowals to the contrary, seems much closer to an idealist existentialist tradition which sees "man's search for meaning" as the primary drive.

How though do Fromm's views of human nature compare with those of Marx? In *Capital*, Marx distinguished between what he called "human nature in general" and "human nature as historically modified in each epoch". In respect of the first point, Terry Eagleton comments:

In his early writings, Marx speaks of what he calls human "species being", which is really a materialist version of human nature. Because of the nature of our material bodies, we are needy, labouring, sociable, sexual, communicative, self-expressive animals who need one another to survive, but who come to find a fulfilment in that companionship over and above its social usefulness... Because we are laboring, desiring, linguistic creatures, we are able to transform our conditions in the process we know as history. In doing so, we come to transform ourselves at the same time. Change in

---

23: Fromm, 1956, pp27-28.
24: For a fuller discussion of the issues involved see Frosh, 1999.

other words, is not the opposite of human nature; it is possible because of the creative, open-ended, unfinished beings we are.[25]

In other words, it is precisely our potential for development, for what Aristotle referred to as "flourishing", that makes us human, is our "essence"; as Marx argued, "freedom is so much the essence of man that even its opponents realise it in that they fight its reality".[26] That essence is not realised in isolation. Rather, as Marx also argued in the sixth of his *Theses on Feuerbach*, it is inextricably bound up with, and shaped by, the social relationships in which people exist: "the human essence is no abstraction inherent in each single individual. In its reality it is the ensemble of the social relations".[27]

For that reason, Eagleton argues, the Marxist notion of social justice "does indeed possess an 'absolute' moral criterion: the unquestionable virtue of the rich, all-round expansion of capacities for each individual. It is from this standpoint that any social formation is to be assessed".[28] And similarly, Fromm argued, it was from that standpoint that we can assess the extent to which a society could be assessed as sane.

The great achievement of Marx and Engels over their utopian socialist predecessors, however, was not that they provided a more convincing moral critique of capitalism (although arguably they did) but that they analysed the economic and political workings of the system and, crucially, identified the force—the working-class—which could act as the gravedigger of the system through its own self-emancipation.

By contrast, while Fromm recognises that different types of society (or modes of production) modify that human nature considerably (reflected in his concept of social character), as we shall see there is no recognition in his writings of the dynamic role of class and class struggle in that process. The focus instead is on "Man" or "humanity". Here, as in his writings on religion, Fromm often seems closer to Feuerbach than to Marx.[29]

Social character

The concept of social character is Fromm's alternative to Freud's drive theory and was seen by him (and by most contemporary commentators) as his most important theoretical contribution. *Individual* character structure, Fromm argues following Freud, is a persistent, enduring, relatively

---

25: Eagleton, 2011, p81.
26: Cited in Blackledge, 2012, p56.
27: Marx, 1947.
28: Eagleton, 1990, p23.
29: Friedman, 2014, p154.

fixed entity. People frequently behave in specific, often predictable, almost automatic ways. By extension, *social* character refers to the "nucleus of the character structure which is shared by most members of the same culture, in contradistinction to the individual character in which people belonging to the same culture differ from each other".[30]

While for Freud social behaviour had its roots in the interaction between the biological drives of individuals and their formation in social structures such as the family, Fromm argued that "the most important conditioning factor in the creation of social character, the context in which it is shaped, is the mode of production".[31]

What, then, are the key elements of Fromm's concept of social character? Firstly, it is a wider concept than ideology in that, while it includes conscious ideas, it also includes unconscious thoughts, feelings and behaviours (in this respect social character bears some resemblance to Pierre Bourdieu's concept of *habitus*, a point also noted by Kieran Durkin.[32])

Secondly, Fromm argued, psychoanalytic concepts that were employed in the analysis of individual behaviour were applicable, with some modification, to explanations of the social character of groups or classes. So, for example, the concept of sado-masochism played an important role in his explanation of the role of the German middle classes in the rise of Nazism. By this, however, Fromm meant not neurosis or perversion but rather an attitude towards authority rooted in social character: "He [the petty-bourgeois] admired authority and tends to submit to it, but at the same time he wants to be an authority himself and have others submit to him".[33]

Thirdly, for Fromm social character plays an important role in the smooth functioning of the capitalist system. In the same way as individual character means that people behave in "characteristic" ways without having to deal with each new situation afresh, so too the social character of the working class means that its members tend to behave in fairly predictable ways, suited to the needs of capital:

> Modern, industrial society, for instance, could not have attained its ends had it not harnessed the energy of free men in an unprecedented degree... It would not have sufficed if each individual had to make up his mind consciously every day that he wanted to work, to be on time, etc. since any

---

30: Fromm, 1962, p74.
31: Sagall, 2013, p69.
32: Durkin, 2014, p124.
33: Cited in Friedman, 2014, p112.

such conscious deliberation would lead to many more exceptions than the smooth functioning of society can afford. Nor would threat and force have sufficed as a motive since the highly differentiated tasks in modern industrial society can, in the long run, only be the work of free men and not of forced labour. The social *necessity* for work, for punctuality, and orderliness had to be transformed into an inner *drive*. This means that society had to produce a social character in which these strivings were inherent.[34]

The same example is fruitfully employed by E P Thompson in his classic *The Making of the English Working Class* in exploring the role of Methodism in imposing a new work discipline on the growing working class in the late 18th and early 19th century.[35] The issue of discipline, or rather the lack of discipline, of the semi-industrialised workforce, was a major challenge for the new factory owners. The extent of the problem was emphasised by Dr Andrew Ure (a popular target of Marx and Engels) in his *Philosophy of Manufactures* (1835):

Even at the present day, when the system is perfectly organised, and its labour lightened to the utmost, it is found nearly impossible to convert persons past the age of puberty, whether drawn from rural or from handicraft occupations, into useful factory hands. After struggling for a while to conquer their listless or restive habits, they either renounce the employment spontaneously, or are dismissed by the overlookers on account of inattention.[36]

Methodism, Thompson argued, which attracted a huge following in working class districts in the late 1790s, provided one key ideological mechanism through which this "problem" could be addressed. Combining a "religion of the soul" that allowed for the expression of intense emotion within the church walls with a strict emphasis on discipline and respectability in daily life, Methodism:

weakened the poor from within, by adding to them the active ingredient of submission; and they [the Methodist leaders] fostered within the Methodist Church those elements most suited to make up the psychic component of the work-discipline of which the manufacturers stood most in need.

34: Fromm, 1962, p75.
35: Thompson, 1968; also discussed by Sagall, 2013, p83.
36: Cited in Thompson, 1968, p360.

In language drawn from Fromm (whom he cites in a footnote but does not refer to directly), Thompson argues: "Men came to be driven to work not so much by external pressure but by an internal compulsion… The inner compulsion was more effective in harnessing all energies to work than any outer compulsion could ever be…man was turned into his own slave-driver".[37]

Thompson presents a persuasive argument for the role of Methodism in shaping working class character but as he himself recognises, it is one which needs some contextualisation. First, the mid to late-1790s was a period of counter-revolution when England was at war with revolutionary France and the hopes that had been raised by the French Revolution had been crushed. It was precisely in this context of defeat and despair that Methodist ideas could take on the hold that they did. As he comments:

> Methodism *may* have inhibited revolution; but we can affirm with certainty that its rapid growth during the wars was a component of the psychic processes of counter-revolution. There is a sense in which any religion which places great emphasis on the after-life is the chiliasm of the defeated and the hopeless.[38]

Secondly, this was also a period of enormous state repression, culminating in the Combination Acts banning trade unions introduced in 1799. Methodism, and its shaping of social character, was undoubtedly an element in the disciplining of the working class but only one among many others in the armoury of the ruling class during this period.

Thirdly, even if Methodism did help to contribute to a particular form of working class social character, it would be wrong to overestimate the role that that character played in inhibiting struggle. As Thompson admits:

> Even in the darkest war years the democratic impulse can still be felt at work beneath the surface… The Combination Acts (1799-1800) served only to bring illegal Jacobin and trade union strands closer together. Even beneath the fever of the "invasion" years, new ideas and new forms of organisation continue to ferment. There is a radical alteration in the sub-political attitudes of the people to which the experiences of tens of thousands of unwilling

---

37: Cited in Sagall, 2013, p83. One is reminded of the joke about the Arab sheik who came to Britain to buy guns to keep his workers in line but who, having witnessed the way in which thousands of workers arrived and left their factory promptly in response to the factory hooter, ordered a hundred hooters instead.
38: Thompson, 1968, pp381-382.

soldiers contributed. By 1811 we can witness the simultaneous emergence of a new popular radicalism and of a newly-militant trade unionism.[39]

A more problematic use of the concept of social character occurs in Sabby Sagall's ambitious and fascinating study of genocides and the roots of human destructiveness.[40] Space (and lack of knowledge on my part) precludes a discussion of three of the four genocides discussed by Sagall (the Rwandan, Native American and Armenian genocides) or of his main thesis that some types of genocide ("irrational" as opposed to "rational" genocides) require the use of psychoanalytic categories in order to explain them. Here I shall only address his argument that the classical Marxist analysis of the rise of Nazism developed by Trotsky, which emphasised the economic and political factors fuelling the growth of the Nazis, needs to be supplemented by a "theory of subjectivity", based on the social character of the German middle classes.

Sagall's argument draws on Fromm's account of the rise of Nazism in *Escape from Freedom*, where he set out to analyse "those dynamic factors in the character structure of modern man, which made him want to give up freedom in fascist countries and which so widely prevail in millions of our own people".[41] In similar fashion Sagall aims to "uncover the links between the objective development of German industrial capitalism and the subjective ideas and feelings of fear, hatred and destructive rage of the Nazi perpetrators".[42] His general analysis closely follows that of Trotsky in emphasising the impact of the Great Depression on the middle classes, the role of Nazi ideology, and so on. Where it begins to diverge, however, is when he argues that "no analysis of the rise of Nazism can be complete without an understanding of the psychological dimension of the crisis of Germany's middle classes".[43]

If by this was meant the frenzied rage of the middle classes and their search for scapegoats in the wake of their loss of savings and social position due to economic crisis, hyper-inflation, and so on, then that would be consistent with the general argument he is pursuing. But it is clear Sagall means more than this:

> As a result of their historical experience as a social class in the development of German capitalism, the middle classes developed within the family a typical social character which some psychoanalysts have described as an authoritarian

---

39: Thompson, 1968, pp181-182.
40: Sagall, 2013.
41: Fromm, 2013, p4.
42: Sagall, 2013, p181.
43: Sagall, 2013, p200.

personality... This social character has been described as the simultaneous presence of sadistic and masochistic drives.[44]

The authoritarian character of the German middle class, Sagall argues, was not simply one more contributory factor to the rise of Nazism; rather, it was a *necessary* pre-condition of the Holocaust, without which the Holocaust could not have happened:

> Could the Holocaust have occurred elsewhere than in Germany? As we have seen, there needed to have been two sets of preconditions that together amounted to necessary and sufficient conditions: 1) the necessary predisposing conditions—an authoritarian or predisposing character and 2) the necessary precipitating conditions [economic collapse, the rise of Nazism, etc].[45]

It is an argument that is open both to empirical and theoretical objections.[46] Thus, did the "social character" of the German middle classes make them all uniquely prone to genocidal murder? Were middle class female children prone, too, to extreme violence? Was it only the middle classes in Germany who harboured such murderous potential? And, if so, does this mean we need a different kind of analysis to explain fascism in other countries?

Theoretically, Sagall is open to the charge of reifying social character, of treating class consciousness (and presumably also the "social unconscious") as fixed and unchanging, unaffected by external factors. This is a problem not just with Sagalls' argument but with the concept of social character more generally. As Durkin comments on Fromm's typology of social characters, "at perhaps the most basic level it must be asked whether the character orientations do not in fact inflate and reify transient, conflicting personality aspects".[47]

In fact Fromm himself was aware of this possibility. In a debate with R D Laing, for example, who argued that there was no "basic personality" or no "one internal system", he wrote:

> I only want to say that the assumption of a basic character system in person A does not exclude the possibility that this system is constantly being affected by systems B, C and D...with which it communicates, and that in this

---

44: Sagall, 2013, pp200-201.
45: Sagall, 2013, p221.
46: Ridley, 2014; see also the reply by Sagall, 2014.
47: Durkin, 2014, pp125-126.

interpersonal process various aspects of the character system in person A are energised and others lose in intensity.[48]

As Durkin comments, "an almost endless number of combinatory possibilities exist. In light of this, it may be legitimately asked how useful for social analysis such designations can be?"[49]

In fact, it was precisely this awareness of the transient and, above all, *contradictory* nature of the class consciousness of the German petty bourgeoisie that formed the basis for Trotsky's argument for a united working class response to the rise of Nazism:

> The daily struggle of the proletariat sharpens the instability of bourgeois society. The strikes and the political disturbances aggravate the economic situation of the country. The petty bourgeoisie could reconcile itself temporarily to the growing privations, if it came through experience to the conviction that the proletariat is in a position to lead it onto a new road. But if the revolutionary party, in spite of a class struggle becoming incessantly more attenuated, proves time and time again to be incapable of uniting the working class behind it; if it vacillates, becomes confused, contradicts itself, then the petty bourgeoisie loses patience and begins to look upon the revolutionary workers as those responsible for its own misery... When the social crisis takes on an intolerable acuteness, a particular party appears on the scene with the direct aim of agitating the petty bourgeoisie to a white heat and directing its hatred and its despair against the proletariat. In Germany, this historical function is fulfilled by National Socialism, a broad current whose ideology is composed of all the putrid vapours of decomposing bourgeois society.[50]

The key factor, in other words, in shaping the consciousness of the German middle class in the late 1920s and early 1930s was not a social character forged in infancy (though this may of course have played a role) but rather the state of the class struggle and above all, the extent to which the working class (and its political organisations) could point a way out of the crisis. Overstating the role of social character can lead to the conclusion that there was something uniquely German about Nazism and the Holocaust. Clearly fascism will take on particular characteristics at different times and in different societies but at its core, then and now it "is a mobilisation of

---

48: Fromm, 1992.
49: Durkin, 2014, p126.
50: Trotsky, 1975, pp272-273.

large layers of the petty bourgeoisie in a violent mass movement that aims to destroy the working class's capacity to wage struggle".[51] It was that understanding that underpinned Trotsky's observation that had the Whites won the civil war, the word for fascism would have been introduced to the world in the Russian language, not the Italian.

A final criticism of Fromm's concept of social character came from his contemporary and fellow Freudian Marxist, Wilhelm Reich. While Fromm argued that psychoanalytic categories could be applied to social phenomena as well as to individuals, Reich argued that the opposite was the case:

> There are plenty of instances of human social behaviour in which the unconscious instinctual mechanisms interposed in human action, which psychoanalysis has described and which are of decisive importance in other phenomena, play virtually no part at all. The point I want to make is that, say, the behaviour of people with small savings after a bank failure or a peasants' uprising after a sudden drop in wheat prices cannot be explained by unconscious libidinous motives or as a case of rebellion against the father. It is important to realise that in such cases psychology can indeed have something to say about the effects of this behaviour but not about its causes or background.[52]

Whatever Reich's later eccentricities, his position in the 1930s arguably provides revolutionaries with a better guide to the relationship between individual psychology and class struggle than that of Fromm.

The politics of socialist humanism

Fromm's main period of political activity began in the late 1950s when he played a leading role in the socialist humanist movement that developed in these years in the wake of Nikita Khrushchev's secret speech revealing the crimes of Stalin, and also the crushing of the Hungarian workers' uprising of 1956. Chris Harman described socialist humanism as "an intellectual staging post for those recoiling from Stalinism in 1956".[53] Drawing heavily on Marx's early writings, it was an attempt to rescue the humanist kernel of Marxism from its brutal Stalinist caricature and to develop a "third road" alternative to the "managerial free enterprise system" of the west and the "managerial communist system" of the Soviets and their allies. Its theoretical underpinning was provided by a radical humanism, the essence of which (in

---

51: Alexander and Cero, 2015, p186.
52: Reich, 2012, pp66-67.
53: Harman, 1983.

Fromm's own words) was "in simplest terms, the belief in the unity of the human race and man's potential to perfect himself by his own efforts".[54]

The first point to make is that in important respects Marxism is indeed a humanism. As Harman observed:

> It is an account of how, in its efforts to maintain itself against the rigours of nature a certain animal—*homo sapiens*—cooperates with others of its kind, creating societies which then come to dominate the lives of the species. In this way there arise different forms of economic and social organisations—and beyond a certain point in history—classes and states.[55]

Marxism is also a humanism in a second sense. Its end goal is not the dictatorship of a particular class but rather the abolition of class society per se; only then, in Marx's words, will the "prehistory" of humanity come to an end and real human history begin.

That said, as a political and theoretical tradition, socialist humanism is very different in key respects from classical Marxism. First, to emphasise only the *unity* of the human race is to ignore what Marx and Engels identified as the overriding feature of human history for at least the past 10,000 years: namely the division of society into antagonistic classes and the fact that since then, "the history of all hitherto existing society is the history of class struggle". By contrast, in Fromm's writings class scarcely figures, other than as a sociological category, and class struggle even less so.

Secondly, linked to his neglect of class was a tendency to substitute sweeping generalisations and moral assertions for any concrete analysis of what was actually happening to the working class or to global capitalism in the post-war period. In this he was not alone; similar criticisms have also been levelled at Marcuse and at the tradition of Western Marxism more generally.[56] Nevertheless, as Friedman notes, Fromm was particularly prone to making generalisations based on very little empirical evidence, often leading to extremely superficial and politically erroneous conclusions. Here, for example, is his description of the situation of the US working class in the mid-1950s:

> Speaking of the economically most progressive country, the United States, the economic exploitation of the masses has disappeared to a degree which would have sounded fantastic in Marx's time. The working class, instead of

---

54: Fromm, 1965, p.ix.
55: Harman, 1983.
56: McIntyre, 1970; Anderson, 1976.

falling behind in the economic development of the whole society, has an increasing share in the national wealth, and it is a perfectly valid assumption that provided no major catastrophe occurs, there will, in about one or two generations, be no more marked poverty in the United States.[57]

In fact, as Michael Harrington's *The Other America*, published just a few years later was to show, the reality was very different indeed.[58] Based on dozens of interviews and visits to working class areas across the country, Harrington found that some 40 million Americans in a nation of 176 million were poor, including half of all American senior citizens. In addition he found that 16 million Americans in a labour force totalling 69.6 million were excluded from the federal minimum wage law.

Thirdly, socialist humanism's emphasis on a common humanity led in practice to a particular type of popular front politics in which class differences and antagonisms were downplayed or consciously discouraged, usually at the expense of working class interests. In a discussion of the work and politics of E P Thompson, for example, Alex Callinicos observed:

A Marxist approach naturally focuses on the classes formed within definite relations of production, and on the struggle between them that is generated by the form of exploitation implicated in these relations. It is this, the most distinctive element of historical materialism which tends to become lost in humanist versions of Marxism... Thompson's populism is a logical consequence of a humanist Marxism which moves directly from a conception of human nature to immediate historical and political questions without passing through the necessary stage of an analysis of the forces and relations of production which structure social formations.[59]

Similar criticisms can be made of Fromm. On the one hand, as Friedman shows, he spent a good deal of time trying to persuade world leaders (including John F Kennedy) to change their ways; on the other, he was in favour of downplaying specifically working class demands so as not to alienate respectable middle class opinion:

In order to gain power, the social democratic parties need to win the votes of many members of the middle class, and in order to achieve this goal,

---

57: Fromm, 1991, p98.
58: Harrington, 1997.
59: Callinicos, 1983.

the socialist parties have had to cut back their programme from one with a socialist vision to one offering liberal reforms. On the other hand, by identifying the working class as the lever of humanistic change, socialism necessarily antagonised the members of all other classes, who felt that their properties and privileges were going to be taken away by the workers.

Socialism, Fromm reassured his readers, "does not threaten to take anybody's property, and as far as income is concerned, it would raise the standard of living of those who are poor. High salaries for top executives would not have to be lowered, but if the system worked, they would not want to be symbols of time past".[60]

The danger of such an approach for organisations such as SANE (The National Committee for a SANE Nuclear Policy) of which Fromm was a founder-member was that it risked sowing illusions in "progressive" Democratic politicians to end war rather than building a movement from below, not least through linking the struggle against both nuclear war and the war in Vietnam to working class concerns around poverty, welfare and conscription. The problem for Fromm was that such a movement, if it were to be effective, would precisely involve threatening the wealth and property of the rich.

Conclusion

The renewal of interest in the ideas of Erich Fromm reflects two key aspects of politics in the 21st century. First, there is the widespread and deeply-felt desire for an alternative to neoliberal capitalism, a desire which found its initial political expression in the protests against the World Trade Organisation in Seattle in 1999 and in the subsequent development of the anti-capitalist movement. Slogans such as "the world is not for sale'" and "another world is possible" mirror almost exactly the core elements of Fromm's thought: first, his ethical critique of materialism and consumerism, responsible for the "marketing" social character that he saw as the dominant social character of our time; secondly, his "prophetic messianism", which expressed a utopian longing for a different, more just society.

Fromm's ideas also fit, however, with another, more negative, feature of much of the current political left: namely, its abandonment of class politics and any notion that the working class can change the world. Missing from his work is a conception of the working class as a collective actor that can emancipate itself and in so doing emancipate humanity. In this sense,

---

60: Fromm, 1978, pp200-201.

Fromm is indeed closer to the utopian socialists of the early 19th century than to Marx himself.

A third factor which may also contribute to Fromm's current popularity is the desire for a social psychology which is more critical than currently dominant "surface" approaches such as cognitive-behavioural psychology, approaches which are increasingly tarnished by their deployment within welfare to work programmes.[61] While in itself this is a positive development, whether Fromm's "trademark" concept of social character is capable of providing that critical alternative is open to question. As I have argued above, it risks reifying working class consciousness and becoming a substitute for a concrete analysis of the factors shaping people's thoughts and feelings.

Yet working class consciousness is not fixed or static. As we have seen in recent years from the revolutions of the Arab Spring to the great movements against austerity in Greece, Spain and Scotland, people's ideas (as well as their deepest feelings) can change on a mass scale, especially when the level of struggle is high. Despite 30 years of neoliberalism in Britain, the electoral successes of the Scottish National Party on a broadly social democratic platform and the election of veteran left-winger Jeremy Corbyn as leader of the Labour Party show the extent to which Margaret Thatcher's dream of changing "the heart and soul" of British workers has failed.[62] And the defeats or setbacks that some of these movements have recently experienced are not the inevitable product of the early individual life experiences of those involved but rather of a current lack of confidence in their ability to change the world and a failure fully to appreciate what is required for a successful revolution. Nevertheless, it is above all through participation in such mass struggles that change, both social and personal can take place; in the words of the young Marx: "The coincidence of the changing of circumstances and of human activity or self-changing can be conceived and rationally understood only as revolutionary practice"[63]—something seldom recognised by Fromm, despite his often incisive critiques of life under capitalism. Let the last word, then, go to a Metro worker in Paris involved in the magnificent (and successful) strikes in 1995 against the Juppe Plan to slash the public sector:

> Strikes completely change a man. People live in their own little corner. They come first, never mind the neighbour. During the strikes individualism was

---

61: Friedli and Stearn, 2015.
62: "Economics are the Method: The Object is to Change the Soul". Interview, *Sunday Times*, 3rd May 1981.
63: Marx, 1947.

completely broken up. Completely! The chains were broken. Spontaneously. Because we were discussing things all the time, we learned to get to know each other. We were at the firm 24 hours a day. In our job we're very isolated and we only see each other during the 10 minute breaks. Here we learned to live together.[64]

References

Alexander, Anne, and Haytham Cero, 2015, "Fascism and ISIS", *International Socialism, 148* (autumn), http://isj.org.uk/fascism-and-isis

Anderson, Kevin B, 2007a, "The Rediscovery and Persistence of the Dialectic in Philosophy and in World Politics", in Sebastian Budgen, Stathis Kouvelakis, and Slavoj Žižek, (eds) *Lenin Reloaded: Towards a Politics of Truth* (Duke University Press).

Anderson, Kevin B, 2007b, "Thinking about Fromm and Marxism", *Logos*, volume 6, issue 3, www.logosjournal.com/issue_6.3/anderson.htm

Anderson, Perry, 1976, *Considerations on Western Marxism* (Verso).

Blackledge, Paul, 2012, *Marxism and Ethics: Freedom, Desire, and Revolution* (SUNY).

Braune, Joan, 2014, *Erich Fromm's Revolutionary Hope: Prophetic Messianism as a Critical Theory of the Future* (Sense Publishers).

Callinicos, Alex, 1983, "Marxism and Philosophy: A Reply to Peter Binns", *International Socialism 19* (spring), www.marxists.org/history/etol/writers/callinicos/1983/xx/binns.html

Collier, Andrew, 1980, "Lacan, Psychoanalysis and the Left", *International Socialism 7* (winter), www.marxists.org/history/etol/newspape/isj2/1980/no2-007/collier.html

Durkin, Kieran, 2014, *The Radical Humanism of Erich Fromm* (Palgrave MacMillan).

Eagleton, Terry, 1990, *The Ideology of the Aesthetic* (Blackwell).

Eagleton, Terry, 2011, *Why Marx Was Right* (Yale University Press).

Friedli, Lynne and Robert Stern, 2015, "Positive Affect as Coercive Strategy: Conditionality, Activation and the Role of Psychology in UK Government Workfare Programmes", *Medical Humanities*, volume 41, issue 1.

Friedman, Lawrence J, 2014, *The Lives of Erich Fromm: Love's Prophet* (Columbia University Press).

Fromm, Erich, 1949, *Man for Himself; An Enquiry into the Psychology of Ethics* (Routledge and Kegan Paul).

Fromm, Erich, 1956, *The Art of Loving* (Thorsons).

Fromm, Erich, 1962, *Beyond the Chains of Illusion: My Encounter with Marx and Freud* (Abacus).

Fromm, Erich (ed), *Socialist Humanism: An International Symposium Garden* (Doubleday), www.marxists.org/archive/fromm/works/1965/introduction.htm

Fromm, Erich, 1978, *To Have or to Be?* (Jonathan Cape).

Fromm, Erich, 1991 [1955], *The Sane Society, 2nd edition* (Routledge).

Fromm, Erich, 1992, *The Revision of Psychoanalysis* (Westview Press).

Fromm, Erich, 2013 [1941], *Escape from Freedom* (Kindle Edition).

Frosh, Stephen, 1999, *The Politics of Psychoanalysis: An Introduction to Freudian and Post-Freudian Theory,*

64: Cited in Wolfreys, 1999, pp36-37.

2nd edition (Macmillan).

Funk, Rainer, 2000, *Erich Fromm: His Life and Ideas* (Continuum).

Harman, Chris, 1983, "Philosophy and Revolution", *International Socialism* 21 (autumn), www.marxists.org/archive/harman/1983/xx/phil-rev.html

Harrington, Michael, 1997 [1962], *The Other America: Poverty in the United States* (Scribner).

James, Oliver, 2008, *The Selfish Capitalist: Origins of Affluenza* (Vermilion).

Löwy, Michael, 2013, "Erich Fromm: From Messianic Utopia to Critical Criminology", in Malloch, Margaret and Bill Munro (eds) *Crime, Critique and Utopia* (Palgrave MacMillan).

Marx, Karl, 1947 [1845], "Theses on Feuerbach", in Marx, Karl, and Frederick Engels, *Collected Works*, volume 4 (Progress), www.marxists.org/archive/marx/works/1845/theses/theses.htm

Marx, Karl, 1976, *Capital*, Volume I (Pelican).

McIntyre, Alasdair, 1970, *Marcuse* (Fontana/Collins).

Miri, Seyed Javed, Robert Lake, and Tricia M Kress (eds), 2014, *Reclaiming the Sane Society: Essays on Erich Fromm's Thought* (Sense Publishers).

Mitchell, Juliet, 1974, *Psychoanalysis and Feminism* (Penguin Books).

Reich, Wilhelm, 2012, *Sex-Pol: Essays, 1929-1934* (Verso).

Ridley, Andy, 2014, "Dark Thoughts: Psychology and Genocide", *International Socialism* 143 (summer), http://isj.org.uk/dark-thoughts-psychology-and-genocide

Sagall, Sabby, 2013, *Final Solutions: Human Nature, Capitalism and Genocide* (Pluto Press).

Sagall, Sabby, 2014, "Marxism, Psychology and Genocide: A Reply to Andy Ridley", *International Socialism* 144 (autumn), http://isj.org.uk/marxism-psychology-and-genocide-a-reply-to-andy-ridley

Thomson, Annette, 2009, *Erich Fromm: Explorer of the Human Condition* (Palgrave).

Thompson, E P, 1968, *The Making of the English Working Class* (Vintage Books).

Thompson, Michael J, 2014, "Normative Humanism as Redemptive Critique", in Miri, Seyed Javed, Robert Lake, and Tricia M Kress (eds), *Reclaiming the Sane Society: Essays on Erich Fromm's Thought* (Sense Publishers).

Trotsky, Leon, 1975, *The Struggle Against Fascism in Germany* (Pelican).

Wolfreys, Jim, 1999, "Class Struggles in France", *International Socialism* 84 (autumn), www.marxists.org/history/etol/newspape/isj2/1999/isj2-084/wolfreys.htm

Half socialist? Leon Trotsky and the Soviet Union

John Rose

A review of Paul Le Blanc, **Leon Trotsky** *(Reaktion Books, Critical Lives series, 2015), £11.99*

Paul Le Blanc faced a daunting challenge when he agreed to write a book about Leon Trotsky and his life in exile for the *Critical Lives* series, which specialises in brief introductions to leading political and cultural personalities. How do you *briefly* introduce one of the greatest leaders of the world's first socialist revolution that then apparently rejected him? How do you summarise all the unanswered political questions that were intensified by Trotsky's expulsion from the Soviet Union in February 1929?[1]

The most powerful chapter of the book is appropriately titled "Revolution Betrayed". This, of course, is also the title of Trotsky's most famous book of the 1930s, written as the crisis of Communism was reaching its climax: *The Book* in George Orwell's *1984*. Le Blanc's discussion of André Malraux, the gifted left wing French novelist, illustrates the difficulty of understanding Trotsky's betrayal by the Soviet Union. Malraux "personally witnessed the debacle of Stalin's policy in China, which resulted in the slaughter in 1927 of many idealistic revolutionary militants. He told their story...in one of the great novels of the 20th century, *La Condition humaine*

1:    Le Blanc, 2015, pp58-62.

(Man's Fate)".[2] The novel was highly valued by Trotsky, and mirrored his own devastating assaults on Stalin and the Comintern's policies in China. Now Malraux is introduced here very effectively to illustrate the great paradox at the heart of the 20th century's crisis of Communism. How could someone like Malraux, who had an unusually refined and detailed grasp of the treachery of Stalin and his policies, nevertheless rally to Stalin and desert Trotsky?

We will return to this question in a moment. But first we need to note critically that apart from two other sentences,[3] this is the only reference to what was nothing less than the sabotage of a potential socialist revolution in China. This was the first major showdown between Stalin and Trotsky over an international question with parallels with the Russian Revolution itself. It was indeed part of the "decisive contest" between the two leaders, to use Isaac Deutscher's words.[4] Failure of the Communist movement internationally to discuss the lessons of China in 1927 meant it was doomed to repeat similar mistakes in the 1930s.

The "Revolution Betrayed" chapter juxtaposes Stalin's "People's Front" perspectives with "The Great Madness", a phrase originating in Prosecutor Vyshinsky's demand during the Moscow Trials that each of the "mad dogs be shot", but evoking the full weight of Stalin's internal policies for the period.[5] Only the madness turns out to have a terrifying rational core. The tremendously positive reception to the People's Front perspectives internationally helped Stalin emphasise the rational core and somehow get away with minimising the scale of the Terror. This was despite the fact that nothing less than the total destruction of the aims and objectives of the October 1917 Russian Revolution, including its core cadre, was at stake, turning communism into its opposite, symbolised of course by the systematic persecution, and ultimate assassination, of the Terror's principal victim, Leon Trotsky.

The complexities involved in this process are impressively explained. So let me write now: buy this book! It provides brief succinct explanations for many of Trotsky's most important writings. It is very stimulating, often beautifully written and highly original. It pulls no punches in criticising

---

2: Le Blanc, 2015, pp100-101.
3: Le Blanc, 2015, p51. The two sentences do touch on the fundamental flaw of Comintern policy. "Close ties" with nationalist leader Chiang Kai-shek which left the Chinese Communists completely unprepared for the nationalists' murderous onslaught on them. But the crushing of the workers' insurrection in Shanghai isn't mentioned, nor is there any wider discussion of Stalin's justification for an all-class alliance of workers and peasants with the Chinese nationalist bourgeoisie.
4: Deutscher, 1959, chapter 5.
5: Le Blanc, 2015, p113.

Trotsky's earlier overcautious approach to Stalin. It describes the influence of workers' movements on the young Trotsky very well, there are rich and thoughtful insights into his personality as well as a good discussion of the continuing obsession with Trotsky among conservative scholars, the wider media and the art world, itself an unintended tribute.

The reader is drawn into and becomes absorbed in the nightmare world of Stalin's sinister and sickening hounding of Trotsky, including the meticulous destruction of Trotsky's family, often with the tacit support of "liberal" governments and Communist Parties everywhere. Notwithstanding the criticisms outlined here, in part driven by the severe restrictions imposed by the publishing format, it succeeds in introducing new readers both to Trotsky and particularly his life in exile.

However, there is one highly significant omission, which cannot be excused, in this case, by the cramped space within which the book was written, namely Le Blanc's failure properly and critically to assess Trotsky's interpretation of Stalinism and the debates this provoked. The issues involved here are of such magnitude that they will dominate this review.

In 1935, at the 7th World Congress of the Communist International, its new head, Georgi Dimitrov, "mapped out before the assembled leaders and representatives of the parties of world Communism a new strategic orientation", the People's Front: "'The toiling masses in a number of capitalist countries are faced with the necessity of making a *definite* choice...not between proletarian dictatorship and bourgeois democracy, but between bourgeois democracy and fascism'".[6] As Trotsky pointed out, this was "the traditional policy of Menshevism against which Lenin fought all his life. It signals the renunciation of proletarian revolution in favour of conservative bourgeois democracy".[7]

Le Blanc points out that:

> The primary purpose of the People's Front was to form electoral coalitions of working class parties (Communists, Socialists or Social Democrats) with pro-capitalist liberal parties for the purpose of winning elections and forming governments that, while initiating social reforms, would preserve a democratic republic along with a capitalist economy, and maintain a pro-Soviet foreign policy—thereby (presumably) blocking fascism. In France and Spain such governments were established. The problem with this, Trotsky argued, is that fascism arose out of the crises of capitalism, just as imperialism

6:   Le Blanc, 2015, p104.
7:   Le Blanc, 2015, p105.

and war arise out of the natural dynamics of capitalism. To preserve the unity of the People's Front, it was necessary to repress the uncompromising militancy of working class struggles—but this was the force needed to end both capitalism and the threat of fascism.[8]

But, Le Blanc argues, Trotsky's critical stance isolated him from the "the broad coming together of progressive forces" that the Popular Front policy produced. Le Blanc hails the historian Paulo Spriano, who describes the "great political turn which was welcomed...by masses of workers, peasants, the middle class (the last term referring to professionals, more or less declassé intellectuals, artists, small business people). Communism had acquired a new countenance: it spoke with a different voice, one which echoed the profoundly humanistic, rational, libertarian and egalitarian qualities of the Enlightenment—emphasising the virtues of 'the people'".[9] Well, yes, "Stalin is better than Hitler,"[10] as Trotsky ruefully observed.

Surely this is the most extraordinary moment in 20th century history? Communism becomes the worldwide rallying point for the defence of Enlightenment values against the threat of fascist barbarism as it openly opposes the politicisation of workers' struggles against capitalism. It is the moment it also intensifies its own barbaric orgy of self-destruction, the political accompaniment to its forced collectivisation of the land and catastrophic concentration of industrial development, literally only achievable at gunpoint.

The infamous "Moscow Trials" were triggered by the assassination in late 1934 of Sergey Kirov, a pro-Stalin Communist leader linked to oppositionists associated with Grigori Zinoviev. Zinoviev and Lev Kamenev headed a list of 50 people accused of being part of a "Trotskyite-Zinovievite Centre". A new *History of the Communist Party of the Soviet*

8: Le Blanc, 2015, pp105-106. Trotsky predicted with astonishing accuracy that the Popular Front "experiments" in France and Spain would end in disaster, precisely because of Stalinist connivance in the repression of working class activity. The restricted space in the book means that the example of France is ignored completely, while the three pages on Spain, the curtain-raiser to the Second World War (pp135-138), frustrate because of all the tantalising questions it raises that demand answers. To give just one example, Trotsky had a mass following in Spain. In 1936 a socialist revolution appeared momentarily to be gathering pace in response to Franco's attempted fascist coup. But Trotsky had a bitter falling out with the POUM, the organisation that contained many of his supporters but which nevertheless joined the Popular Front government. In fairness, the author partly resolves this problem with a strong recommended bibliography. I would like to add one reference to it, Andy Durgan's article "Trotsky and the POUM" (Durgan, 2006).
9: Le Blanc, 2015, p105.
10: Deutscher, 1963, p380.

Union would explain how the Trotskyite-Zinovievites were aiding both the Nazis and the Western capitalists, "fascism found faithful servants," ready to commit "acts of terrorism...to defeat the USSR in order to restore capitalism".[11]

Further public trials would include Nikolai Bukharin, Karl Radek, Alexei Rykov and various other Bolshevik leaders of both the "right" and the "left", all accused of similar conspiracies. But Conspirator No 1, Leon Trotsky, though constantly denounced as linked to all the different groups of traitors, couldn't be brought to trial because for the moment at least he had a degree of protection abroad.[12]

The public confessions of the accused were and remain truly disturbing. True, the extreme methods of torture, the threats to family members—often carried out, the promises to avoid the firing squad—always broken—partly explain it, but not fully. Whatever their differences and earlier political weaknesses, these former Bolshevik revolutionaries had devoted their lives to the overthrow of capitalism and had often demonstrated unparalleled courage in the long years in the underground struggle against the Tsar. Victor Serge's poem, *Confessions*, caught something in addition about their broken personalities: "We have never been what we are/The faces of our lives are not our own/Today our only truth is despair".[13] Trotsky developed this theme, describing the Stalinist "art" of breaking revolutionaries.[14]

The scale of the repression reached genocidal proportions: "It has been estimated that more than 2 million people were condemned from 1934 through 1938—with more than 700,000 executions and over a million were sent to increasingly brutalised labour camps where many more perished".[15]

The "Revolution Betrayed" chapter, which so successfully contrasts Stalin's People's Front perspectives with the "great madness", nevertheless disappoints when it comes to its discussion of Trotsky's politics, which informed his book of the same name. Inexplicably, Trotsky's argument is split into two separate parts of this chapter, which inevitably builds in quite unnecessary confusion for the reader wanting to grasp difficult and highly controversial arguments. Even more inexplicably, while the first part rests upon some very important passages from Trotsky's *Revolution Betrayed*,[16] the

11:   Cited in Le Blanc, 2015, pp111-112.

12:   In Norway—but hounded out even there—Le Blanc, 2015, pp125-126.

13:   Serge cited in Le Blanc, 2015, p113.

14:   Quoted in the fourth volume of Tony Cliff's biography of Trotsky—Cliff, 1993, p347-348.

15:   Le Blanc, 2015, pp114-115. See also the author's chilling description of the extraordinary mass hunger strike at the Vorkuta labour camp, led by Trotskyists (pp121-124).

16:   Le Blanc, 2015, pp106-109.

second part dispenses with Trotsky altogether, instead relying on a recent Stalin biographer Robert C Tucker and the author's own commentary.[17]

In the first part of the chapter we have Trotsky's analysis, which is partly based on Marx's writings in *The German Ideology*: "A development of the productive forces is the absolutely necessary practical premise [of communism], because without it want is generalised, and with want the struggle for necessities begins again, and that means all the old crap must revive".[18]

The unanticipated isolation of the socialist revolution in economically backward Russia meant exactly the old crap reviving. Trotsky provided the memorable example: "When there is little goods, the purchasers are compelled to stand in line...when the lines are very long, it is necessary to appoint a policeman to keep order...the starting point of the power of the Soviet bureaucracy".[19] Trotsky added that nobody who has wealth to distribute ever omits themself. He shows the new bureaucratic elite enriching itself, "limousines for the 'activists,' fine perfumes for 'our women'", to such an extent that such "socialism" could "seem to the masses a new refacing of capitalism, and they are not far wrong".[20]

Yet Trotsky insisted that capitalism had not been reinstated:

> The Soviet Union is a contradictory society halfway between capitalism and socialism, in which (a) the productive forces are still far from adequate to give state property a socialist character; (b) the tendency towards primitive accumulation created by want breaks through innumerable pores of the planned economy; (c) norms of distribution preserving a bourgeois character lie at the basis of a new differentiation of society; (d) the economic growth, while slowly bettering the situation of the toilers, promotes a swift formation of a privileged strata; (e) exploiting the social antagonisms, a bureaucracy has converted itself into an uncontrolled caste alien to socialism; (f) the social revolution, betrayed by the ruling party, still exists in property relations and in the consciousness of the toiling masses; (g) a further development of the accumulating contradictions can as well lead to socialism as back to capitalism; (h) on the road to capitalism the counter-revolution would have to break the resistance of the workers; (i) on the road to socialism the workers would have to overthrow the bureaucracy.[21]

17: Le Blanc, 2015, pp115-120.
18: Cited in Le Blanc, 2015, p106.
19: Trotsky, 1936, cited in Le Blanc, 2015, p107.
20: Trotsky, 1936, cited in Le Blanc, 2015, p108.
21: Trotsky, 1936, cited in Le Blanc, 2015, p108-109.

To help prepare for the overthrow of the bureaucracy would be the "task of the Soviet section of the Fourth International".[22]

But was the Soviet Union a contradictory society halfway between capitalism and socialism? The second part of the chapter, intentionally or otherwise, casts doubt on this perspective". There was, as Le Blanc says, "a method in the madness. What Marx called *primitive capitalist accumulation* [emphasis in the original]—involving massively inhumane means (which included the slave trade and genocide against native peoples, as well as destroying the livelihood of millions of peasants and brutalising the working class during the early days of industrialisation)—had created the basis for a modern capitalist economy".[23]

It's left for Tucker to explain that Stalin had undertaken something similar, "a policy of revolutionary advance in the construction of socialism, for which the speedy collectivisation of the peasants was a necessity. He thereby steered the state into a revolution from above". Tucker is then quoted as showing how long it took for Stalin's comrades to "divine what the apostle of socialism in one country" intended.[24] This is hardly surprising because Stalin hoped to achieve, in just a few years, an industrialisation programme which had taken capitalism at its origins centuries! A paragraph or two can hardly capture the impact this would have but they do at least underline that if this was indeed "socialism" then something had gone radically wrong:

> Stalin's "revolution from above"...remorselessly squeezing the working class, choking intellectual and cultural life, killing millions of peasants and culminating in purge trials, mass executions, and a ghastly network of prison camps (the infamous Gulag)... At the same time, an immense propaganda campaign proclaimed that socialism was being established...which involved a personality cult glorifying Stalin.[25]

In the last part of the book we are introduced to Rae Spiegel or Raya Dunayevskaya, Trotsky's "devoted secretary" during his final exile

---

22: Trotsky, 1936, cited in Le Blanc, 2015, p109. As Le Blanc says this was highly problematic. Unfortunately lack of space prevents a proper discussion of the Trotskyist Fourth International, except to note that its chronic weakness worldwide was partly attributable both to the success of Stalin's People's Front policies and the witch-hunts of "trotskyite-fascists" by Communist Parties everywhere. Nevertheless, however tiny, it helped carry the true significance of the Bolshevik revolution beyond Hitler and Stalin and the Second World War to a new generation of revolutionary socialists.

23: Le Blanc, 2015, p116.

24: Le Blanc, 2015, p115.

25: Le Blanc, 2015, p116-117.

in Mexico,[26] as well as the great Trinidadian intellectual C L R James.[27] What we are not told is that Dunayevskaya and James developed an important criticism of Trotsky's analysis, insisting that Stalin's "revolution from above" had indeed reintroduced capitalism albeit in the novel form of state capitalism. In 1942 Dunayevskaya, using official Russian statistics, argued that "the reality of the world market...would not permit Russia to tear itself out of the vortex of the world economy and build 'socialism in one country'".[28] She would later insist that the law of value operated in Russia because its state-run industries exploited alienated labour. The arguments were more fully developed in the book *State Capitalism and World Revolution* that she wrote with James and Grace Lee Boggs, published in 1950. At the same time Tony Cliff was developing his own theory of state capitalism.[29]

This is, frankly, a startling omission particularly because the state capitalist analysis fits so well with Tucker's discussion of Stalin's "revolution from above". Tucker argues that the so-called "modernising" Tsar, Peter the Great, captivated by the beginnings of capitalism in Western Europe in the early 18th century, served as Stalin's role model:

> Stalin followed Peter's example in looking to the West for aid in Russia's industrialisation... An exhaustive study concludes that "no major technology or major plant under construction between 1930 and 1945 has been identified as a purely Soviet effort." The foreign companies involved in this massive technological transfer...reads like a Who's Who of world capitalism.[30]

Tucker sees the huge iron and steel centre at Magnitogorsk in the Urals as

> a microcosm of the hierarchical new society taking form... The ordinary workers lived in wooden barracks, crowded into minuscule, barely furnished rooms...at the bottom, an underclass of convict labourers...went to work

---

26: Le Blanc, 2015, p147.
27: Le Blanc, 2015. p150.
28: Cited and sourced in Birchall, 2011, p105.
29: For a good introduction to this subject as well as the relations between Dunayevskaya, James and Cliff, see Birchall, 2011, pp105-108, and Callinicos, 1990, pp73-85. Cliff revisited his own theory of state capitalism in great detail in his own chapter "Revolution Betrayed" in the fourth volume of his Trotsky biography. It's an additional puzzle that Cliff isn't referred to by Le Blanc, especially as Duncan Hallas's *Trotsky's Marxism*, which relies heavily on Cliff's analysis, is referenced.
30: Tucker, 1990, p97.

under police guard, and did the heaviest work...for next to no pay... Five miles away, in a small suburban world of which the workers had hardly any knowledge, lived the elite, and the foreign engineers working on contract, in...houses equipped with running water and central heating, served by a well-stocked special store... This suburb was informally called "American City"... Bolshevik theory envisioned the withering away of the state, but Stalin the Russian national Bolshevik saw things differently. Statelessness was no part of his intention, and socialist society...was not...classless. The revolution from above was creating a new privileged service class.[31]

Trotsky regarded as Stalin's "greatest crime" not simply that he carried his totalitarian "revolution from above" by smashing the opposition of workers and peasants, but that he did so in the name of socialism, thus potentially compromising the very future of the revolution and communism itself.[32]

Several generations later and well into the start of a new century, we continue to live in the shadow of that awesome prediction. It matters that we report frankly and fully the major controversies sparked by Trotsky and his writings. This is particularly true of the conclusion to the one controversy that might liberate us from a cumbersome and even, arguably, compromising defence that somehow the Soviet Union was "halfway between capitalism and socialism". We have had the luxury of several generations in relatively tranquil circumstances, not afforded Trotsky, to debate this matter fully and reach a conclusion that is arguably intellectually, politically, morally and dare even be said, scientifically, superior to the original. Yes, there is a continuing argument but both sides need to be put. Trotsky would have expected nothing less. One of the greatest lessons politics had taught him was resistance to "dogmatic orthodoxies".[33]

31: Tucker, 1990, p113-114.
32: Deutscher, 1963, p103.
33: Le Blanc, 2015, p185.

References

Birchall, Ian, 2011, *Tony Cliff: A Marxist for his Time* (Bookmarks).

Callinicos, Alex, 1990, *Trotskyism* (Open University Press).

Cliff, Tony, 1993, *Trotsky: The Darker the Night, the Brighter the Star, 1927-1940* (Bookmarks), www.marxists.org/archive/cliff/works/1993/trotsky4

Deutscher, Isaac, 1959, *The Prophet Unarmed, Trotsky 1921-1929* (Oxford University Press).

Deutscher, Isaac, 1963, *The Prophet Outcast, Trotsky 1929-1940* (Oxford University Press).

Durgan, Andy, 2006, "Marxism, War and Revolution: Trotsky and the POUM", *Revolutionary History*, volume 9, number 2, http://fundanin.org/durgan10.htm

Le Blanc, Paul, 2015, *Leon Trotsky* (Reaktion Books).

Trotsky, Leon, 1936, *The Revolution Betrayed*, www.marxists.org/archive/trotsky/1936/revbet

Tucker, Robert C, 1990, *Stalin In Power: The Revolution From Above, 1928-1941* (W W Norton & Company).

Was the German Revolution defeated by January 1919?

Tony Phillips

John Rose argued in his talk at Marxism 2014 that the German Revolution had effectively suffered terminal defeat by January 1919.[1] The National Congress of Workers' and Soldiers' Councils voted in December 1918 to hand power to the National Assembly after elections to be held in January 1919. The outstanding leaders of the revolutionary left, Rosa Luxemburg and Karl Liebknecht, were murdered in January 1919. The following week the SPD, whose leaders were working closely with the army high command to crush the revolution and had ordered the murders, won the overwhelming majority of working class votes in the general election. John argues that Chris Harman and Pierre Broué underestimate the impact of these events in their classic Marxist histories of the revolution.[2] He states that "Chris underestimates the level of the defeat in January 1919 when the councils effectively collapse and the Parliament is elected". He goes on to favourably quote Richard Müller, the leader of the revolutionary shop stewards in Berlin: "He describes this moment in December as the end. I think he is right actually; I think really it does end there".[3]

The events John describes were undoubtedly disastrous blows for

---

1:   Rose, 2014.
2:   Harman, 1982, and Broué, 2006.
3:   Rose, 2014.

the revolution, but I want to agree with Harman and Broué that later developments would show that the German working class continued to show its revolutionary potential after January 1919 and could still have taken power right up to October 1923.

The October Revolution and the November Revolution

It is useful to compare developments in Germany with the Russian Revolution the year before—the only successful workers' revolution in history so far. However, we also need to be careful to emphasise the important differences between the two revolutions. The German Councils of Workers and Soldiers had sprung into existence following the naval mutinies at Wilhelmshaven and Kiel which began the revolution on 4 November and spread rapidly across the country. They were clearly inspired by the Soviets of Workers' and Soldiers' Deputies that had reappeared in Russia following the fall of the Tsar in February 1917.

But in Russia, far from dissolving itself, the Military Revolutionary Committee of the Petrograd Soviet had been the organisation through which the Bolsheviks, in alliance with the left wing of the Socialist Revolutionary Party, had overthrown the capitalist Provisional Government. The new workers' government was based on the soviets as a new higher form of democracy, fully accountable to the masses and combining both representative and executive functions. This was the justification for the dispersal of the Constituent Assembly in February 1918. Elections to the assembly had taken place before the October overturn and it no longer reflected the new reality of workers' power.

Why then did the opposite happen in Germany? There were crucial objective differences between Germany and Russia in the early 20th century. Russia was an overwhelmingly rural society in which the working class, though very militant and class conscious, were a small minority of the population. The political superstructure of Russia was a hangover from its recent feudal past and there was no civil society of mass reformist political parties and trade unions. In contrast Germany was, along with the United States, one of the most advanced industrial societies in the world at the time. While there was still a large rural population, the working class was a much larger percentage of the population than in Russia with much greater social weight. While the German Reich under the Kaiser was not a democracy, a mass workers' party, the SPD, had become the biggest group in the Reichstag and was allied with mass trade unions run by a significant layer of full-time officials.

Workers' and soldiers' councils in Germany

The November Revolution swept away the superstructure of the Reich. Workers' and Soldiers' councils sprang up across Germany. However, there was confusion among the workers about the role of the councils which the counter-revolutionary SPD leadership and the trade union bureaucracy exploited to the full. Unlike their Russian comrades, the German working class had not been through the dress rehearsal of the 1905 revolution in which the soviets had first come into being and played a central role. The councils in places such as the North Sea coast, Bremen and Brunswick were fully conscious of their role as the potential basis of a revolutionary workers' government. Elsewhere, however, less politically sophisticated and experienced workers and soldiers looked to the SPD politicians and even army officers for leadership. They in turn worked hard to poison the workers' and soldiers' minds against the revolutionary left.[4] The council in Berlin appointed a national executive which in turn appointed a government of six drawn from the SPD and USPD leadership all of whom were opposed to socialist revolution.[5]

The Central Congress of Workers' and Soldiers' Councils of December 1918 that, as John points out, voted to subordinate itself to the National Assembly was not at all representative of the revolutionary workers, soldiers and sailors who had made the revolution the previous month. The SPD machine and the trade union bureaucracy made sure that it was packed with their appointees and not composed of delegates from the factories, barracks and naval bases. Neither Karl Liebknecht nor Rosa Luxemburg was a delegate to the congress.[6] Following the elections to the National Assembly, the resulting coalition government of bourgeois parties and the SPD sent squads of counter-revolutionary officers—the Freikorps—to crush the revolutionary workers' councils in the first months of 1919.

The Soviets of Workers' and Soldiers' Deputies in Russia had much deeper roots in the population from the beginning of the revolution. However, they were dominated by the Socialist Revolutionary and Menshevik parties from February until September 1917 who tried to play a similar role to the SPD and USPD.[7] Initially, like Luxemburg's and Liebknecht's Spartacus League in Germany, the Bolsheviks were a small minority in the soviets. Like the Spartacists in January 1919, they were

---

4:   Riddell, 1986.
5:   The USPD was a left wing anti-war split from the SPD that included most of the revolutionaries until December 1918.
6:   Riddell, 1986.
7:   Trotsky, 1977, p191.

subject to repression after the July Days, but thanks to their greater roots and experience they were able to manoeuvre and prove in practice to the masses that only through all power passing to the soviets could the key demands of the people be realised.

Unlike the Bolsheviks, who had formally set up a separate organisation in 1912, the Spartacists did not leave the USPD and set up an independent revolutionary party until the end of December 1918 when they launched the German Communist Party (KPD). The fact that the majority of its members had no understanding of the need for patient work in the organisations of the working class and the tactics required to win over the majority of the working class meant that the new party was unable to intervene as a unit in the uprising in January 1919. It was not able to ensure that the revolutionary movement retreated in good order and paid a terrible price with the loss of Liebknecht, Luxemburg and a few weeks later the key party organiser Leo Jogiches.

But did this mean that the revolution was over? On 15 December Luxemburg argued in *Die Rote Fahne*, the Spartacist paper:

> The councils were not able to resist any of this. They left the entire apparatus forming public opinion in the hands of the cabinet, and therefore the counter-revolution. They watched silently while the cabinet, this counter-revolutionary club, threw firebombs into their homes every day. However, the weakness of the councils is not the weakness of the revolution. The revolution cannot be killed by any of these petty means... Yesterday the workers arose in Upper Silesia, today they will arise in Berlin, tomorrow in Rhineland-Westphalia, Stuttgart and Hamburg.[8]

Luxemburg was premature in her specific examples, but she was absolutely right about the overall course of development of the revolution in the next few months, though she tragically did not live to see it. Despite the defeat in Berlin, the vote of the Congress of Workers' and Soldiers' Councils and the election results, the working class as a whole continued to move to the left. In March there was a general strike and street fighting in Berlin. Workers in the Ruhr, Bremen, Saxony and Bavaria put up armed opposition to the Freikorps, who were only able to pick them off one by one due to their lack of coordination across the country.[9]

In addition, as John Rose mentions in his talk, economic hardship led to a massive strike wave. In 1918 there were five million strike days, in 1919,

8:   Luxemburg, 1918, "Auf die Schanzen (To the Entrenchments)" in Kuhn, 2012, p111.
9:   Broué, 2006, chapter 13.

48 million and in 1920 over 54 million.[10] Compare these figures with the 11,703,000 strike days during the British upturn of 1968-74. German workers went on strike over political issues as well as the cost of living, including the right to strike, powers of factory councils and the socialisation of the mines. As Luxemburg wrote about the 1905 Russian Revolution, "the economic struggle was not here really a decay, a dissipation of action, but merely a change of front...after the possible content of political action in the given situation and at the given stage of the revolution was exhausted, it broke, or rather changed, into economic action".[11]

Contrary to John's suggestion in his talk, although there were attempts at incorporation, the factory councils had nothing in common with the bureaucratic works councils of Germany today.[12] They were militant bodies of struggle at the point of production with far more in common with the shop stewards' committees of Glasgow and Sheffield of 1914-21. Like the shop stewards' committees, they had grown up in conditions of wartime illegality outside the official union structures and were highly democratic and accountable to the rank and file. It was through these bodies that the strikes were built and resistance to the Freikorps coordinated. They were the basis for the potential revival of the workers' councils.

The experience of the use of troops by the SPD against the workers, whether Communists or not, and continuing economic hardship despite the end of the war led millions of workers to shed their illusions in the SPD as the party that defended their interests. In the general election of June 1920, the first since January 1919, the USPD vote increased from 2.3 million to 4.5 million and the SPD vote fell from 11.5 million to 5.5 million.[13] The KPD, standing in its first election, won 590,000 votes and four Reichstag deputies.[14]

The Kapp putsch

The German ruling class had certainly learnt from the experience of Russia and moved ruthlessly to crush the Spartacists by force at the beginning of the revolution. It had used the SPD's false image as a socialist party to outmanoeuvre the revolutionary left and ride out the initial phase aided by the centrist USPD leadership. However, the reparations imposed by the Allies on Germany only exacerbated the country's economic problems of which

---

10: Harman, 1982, p145.
11: Luxemburg, 1970, p172.
12: See Rose, 2014.
13: Harman, 1982, p146.
14: Broué, 2006, p380.

the workers were the main victims. The vast sea of bitterness engendered by the sufferings of war and the hope inspired by the Russian Revolution and the post-war revolutionary wave affected growing sections of the working class.

In this situation, the ruling class overplayed its hand by moving to crush the Weimar Republic, as the parliamentary democracy that had emerged from the November revolution became known. The Kapp-Lüttwitz military coup (the Kapp putsch) of March 1920 resulted in a crushing defeat for the forces of reaction. Union bureaucrat Carl Legien, whom the leading industrialist Hugo Stinnes named a ship after in gratitude for services rendered to the ruling class, was forced to call a general strike that completely paralysed the country. Determined, unified action by the working class pulled even the workers of rural East Prussia and conservative white collar employees into the strike.

John argues in his summing up in his Marxism 2014 talk that "the Kapp putsch strengthened the parliamentary process".[15] The truth is more contradictory. The equivalent event during the Russian Revolution was the Kornilov coup of August 1917, which, by exposing the counter-revolutionary role of the Provisional Government, pushed the majority in the soviets towards a seizure of power led by the Bolsheviks. The balance of class forces in Germany in March 1920 was less favourable due to the events sketched above, but the response of the mass of workers to the coup showed that with correct intervention by revolutionaries the defeat of the coup contained the potential to turn the tables on the ruling class.

In the Ruhr and Saxony where workers' councils had been put down by the Freikorps the previous year, resistance to the coup went far beyond strike action. In the Ruhr, the army was driven out in pitched battles with armed workers and a Red Army set up with mass support. Workers' councils took power in most major towns, often excluding the local SPD leadership. In Saxony and Thuringia armed workers took over all the major towns, defeating the army and reactionary militias. A workers' council was elected from factories in the region based in Chemnitz. The KPD was the biggest party in the council, having built up support through united front work with the USPD and avoiding premature bids for power. Workers' councils were also set up on the northern coast where there had been no previous experience of revolutionary struggle. Rural workers east of the river Elbe where there was no Communist presence also armed themselves against reactionary militias to enable themselves to join the strike.

The military and the bourgeois parties now realised that they could

---

15: See Rose, 2014.

not defeat a united and determined working class and the coup's leaders ran for cover. This was a great victory for the workers. However, the events in the Ruhr, Saxony and the north showed that with determined centralised leadership, the workers could have gone over to the offensive against the ruling class and the SPD.

Broué notes that:

> While this time Germany was not covered by a network of workers' councils…it was nonetheless covered by a tight network of executive committees or action committees formed by the workers' parties and trade unions. The struggle against the putschists…led these committees to play the role of revolutionary centres and this posed in a practical way…the problem of power in general.[16]

As Harman puts it, "The situation was rather similar to that in Spain in July 1936 after Franco's coup. The right wing army coup provoked a rising of the workers".[17]

Tragically, the KPD was still not in a position to provide the leadership needed. It had grown over the previous year, but had expelled half its membership for holding ultra-left positions rather than trying to win them over. This had severely weakened the party in key cities such as Berlin and Hamburg. Following the coup the party's national leadership vacillated and did not offer a clear lead. The centrist USPD also dithered and the general strike was allowed to peter out without decisive action against the right. This allowed the SPD leadership to let the army leaders take revenge on the armed workers.

The impact of the events of 1919 and 1920 on the USPD rank and file was profound. The civil war and the Kapp putsch had shown millions of workers that the ruling class was determined to reverse the November Revolution. The Weimar Republic had not delivered on the vital needs of the workers. The counter-revolutionary role of the SPD was very clear; as was the need for a mass, centralised combat party of the working class instead of the centrist leadership of the USPD, who in practice shared the politics of the SPD, and the ultra-leftism of large sections of the KPD. There was now much greater understanding of events in Russia and the lessons for Germany and sympathy for the German Communists based on the experience of common struggle.

16: Broué, 2006, p360.
17: Harman, 1982, p170.

The USPD was a very significant organisation with 800,000 members in 1920, including many working class activists with deep roots in the unions, factories and pits. As mentioned above, it doubled its vote in the 1920 elections, nearly equalling that of the SPD. The leadership now came under massive pressure to affiliate to the Communist International. At its congress at Halle in November 1920, delegates voted overwhelmingly to support an appeal delivered in person by Grigori Zinoviev, the president of the Communist International, to join the International and for the USPD and KPD to merge to form the United Communist Party of Germany. At last German workers had a mass revolutionary organisation with serious roots in the key organisations of the class.

Was defeat in October 1923 inevitable?

But it was the events of the year of crisis 1923 that showed most clearly that the German Revolution could still have ended in victory for the workers. The invasion of the Ruhr, Germany's most important industrial area, by French troops and the raging inflation that destroyed the living standards of the middle class let alone the workers, threw the ruling class into a deep crisis. Chris Harman quotes the minister of finance as saying, "the dissolution of the social order was expected by the hour".[18]

Initially the government, led by Wilhelm Cuno, was able to unite all classes in a wave of patriotic fervour behind its policy of passive resistance to the invader. But by April its credibility was in tatters as it was clear the big industrialists of the Ruhr were using passive resistance for their own ends. Inflation really began to take hold stimulated by currency speculation by Stinnes. Soaring prices were met by a massive wave of strikes that quickly got out of the control of the union bureaucrats. Tried and tested methods of reaching a compromise to get workers back to work no longer worked in a situation in which prices were doubling weekly. The unions' bureaucratic machine was disintegrating as officials' salaries were becoming worthless and the unions could not afford strike pay. In June, Rudolf Wissell, a member of the government's Provisional Economic Council, wrote, "I tell you quite clearly that a revolutionary and activist spirit is rising in the most quiet and most stable of the masses... It only needs a little excitement to explode everything".[19]

Workers were increasingly ignoring the union structures and organising their struggles through the factory and pit councils. In the revolutionary

---

18: Harman, 1982, p222.
19: Quoted in Harman, 1982, pp246-247.

situation that was now developing in Germany, the factory councils, linked up nationally, had the potential to become the basis for a revolutionary workers' government that could replace the capitalist state. As the economic crisis deepened during 1923, the factory councils launched bodies known as control committees that fought to control prices by regulating markets and requisitioning foodstuffs. They involved housewives, spreading the power of the factory councils into working class communities.[20] On top of this, in response to the growth of the far-right, the leadership of the factory councils called in April for the formation of armed workers' detachments known as the proletarian hundreds. These became particularly strong in the Ruhr and Central Germany, amounting to 100,000 men nationally by October.[21]

These developments show that despite the absence of soviets as such, organisations of working class power were developing rapidly. In his critical notes on Zinoviev's "Foundations of the Third International: Theses", Lenin corrected the sentence: "The real organs of mass revolutionary struggle which will be transformed after the insurrection into organs of power are the soviets of workers' deputies" with the words, *"of the type of the Commune and the Soviets"*.[22] This reflects his understanding that the organs of workers' power do not have to replicate exactly the soviet form thrown up by the Russian Revolution.[23] Leon Trotsky wrote a year later:

> It was in Germany that soviets were several times created as the organs of insurrection without an insurrection taking place—and as organs of state power—without any power. This led to the following: in 1923, the movement of broad proletarian and semi-proletarian masses began to crystallise around the factory committees which *in the main* fulfilled all the functions of our own soviets in the period preceding the direct struggle for power.[24]

He noted that in 1917 "Lenin had indicated the factory councils as the organisations of the struggle for power" in the period when the soviets were dominated by the counter-revolutionary Menshevik and Socialist Revolutionaries.[25]

Even before the crisis, the KPD had begun to recover from its own disastrous putsch of March 1921, which had severely damaged its credibility.

20: Harman, 1982, p238.
21: Broué, 2006, p770.
22: See Riddell, 1986, p608, my emphasis.
23: Riddell, 1986, p608.
24: Trotsky, 1975, p249, Trotsky's emphasis.
25: Trotsky, 1975, p249.

Careful application of the united front policy had led to a gradual rise in support and influence at the expense of the SPD. When the unions had refused to call a national conference of factory councils at the end of 1922, an unofficial conference had been held which showed strong support for the KPD. Now the SPD was in crisis because the police in the states it controlled were shooting down workers and like the unions, its apparatus was bankrupt. By August prices were doubling and trebling daily. Normal daily life was now impossible for the working class and much of the middle class. The factory councils called a general strike which swept across Germany demanding not only action on living standards, but the replacement of the Cuno government by a government of the workers' parties and legalisation of the proletarian hundreds. The government fell within days. The ruling class was in deep crisis.

The KPD leadership and the Communist International leadership in Moscow belatedly realised that workers' power was now on the agenda. For months, the KPD leadership had maintained a defensive posture, lagging behind events. It had lost confidence in its own judgement, paralysed by its own previous mistakes. The date was set for the seizure of power and feverish military preparations began. Tragically, the KPD called off the rising and missed the boat.

Conclusion

The purpose of this article is to reaffirm the view of Broué and Harman that workers' power was on the agenda between 1918 and 1923. I attempt to refute John Rose's claim that once the workers' councils acquiesced in their own effective dissolution in December 1918 and the SPD won a majority of workers' votes in the general election the revolution was all but over. I also dispute John's claim that the outcome of the defeat of the Kapp putsch was the strengthening of the Weimar Republic and his dismissal of the importance of factory councils.

In his talk John leans heavily on the documents contained in Gabriel Kuhn's book *All Power to the Councils!,* which, although containing excellent material by Rosa Luxemburg, also relies heavily on materials by ultra-lefts and anarchists who were pessimistic about the prospects of revolution in Germany and hostile to the Bolsheviks and the KPD. As this journal has repeatedly argued, revolution is a process not an event or series of discrete events. The German workers were inexperienced and confused in 1918 and fell prey to the manoeuvres of the SPD leaders and trade union bureaucrats. By the summer of 1923, five years of revolutionary struggle had taught them many hard lessons. Now they looked to the KPD to lead them in giving capitalism the knock-out blow. Tragically they were let down with consequences of world historic proportions. As Trotsky put it:

> Why did the German Revolution fail to lead to victory? The causes for this lie wholly in tactics and not in objective conditions... In the course of 1923 the working masses realised or sensed that the moment of decisive struggle was approaching. However, they did not see the necessary resolution and self-confidence on the side of the Communist Party.[26]

References

Broué, Pierre, 2006, *The German Revolution 1918-23* (Haymarket).

Harman, Chris, 1982, *The Lost Revolution: Germany 1918-23* (Bookmarks).

Kuhn, Gabriel (ed), 2012, *All Power to the Councils! A Documentary History of the German Revolution of 1918-1919* (Merlin Press).

Luxemburg, Rosa, 1970, "The Mass Strike, the Political Party and the Trade Unions", in Mary-Alice Waters (ed), *Rosa Luxemburg Speaks* (Pathfinder).

Riddell, John, 1986, *The German Revolution and the Debate on Soviet Power: Preparing the Founding Congress* (Pathfinder).

Rose, John, 2014, "Workers' and Soldiers' Councils in Germany, 1918-19", talk at Marxism 2014, http://swpradiocast.bandcamp.com/track/workers-and-soldiers-councils-in-germany-1918-19-marxism-2014

Trotsky, Leon, 1972, *The First Five Years of the Communist International*, Volume I (Monad Press), www.marxists.org/archive/trotsky/1924/ffyci-1

Trotsky, Leon, 1975, "Lessons of October", in *The Challenge of the Left Opposition 1923-25* (Pathfinder Press), www.marxists.org/archive/trotsky/1924/lessons/

Trotsky, Leon, 1977, *The History of the Russian Revolution* (Pluto Press).

26: Trotsky, 1972, pp2-3.

MARXISM AND WOMEN'S LIBERATION

JUDITH ORR

Out now!

"A tour de force. Wide ranging, tackling complex issues with a sure grasp, and deeply informed both historically and in the present."
Hester Eisenstein, professor of sociology, City University of New York

"A powerful and urgent call to action." **Sinead Kennedy, abortion rights campaigner with Action for Choice, Ireland**

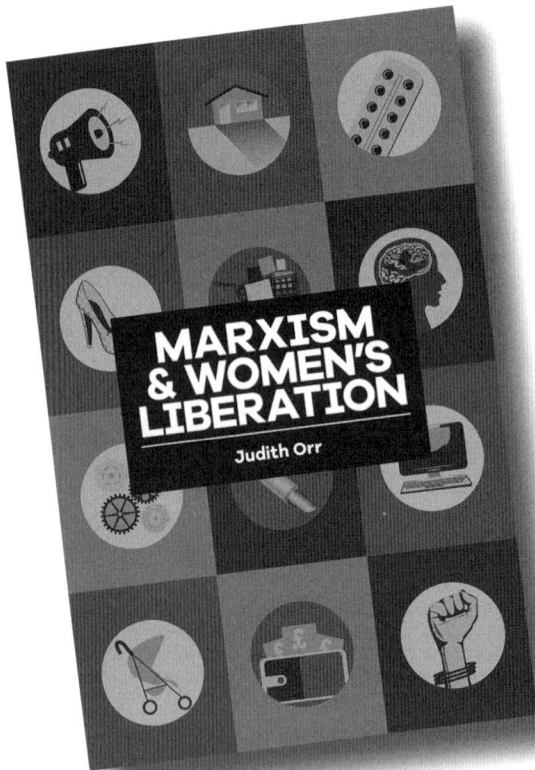

MARXISM & WOMEN'S LIBERATION
Judith Orr

As austerity bites and new debates about oppression rage, Judith Orr steers a path through the history and future of the fight for women's liberation.

Price £9.99

Published by
Bookmarks Publications
1 Bloomsbury Street,
London
WC1B 3QE
0207 637 1848
bookmarksbookshop.
co.uk

Paul Mason's PostCapitalism: A response to Joseph Choonara

Pete Green

It came as no surprise that *International Socialism* could publish, in the last issue, such a dismissive review of Paul Mason's fascinating and thought-provoking new book.[1] Certainly Mason has moved a considerable distance from the Leninism of his youth and now advocates a politics which uneasily combines elements of left reformism with an autonomist focus on the emergence of alternative forms of cooperative endeavour within contemporary capitalism. Mason's provocative thesis that Wikipedia and the Anonymous network, rather than the Petrograd Soviet of 1917, anticipate the future of a "post-capitalist" society has predictably met with obdurate rejection by all who still think that the Bolshevik revolution provides us with a model for the path to socialism. But if that was all that Mason's book had to say I would not have bothered to write this response to Joseph Choonara's review.

Choonara, to be fair, focuses much of his review on the economic analysis in Mason's book and attempts to deal with that on its own merits. Nevertheless, I was disappointed that his review either failed to acknowledge, or seriously misread, Mason's illuminating if sketchy observations on the relevance of Marx's theory of value to exploring the deeply contradictory character of contemporary capitalism in general and the impact of IT in particular. Instead Choonara simply assimilates Mason's position to that of

---

1: Mason, 2015, reviewed by Joseph Choonara—Choonara, 2015a.

Michael Hardt and Antonio Negri, who maintain that the labour theory of value is no longer applicable in a world where labour has supposedly become "immeasurable".[2] It is that mistake which prompted this response and on which I want to focus most of what follows. I will not dwell on the more problematic character of Mason's conception of historical agency because that raises questions of analysis and strategy which would demand a much longer response than is possible here.

Certainly Mason draws on earlier work by Negri as well as such deviant Marxists as André Gorz and Manuel Castells. One could extend the eclectic list of influences considerably because Mason is a magpie type of thinker whose work as a globe-trotting journalist has somehow been combined with dipping into an impressively wide range of Marxist and non-Marxist writers. But the review's sweeping comment, that there is little here that has not appeared elsewhere, is comparable to saying that there was nothing new in John Heartfield's photomontages because he cut out all the photographic elements from somewhere else and just added a caption.

To give just one example, Choonara ignores completely the juxtaposition towards the end of Mason's book of two quite distinct processes. Firstly, there is a discussion of the transition from feudalism to capitalism in Western Europe which emphasises the interplay between internal and external factors. One critical external factor, contributing to what historians call the "general crisis of feudalism", was the Black Death, the plague that swept across Europe after 1347. In Mason's summary this was an "external shock that helped to collapse an internally weakened system".[3] New technologies such as the printing press, the development of banking and trade and the conquest of the Americas all played a role in a "complex interplay of factors". All of that is certainly derivative from the work of economic historians. But Mason then proceeds to suggest in his next chapter that climate change, along with related issues such as energy depletion and migration, is likely to be our equivalent of the Black Death, putting "the whole global system under strain" and "democracy itself in danger". Of course, one can disagree with the details of the historical analysis, and it would be wrong to identify climate change as "external" to capitalism; Mason could have been a little more careful in his presentation in that respect because he manifestly does hold capitalism responsible for carbon emissions. But the historical analogy is imaginative, thought-provoking and certainly not "passé".

2:   My own critical comments on Hardt and Negri's *Empire* can be found in a review—Green, 2002.

3:   Mason, 2015, p239.

Choonara neglects even to mention in passing Mason's icono-clastic (for contemporary Marxists) attempt to draw a parallel between the transition from feudalism to capitalism and the projected transition to "post-capitalism", which is one of the central themes of the book. Instead he critiques Mason's use of historical stories to "buttress arguments about the contemporary world", as if writers in this journal have always been completely innocent of such discursive manoeuvres.

That comment followed one piece of criticism where Choonara gets it right. Mason's account of Lenin's split with Alexander Bogdanov is mis-leading and does ignore the rather important point that Bogdanov led the "left" opposition to Lenin after the defeat of the 1905 revolution. Yet in his rush to the defence of Lenin, Choonara himself ignores Mason's revelatory account of Bogdanov's utopian science fiction novel *Red Star*, which is why its author features in Mason's narrative. The omission is sadly symptomatic of Choonara's reluctance to engage seriously with the utopian and visionary dimension of Mason's book.

Rather than dwelling on that issue, however, I want to address the two critiques at the core of Choonara's review. In both cases I think Choonara has seriously misread what Mason is saying, in part because he has not read the book carefully enough and in part because he has simply amalgamated Mason's ideas with those of Hardt and Negri and other autonomists.

The first critique concerns Mason's use of the Russian economist Nikolai Kondratiev and the question of long waves of expansion and decline (or stagnation) in the history of capitalism. Choonara's critique runs along the following lines. He agrees that there are long periods of expansion and stagnation evident in the historical record but, like Leon Trotsky, questions their regularity. He acknowledges that Mason also references Trotsky but notes that Mason later uses the phrase "fifty-year cycle" repeat-edly in his discussion of crisis theory. The danger of this is that it appears "to reduce the complexity of capitalism as a historical system to the sim-plicity of a mathematical formula". On that we can agree. But then so does Mason in passages such as the following:

> The long-wave pattern has been disrupted. The fourth long cycle was prolonged, distorted and ultimately broken by factors that have not occurred before in the history of capitalism: the defeat and moral surrender of organised labour; the rise of information technology and the discovery that

once an unchallenged superpower exists, it can create money out of nothing for a long time.[4]

Whatever else you may want to say about that analysis it is certainly not one that reduces history to a simple mathematical formula.

Choonara then praises Mason for placing profit rates at the centre of his analysis and not simply relying on Kondratiev's own explanation of long waves as a function of very long-term capital investments. Both Choonara and Mason stress that there are tendencies and counteracting tendencies at play as Karl Marx himself identified. This is an approach I also share. Where he disagrees with Mason at this point is simply over the issue of whether the turn to neoliberalism "restored profit rates from the late 1980s onward".[5] This of course touches on an extensive debate among Marxist economists which I cannot explore in any depth here but on which I tend to agree with Mason and the writers he references.

One can of course argue about how far profit rates were restored, and the usual comparison by writers such as Michael Roberts and Guglielmo Carchedi, on whom Choonara relies, is with the historically very exceptional peak of the mid-1960s for the United States economy alone. Anwar Shaikh certainly suggests that the recovery of profit rates from the early 1980s in the US did not take them back to the level of the earlier peak. But in the same article Shaikh also reasserts his own version of long-wave theory which is why Mason uses him in the book.[6]

Where Mason is absolutely correct in my view is his insistence that there have been critical periods when capitalism could only survive through deep structural adaptation or mutations. These are the transitions from one phase to another which earlier Marxists located in the long depression of the 1870s and 1880s leading to a new wave of imperialist expansion, and of course in the inter-war period which led to a new phase of state-managed capitalism. The crisis of the 1970s resulted in another mutation with the emergence of neoliberalism and renewed globalisation of capital. Mason suggests that this phase has now reached its limits, exposed not just by the financial crisis of 2008 but also by contradictions specific to the era of information technology. Mason is also correct to locate the gap between a rising mass of profits and the relative stagnation of investment as indicative of a

---

4:   Mason, 2015, p78.
5:   Mason, 2015, p71.
6:   Shaikh, 2011. I am however sceptical of the use of US national income accounts (by Carchedi, Roberts and Robert Brenner as well as Shaikh) for figures which, among other deficiencies, exclude the increasing share of profits from overseas accruing to US multinationals.

contradiction specific to neoliberal capitalism with its prioritisation of share-holder value and preference for piling up cash reserves rather than making risky investments in what we call the productive economy.[7]

The most problematic implication of Choonara's argument is that neoliberalism, and all that has accompanied it, including a transformation of the global division of labour with the growing share of manufacturing located in East Asia, had little impact on profitability globally (as distinct from the domestic US economy). Choonara relies on the argument developed by Chris Harman (from an original idea of Mike Kidron's) back in the early 1980s that the size of capitals and state intervention have prevented the clearing out of the system and the devaluation of existing capital which characterised earlier crises. It is an argument which I endorsed at the time when it had a certain validity. But the most cursory examination of the scale of the protracted restructuring of capital since the early 1980s, alongside the disappearance of large sectors of the engineering, mining, shipbuilding and steel industries of countries such as Britain, confirms that thesis has long since ceased to adequately capture the dynamics of contemporary capitalism.

Mason, by contrast, takes seriously, with lots of data, the trends towards globalisation of capital, financialisation and what he terms, a little casually, the "doubling of the world's workforce" with China's move from autarchy to a major participant in world markets. Choonara pays little attention to this section of the book—perhaps because it reveals just how dated the orthodoxy of the Socialist Workers Party on these matters has become.

More surprising, however, is Choonara's misreading of Mason's position at the end of this section of his review. There he claims that "Mason argues that we are now seeing the combination of the end of the neoliberal solution to the downswing, and the embryonic beginnings of a new economic paradigm, the 'fifth wave', whose 'core technology' is 'information'".[8] Now Mason may be a bit fuzzy on certain issues but on this point he is clear and it is pivotal to his core argument. Towards the end of his second chapter he notes that the so-called fifth wave began to emerge in the 1990s driven by network technology, a global marketplace and information goods. But he says that wave never got going—"it has stalled".[9] The reasons he gives for this are in many respects more interesting than the periodisation. Here we arrive at the focus of Choonara's second critique.

7: Although Mason doesn't mention their work, studies by Erdogan Bakir and Al Campbell confirm this argument in detail (see for example Bakir and Campbell, 2010, and Bakir, 2015). Thanks to Jim Kincaid for these references.
8: Choonara, 2015a, p166.
9: Mason, 2015, p48.

Choonara claims that "the central notion in Mason's book is that we are moving to an epoch in which information is rendering value irrelevant".[10] But that is to conflate two quite different notions. Certainly Mason envisages a postcapitalist future in which the law of value would no longer be central to the allocation of resources—but then so did Marx. Mason sees the seeds of such a future in the free labour expended on Wikipedia and opensource software to which the law of value obviously does not apply. But Mason is also defending the relevance of Marx's theory to exposing the deep contradictions of "cognitive capitalism". It is precisely because of the fact that information goods such as computer software can be *reproduced* (or copied!) with a minimal amount of labour that the marginal cost (the cost of producing an extra item) is driven towards zero.

This is a confirmation of Marx's theory, not a critique of it. Choonara conflates this with a related but quite distinct question about the valuation of fixed capital. Some types of fixed capital such as computers are much cheaper but that's not the critical argument. The threat to companies such as Microsoft, Apple and Google is that their massive investment in fixed capital, including all their research and development costs, will not be recovered in a competitive market. Only their ability to maintain a high degree of monopoly, protected above all in this epoch by so-called intellectual property rights globally, enabled them to make the vast profits they have stacked up over recent decades. Where hardware devices such as the iPhone are concerned, that profit derives in large part from the labour of super-exploited workers in Asia. Mason could have said more about that here as he has done elsewhere.[11]

Mason could also have elaborated more on the critical point that, as with all monopolistic structures, the profits of companies such as Google derive less from their own workers than from a transfer of surplus value via the pricing mechanism at the expense of other capitals in the system. When Choonara suggests in a footnote that "there is no reason in principle why other search engines could not in time erode this advantage"[12] he is right, but that's precisely the threat Mason is referring to. As the US Marxist Michael Perelman has explored in detail, the same clash between the high costs of fixed capital and low marginal costs threatened the viability of privately owned railroads in the US in the 19th century and monopolisation was the necessary response.[13]

10:   Choonara, 2015a, p167.

11:   Mason, 2013.

12:   Choonara, 2015a, p171.

13:   Perelman, 2006. Perelman is a writer whom Mason doesn't reference but whose earlier work (Perelman, 2003) on intellectual property rights is also very relevant to his argument

Unfortunately Hardt and Negri, with whom Mason shares an interest in Marx's fragment on machines in the *Grundrisse,* muddle things up by claiming that the categories of labour time and value are no longer relevant because the productivity of "mental" labourers is immeasurable. But that's manifestly not Mason's claim. Even if he echoes Negri with his references to "cognitive capitalism", his core thesis is a derivation from Marx's theory of value, not a break with it.

There is another objection to Mason's argument which has more weight. Visions of a world of completely automated industrial production with most jobs eliminated remain just that—visions of a world which could only be realised in a post-capitalist society. That was Marx's point in the fragment of the *Grundrisse* that Choonara himself quotes. When Marx anticipated the liberatory potential of capitalism's development of technology he certainly wasn't envisaging a smooth process of transition. Nor, to be fair, is Mason.

Moreover, while the global waged labour force has continued to expand, its composition and location has changed dramatically. To sum up a complex process rather crudely—the equivalents of the Petrograd factories of 1917 are today to be found in China and on the Mexican border rather than in Britain or the US. Outsourcing, offshore production and networks of sub-contractors are precisely the tendencies that Marx would have been examining if he was to rewrite those central chapters of *Capital* volume 1 on the organisation of production in Victorian Britain, which emphasised not the statistical average of the time of writing but the underlying tendency of capitalist development.

Choonara also dismisses Mason's reference to the precariat, another topic that requires more space than is available. But the figure quoted by Choonara, that only 6 percent of workers in Britain are on temporary contracts, is grossly misleading. This excludes, for example, agency workers, who are classified as self-employed. The number of self-employed has risen rapidly in recent years to 15 percent of the labour force, with an average income of £11,000, which suggests that for most of them life is very precarious indeed.[14] Nor does possession of a permanent contract in much of the non-unionised private sector offer much protection in this period.

---

about the Googles and Microsofts of our period .

14: Choonara has addressed the issue of self-employment in the December 2015 issue of *Socialist Review* and rightly notes its diverse components—Choonara, 2015b. His claim that the percentage of the labour force in the category has only risen from 13 to 15 percent since 1993 is correct but ignores the sharp fall after 1993 and rise since 2008. These fluctuations are reminiscent of Marx's characterisation of one element of the reserve army of labour, an analysis of the precariat of his day.

In his conclusion, however, Choonara makes one argument with which I agree. The point of production remains a critical location of struggle even if that is not readily apparent from recent strike figures. Mason's impressionistic invocation of a "networked humanity" as the agent of change is also far too fuzzy for my taste although its great merit is its resolute internationalism. I can only conclude by urging readers of *International Socialism* not to be deterred by Choonara's review from reading Mason's book for themselves.

References

Bakir, Erdogan, 2015, "Capital Accumulation, Profitability and Crisis: Neoliberalism in the United States", *Review of Radical Political Economics*, volume 47, number 3.

Bakir, Erdogan and Al Campbell 2010, "Neoliberalism, the Rate of Profit and the Rate of Accumulation", *Science and Society*, volume 74, number 3, http://content.csbs.utah.edu/~al/articles/Sub_Neo_RP_Acc.pdf

Choonara, Joseph, 2015, "Brand New, You're Retro", *International Socialism* 148 (autumn), http://isj.org.uk/brand-new-youre-retro

Choonara, Joseph, 2015b, "Little Joy in Being Your Own Boss", *Socialist Review* (December), http://socialistreview.org.uk/408/little-joy-being-your-own-boss

Green, Peter, 2002, "The Passage from Imperialism to Empire: A Commentary on *Empire* by Michael Hardt and Antonio Negri", *Historical Materialism*, volume 10, issue 1.

Mason, Paul, 2013, *Why It's Still Kicking Off Everywhere: The New Global Revolutions* (Verso).

Mason, Paul, 2015, *PostCapitalism: A Guide to Our Future* (Allen Lane).

Perelman, Michael, 2003, *Steal This Idea: Intellectual Property Rights and the Corporate Confiscation of Creativity* (Palgrave).

Perelman, Michael, 2006, *Railroading Economics: The Creation of the Free Market Mythology* (Monthly Review Press).

Shaikh, Anwar, 2011, "The First Great Recession of the 21st Century", *Socialist Register 2011: The Crisis This Time*, available at www.anwarshaikhecon.org/index.php/publications/political-economy

Letter to the editor

The autumn 2015 issue of *International Socialism* contained two extremely important and erudite articles concerning the issue of the European Union and which way socialists should vote in any potential referendum. In order of appearance they are: "The EU Referendum: The Case for a Socialist Yes vote" (John Palmer), and "The Internationalist Case against the European Union" (Alex Callinicos). Both of these contain a great deal of empirical and historical detail and repay careful consideration.

Having said that, I found myself wondering whether in responding in simple "yes or no" terms we are missing the opportunity to resist what is at best a silly question and at worst a poisonous question. I will do my best to elaborate below.

Taking the latter article first, Alex offers a comprehensive political history of the development of the EU illustrating its neoliberal and imperialist nature. In essence he puts it like this:

"The EU does not represent the transcendence of nationalism, but rather has provided a framework in which the larger European capitalisms could pursue their interests. Secondly, for the past 30 years the EU has functioned as an engine promoting neoliberalism both within and beyond its borders" (p104).

"The EU today is best understood as a dysfunctional would-be imperialist power. We can see its imperialist character most clearly in its promotion of neoliberalism—through its expansion to incorporate Central and Eastern Europe, in its policies towards neighbouring states in the Mediterranean and Eastern Europe and now, within the EU, through the disciplinary mechanisms enforcing permanent austerity. But the dysfunctional nature of this imperialism is evident both internally (the eurozone) and externally (Ukraine)" (p105).

Clearly, if one accepts this analysis then it would be contradictory in the extreme to vote yes in any referendum on the subject. How could any socialist possibly actually vote for this? Of course they couldn't. As Alex puts it: "Yes supporters must either refute this analysis or abandon their position" (p131).

However, rejecting a Yes position need not mean adopting a No position. There is a problem with a No position that John Palmer puts very clearly. It is that our politics, as part of the No campaign, would simply (in the main) be unheard. He suggests that:

"Of course socialists will want to campaign on a wide range of other questions, while voting Yes in the referendum. They will campaign for the broadest possible opposition to EU austerity policies and campaign for a different, socialist Europe. But, as part of the No camp, these politics would be rendered virtually inaudible in the cacophony generated in the referendum debate by the campaign of the Tory right and UKIP" (p95).

This point concerning our campaigning being simply "drowned out" if we are part of the No camp is a vitally important one.

An Alternative Europe is Possible

If the Yes campaign wins, the main beneficiary will be David Cameron who will have negotiated an even more neoliberal EU. If the No campaign wins, the main beneficiaries will be UKIP, right wing Tories, and racist nationalists. Neither of these scenarios could reasonably appeal to us.

In the current political situation the main responsibility of the Socialist Workers Party is to grow, while remaining principled and honest. In other words we tell the truth as we see it. This is what we do week in and week out on our stalls on the streets around the country. How we campaign in the referendum is a tactical question.

In the past year we have run spirited campaigns against UKIP under the banner of "Stand Up to Racism"; our stalls have often been surrounded by well-wishers and people prepared to work with us. Will such people understand us if we become part of the No campaign? If we have stalls campaigning for a No vote, our stalls will be approached by UKIP supporters and assorted little Englanders and racists. Are these the people we wish to attract?

If, in contrast to the above, we were inviting people to join us at public meetings with a focus on the alternative Europe that we envisage we would be clearly differentiating ourselves from both camps while maintaining an internationalist focus. If we were saying clearly: "A plague on both your houses", then most people would understand us saying no to neoliberalism and no to UKIP and racism. Of course we would also explicitly support Antarsya in their policy of support for the withdrawal of Greece from both the EU and the eurozone.

The referendum question is too closed and restrictive a question and offers only an illusion of choice. Do we want neoliberal Tweedledee or a racist Tweedledum? Of course we want neither because a better Europe is both possible and necessary—a plague on both their houses!

Dave Merrick
Bristol South SWP

Book reviews

Face to face with the minotaur
Nikos Lountos

Kevin Ovenden, **Syriza: Inside the Labyrinth** *(Pluto Press/Left Book Club, 2015), £11.50*

I'm writing this review on the eve of a general strike (3 December) in Greece, the second against the Syriza government since it was re-elected in September. Alexis Tsipras is eager to find allies among the leaders of the pro-austerity opposition, feeling already that the majority he enjoys in the parliament, along with his nationalist allies, the "Independent Greeks", will not be enough to push through measures such as a massive cut in pensions. Interestingly, Tsipras's hopes are being complicated because of the deep internal crisis the biggest opposition party, the right wing New Democracy, has got itself into. After the resignation of its leader Antonis Samaras in the aftermath of the referendum on the bailout in July, and the prolonged stay of an interim president, New Democracy failed to stage its own primaries. Now all the candidates are rowing about whether to try again to elect a leader or to split the party altogether.

So, those who predicted that Syriza's second electoral victory would put an end to the political turbulence in Greece have been proved wrong. Yes, on the surface it might appear that the revolt expressed in the "No" vote in the referendum has been aborted. The triumph of the 61.3 percent vote for "No" in July was converted into an overwhelming 90 percent majority in favour of "Yes" to austerity in the parliament elected in September. But, the unsettled account between class forces goes deeper than the parliamentary balance of forces.

Big events can act as blasts of light revealing to us hidden aspects of reality. But the reality is there, ever-changing in between the big moments, be they elections, referendums or general strikes. As we enter 2016, and the anniversary of Syriza's first election victory approaches, Kevin's book is indispensable for anyone trying to grasp this deeper, hidden engine of the Greek turmoil.

This is the first merit of the book. Although formally written about Syriza, its route towards power and its tempestuous first semester, it is actually an insight into the dynamics of the class struggle in Greece in the last decade, thus not a book merely about analysing the past, but, more importantly, about shaping the future. Kevin analyses Syriza as a product of the experience of the bitter struggles and political conundrums through which the movement in Greece has passed—as much as it is an independent political actor in this process. But, contrary to a view of the political actors as ready-made entities, coming out of the blue, like Minerva born already armoured, Kevin advises that: "political crisis and succession of massive popular mobilisations were not simply raw materials to be worked upon by leaders of the radical left to sculpt a victory at the polls of 2015. They comprised the actions and political choices of millions of people concentrated at key moments in the crisis and also the collapse of various strategies by the traditional parties of government to weather the storm" (p21).

In order to strengthen his position, Kevin offers a concise history of the Greek left over the last three decades. Few people outside Greece remember, for example, that the leadership of Synaspismos (the main party behind the creation of Syriza) was ideologically very close to the Blairite prime minister Costas Simitis in the 1990s. Kevin reminds us: "When Simitis spoke as a guest at the 1996 Synaspismos conference, around half the delegates gave him a standing ovation". How did Syriza go from this to being the carrier of hope for radical change? Kevin answers that it was the movement against corporate capitalism that erupted after Seattle in 1999, and following that, the movement against the war in Iraq, that pushed Syriza in a more radical direction. That was not the end of it. In what he calls the "Resisted Rise of Syriza" Kevin traces the key moments in its transformation, including the wave of university occupations in 2006 and 2007, the revolt against austerity and police violence in December 2008 and then the full-blown economic crisis.

A second merit of the book is that it avoids the trap of the "theories" of Greek exceptionalism. It is written both from an insider's and from an outsider's perspective. The *inside* part is due to the author's careful observations of developments in the country in the last decades. He has a *feel* for the events, and for the specific impact some moments have had even if they didn't make headlines. But the *outside* part is equally important. Many commentators have referred to the exceptional character of the situation, whether they are the European Union's elites with their propaganda

that describes the Greeks as a problematic people, unwilling to reform, or those of the international left who have taken superficial approaches in the weeks after the elections, seeing Greece as the promised land. Kevin, on the contrary, is not afraid to use British examples and analogies in order to give colour to persons, events and political forces. He doesn't use the phrase "left reformism" but his conclusions open the way to dealing with Syriza's rise as a phenomenon in the same category as that of Podemos in the Spanish state or Jeremy Corbyn's ascent in Britain. There are strategic lessons coming out of the process that led to Syriza's victory, as much as out of the defeat of its governmental strategy and its retreat after the showdown with the Troika last summer. These strategic lessons, which come out of each one of the book's eight chapters, have a universal value, wherever we may live and fight.

This doesn't mean that Kevin neglects to go into the specificities. On the contrary, a third strong point of the book is the clever use of Greek history to help the English reader understand the specific *weight* of places, words, names and events. The impact of an electoral victory for the left in Greece bears the weight of December 1944 when British tanks suppressed the revolt after the liberation from the Nazis. For Greeks it also brought memories of the 1958 elections when, despite the Communist Party being forced to operate under conditions of illegality with thousands of militants exiled or imprisoned, a left wing party, the "United Democratic Left" polled second, becoming the opposition party in parliament.

But, although Kevin stresses the importance of the movement as a shaping factor, this does not mean that he separates the "social" struggle from the "political" struggle. Actually, the thread of Kevin's argument is one of the "primacy of politics". The political sphere is where the contradictory pressures, the antagonising interests, the burden of the past, the hopes for the future and the urgency of the moment are concentrated. The way these disruptions are resolved—or not—influences consciousness on a massive scale and, through that, the next wave of struggle. Because of this inter-relation, the political aspects of the struggle, and more concretely the political challenges the movement in Greece has faced in the last 15 years, are given specific care by Kevin. This crucial series of arguments adopts an approach that is, if we leave aside articles written for this journal, very difficult to find in other writings in English about Greece.

In this sense, one of the most important parts of the book is Chapter Four, "The monstrous legacy of racism". In 2012, Andreas Loverdos, an arch-bigot Pasok health minister, offered to the sensationalist press the faces of HIV positive women, labelling them as criminal migrants and responsible for the spread of AIDS in Greece. Is there a relation between this incident and the victory of the left in 2015? What did a demonstration of Pakistani immigrants in late August 2012 have to do with the anti-austerity struggle? Kevin answers that these moments have been crucial. The political questions around racism, bigotry and nationalism haven't been optional extras in the struggle of these years. These have been the questions around which the ruling class tried to reorganise itself in order to confuse—to divide and conquer. The outcome was not predetermined. It was up to the forces of the left and, in many cases, of the anti-capitalist left to take initiatives in order to block these attempts in circumstances anything but easy.

Kevin's analysis of the fascist threat is at the same time nuanced and concrete. There are three simplistic views of the rise of the fascist Golden Dawn. It was seen as an automatic consequence of the economic crisis, or as a foreordained fate for a failed left government, or as totally irrelevant to the "primary" battle against austerity. Kevin stresses the fact that there have been specific actors fomenting racism and pushing the mainstream political discourse towards the extreme-right, and these factors didn't come from the margins, but from inside the "liberal" establishment, and even from social democracy in the moments of its decay. The fascists didn't get to their position in parliament by fighting in the streets—they found the streets prepared by the police and the ideological machine of the mainstream parties.

Antonio Gramsci distinguished between the wars of "manoeuvres" fought by revolutionaries when revolution is imminent and the wars of "position" to try to win over sections of the working class at other times. Anyone having in mind a caricatured version of this duality, with the reformists fighting a "war of position" and the revolutionaries only expecting a "war of manoeuvres" will see this turned upside down. Kevin explains that the fight against racism has been a "war of position" fought by the anti-capitalist left in the last decades, who made anti-racism a feature of every struggle, while at some key moments the reformist left shied away from these battles, considering them an obstacle in the way to electoral victory. If the anti-war movement hadn't incorporated the fight against Islamophobia, giving voice to a new generation of Muslim migrants at the start of the 2000s, these same migrants wouldn't have the tools and the networks to fight against racist police violence, against discrimination and at the end against the fascists themselves, and actually frame their struggle as part of the struggle of the left.

Kevin says: "it is to the enormous credit of that section of the Greek left which imaginatively bridged those domains that such a cross-fertilisation took place. The result was little noticed a decade ago. Today it is an unprobed assumption that there are so many Greek young people and activists whose response to the throttling of their country at the hands of the Troika is to see themselves as of a piece with Muslim women in Tahrir square or Palestinian fighters in Gaza" (p76).

Accordingly, Kevin employs arguments specific to the Greek context when he deals with the dead-end of Syriza's first months in government. He does this in two ways. First, Kevin says that instead of focusing on the hypothetical question of how the deep state would react towards a government of the left, we should focus on the concrete choices Tsipras made in his cabinet. Offering us the profile of three ministers, Nikos Kotzias, Panos Kammenos and Yiannis Panousis (ministers for foreign affairs, defence and public order respectively) he shows how the deep state found its way into the government through Tsipras's own appointees. Second, on the issue of the debt on which much has been written, Kevin, without underestimating the important economic debate, puts politics at the centre. Syriza's retreat in front of the Troika was not the result of a wrong economic argument, not even of mere "Europeanism" (whatever this term means), but a consequence of a strategy that hadn't taken into account the necessity of clashing openly with the ruling class—the Greek ruling class—in the first place.

I hope readers won't be discouraged to read Kevin's book by the condensed way I have presented it in these paragraphs. Its 180 pages are easy to read (although he doesn't always follow the promise he gives in the preface not to use advanced political vocabulary) and each and every one of its sections can offer lots of intellectual and factual surprises for the reader who hasn't followed Greek events as closely as Kevin. It is highly recommended not only for understanding Greece, but for orienting ourselves in all our struggles.

Learning the lessons of the past
Shaun Doherty

John Newsinger, **Them and Us: Fighting the Class War 1910-1939** *(Bookmarks, 2015), £7.99*

John Newsinger opens this timely account of working class struggle in the first half of the 20th century with what at first seems an incongruous statement: "We live in a period of unprecedented class warfare". But he argues that the only reason this sounds strange is that the war has been so brutally one-sided in recent years. The Tories' "austerity" agenda has been pursued relentlessly while resistance to it has been sporadic and muted. He ends the book by hoping it will contribute in some small way to "the coming fightback". Indeed it will, because any effective response from our side will require a concerted attempt to unite the political dimensions of the struggle to the economic and ideological and it is useful to remind ourselves of the past combativity and resilience of workers and working class communities. The themes of the book will be familiar to readers of this journal—the willingness of the ruling class to use the coercive power of the state apparatus when necessary; their dependence on trade union leaders' ability to exercise control over their members; the speed with which Labour politicians can transform themselves from socialist firebrands to fawning sycophants of the established order; the gap between abstract general propaganda and specific material struggle and, above all, the inevitability of a barbaric capitalist system forcing a multiplicity of responses from those it seeks to exploit.

Newsinger is right to remind us that this is war. A crucial aspect of this war is that our ruling class wants the history of working class resistance to be buried in the past while we want to absorb it in order to prepare for future struggles. He begins by describing the Great Unrest (1910-1914), when union membership nearly doubled rising to 4.5 million. It began in the South Wales coalfield with miners demanding 2s and 6d per ton for working in abnormal conditions and the coal owners offering only 1s 9d. A strike was called in the Cambrian Combine and the owners responded with lockouts. The police were put at the disposal of the mine companies and fierce fighting broke out in response to police attacks. Winston Churchill, the home secretary at the time, sent in the army under General Macready to provide "a little gentle persuasion with bayonets". Keir Hardie wrote in the *Labour Leader* that: "the valleys are thronged with police...detachments of soldiers are billeted in farm houses...the entire district looks like a besieged district in war time". (Events found their echo in the Great Miners' Strike of 1984-5.)

In 1911 the strike-wave was initiated by seamen and spread to the dockers causing fear and desperation among ruling politicians—"the local unrest in Hull is akin to a revolutionary outbreak"—and memories of the Paris Commune were invoked. In Liverpool on "Bloody" Sunday 13 August police attacked a demonstration of 80,000 in support of the dockers and pitched battles continued for days. Shots were fired by troops on a crowd trying to free protesters from police vans taking them to Walton prison. King George, abandoning any pretext of being above politics, told Churchill that the troops "should be given a free hand and the mob should be made to fear them".

A key element in future struggles was the emergence of workplace organisations like the Clyde Workers' Committee—arising out of the strikes of shipbuilders and engineers in Glasgow in 1915 against dilution (the opening up of skilled jobs to unskilled workers reducing wages and conditions). Its manifesto denounced union leaders' support for the Munitions Act and famously declared: "We will support the officials just so long as they represent the workers, but we will act independently immediately they misrepresent them." David Lloyd George as Munitions Minister accompanied by the Labour leader Arthur Henderson came to Glasgow to reason with the strikers, but was given a dusty response. At that point conciliation went out the window and the courts and imprisonment of the key activists took its place. But the lesson that the ruling class learnt for future struggles was not that the unions should be smashed, but that the officials of the unions should be incorporated and strengthened against the shop floor.

After the end of the war the ruling class was gripped by fear that unrest would spread into the armed forces and the virus of "Bolshevism" would infect the masses in Britain. This was exacerbated by the use of British troops against the new revolutionary government in Russia. When the chief of the army Henry Wilson met a delegation of soldiers, he told Lloyd George "they bore a dangerous resemblance to a soviet". Indeed the end of the war from November 1918 until late 1921 "saw the most prolonged phase of union militancy and class confrontation ever experienced in Britain"—union membership rose to 8.5 million.

A key dispute of this period was the 1919 miners' strike in South Wales, Nottinghamshire and Derbyshire demanding a 30 percent wage increase, a 6 hour working day and the nationalisation of the mines to boot. The government was terrified that this would resonate with other struggles and raise the spectre of a general strike. Lloyd George reputedly told the union leaders that the government could not hope to defeat the Triple Alliance of miners, dockers and transport workers, the strikers could have caused a constitutional crisis—but had they thought of the consequences of defeating the government? Robert Smillie, the left leader of the miners, reflected: "From that moment on we were beaten and we knew we were." The unions were willing to take action on economic issues but did not want political control. Not even the most militant of union offensives was prepared to reckon with the consequences of assuming state power!

This was manifest again in the Hands Off Russia campaign that opposed intervention against the revolutionary government. Local Councils of Action mobilised around the issue and the government backed off, but crucially for the ruling class union leaders put themselves at the head of the campaign against intervention partly to ensure it did not get out of their control. Andrew Bonar Law expressed the view that "the trade union organisation was the only thing between us and anarchy" and even Churchill could remark that "the curse of trade unionism is that there is not enough of it".

This review does not have space for more than these few snapshots of a phase of struggle that continued through the General Strike of 1926, the unemployment agitation of the 1930s and the fight against the rise of fascism and the defeat of the blackshirts. But this succinct and accessible book provides us with an antidote to those who today are looking solely to "movements" and new forms of organisation. Of course historical circumstances have changed and we need to be open to innovations in the way we organise, but Newsinger reminds us of the foundations that any effective resistance will be built on: "The lessons of the past are clear: what is needed to turn the tide is workplace organisation, militancy and most important of all working class solidarity."

Understanding Islamophobia
Brian Richardson

*Arun Kundnani, **The Muslims are Coming! Islamophobia, Extremism, and the Domestic War on Terror** (Verso, 2015), £9.99*

Arun Kundnani's book about Islamophobia deliberately references the 1966 Hollywood movie, *The Russians are Coming! The Russians are Coming!* With its repetitive title and exclamation marks, it was indicative of the anti-Communist hysteria lying at the centre of that film's plot. *The Muslims are Coming!* begins with an episode that, although all too real, reads like something out of a Hollywood studio. Kundnani describes how Luqman Ameen Abdullah, the Imam of at the Al-Haqq mosque in Detroit, was framed by the authorities and then assassinated by four FBI officers in October 2009. Luqman's death was indicative of the excesses of the war on terror.

This is a timely and important book which describes how Muslims, with their distinctive religion and appearance, became an "ideal enemy" to replace the Russians in the aftermath of the Cold War. Focusing on the development of the War on Terror in both the UK and United States, its historical breadth is hugely impressive.

Kundnani locates much of the current discourse around extremism in the analyses of totalitarianism that emerged in the post-war period. He argues that while the authors of such theses were happy to denounce the tyranny of Nazi Germany or Soviet Russia, they did so without any reference to American capitalism and its role in pushing people towards accepting extreme solutions. He writes: "The anti-totalitarian discourse obscured the ways in which the domestic successes of liberal America were dependent on an illiberal foreign policy of using state terror to secure the international arteries of US-led capitalism" (p103). The concept of totalitarianism developed in that era is now being applied to Islamic extremism.

Kundnani suggests that the growing pre-occupation with terrorism from the 1980s onwards provided: "ideological cover for state violence directed at those resisting US and Israeli power, whether they happened to be terrorists or not; a selective use of the term "terrorism" to exclude all those state and non-state actors using violence to achieve our political ends (such as the Contras in Nicaragua); and a suturing of Israel and the US as defenders of 'Western values' against Islamic fanaticism" (p45).

Of course, in one very significant sense, the Muslims aren't coming. Both in Britain and the US sizeable Muslim communities have already existed for decades. Kundnani quotes a famous formulation of his mentor at the Institute of Race Relations, Ambalavaner Sivanandan,

to remind us why that is: "We are here because you were there".

As it happens many Muslims have tried to fit in. Kundnani cites a 2011 Pew survey which indicated that 44 percent of Muslims display a US flag at home, on their car or at the office. Some 80 percent of American Muslims do not attend mosques and have a secular outlook. Regardless of these facts, Muslims of whatever background or outlook are regarded with a hostility and suspicion that is neatly summed up by the comedian Dean Obeidallah: "It's so weird. Before 9/11, I am just a white guy, living a typical white guy's life. All my friends had names like Monica, Chandler, Joey and Ross...I go to bed September tenth white, wake up September eleventh, I am an Arab" (p51).

Kundnani shows how the war on terror theorists adopt a crude and a monolithic view of Muslims and develop theories of radicalisation based upon unfounded assumptions regarding "Islamist ideology". He distinguishes between two types of critics, culturalists and reformists. The culturalists regard Islam as a backward ideology that has failed to adapt to modern society. Culturalists believe that, whereas in the West people make culture, in Islam, culture makes people. Thus, the purportedly reactionary ideas that lead its followers into terrorism can be found within the Qu'ran itself.

The reformists reject such arguments and profess to hold out the hand of friendship to responsible and respectable Muslims. They claim that Islam is not the issue in itself; rather, the problem lies in the way in which the ideas have been distorted to serve the interests of those with a totalitarian agenda. It is out of such crude characterisations that bogus theories of radicalisation are developed.

Kundnani is not afraid to examine the declarations of figures who have encouraged or participated in acts of allegedly "Islamist violence". These include Anwar al-Awlaki, who was assassinated in a drone strike in September 2011, and Michael Adebolajo, one of the men responsible for the gruesome murder of British soldier Lee Rigby in Britain in 2013. Time and again these people highlight the impact of Western wars and imperialism in driving them to extremism. But such explanations are dismissed as part of an illegitimate "grievance agenda" and anybody expressing such views is pinpointed as a potential threat. This is what lies behind counter-extremism strategies such as the UK government's Prevent agenda.

On the very day that I began reading Kundnani's book the world witnessed a dramatic event which demonstrated just how counter-productive the "war on terror" has been. Friday 13 November seemed to begin so well. As dawn broke the headline story was the "vaporisation" of British subject Mohammad Emwazi in a drone attack. David Cameron rushed back to Downing Street from Chequers to boast about Britain's involvement in that extrajudicial killing.

Reporting on the assassination of so-called "Jihadi John" for the BBC's 6pm bulletin, North American editor John Sopel noted President Obama's declared aim of "downgrading and destroying" Islamic State. Emwazi's killing had not destroyed ISIS but, Sopel suggested, it had gone a long way towards downgrading the menace. Before the next scheduled broadcast at 10pm, news of the attacks that killed 130 people in Paris was coming through. In their wake, we are once again told that counter-extremism is "one of the great struggles of our generation".

Kundnani's book was originally published in 2014. In an afterword written for the paperback edition in 2015 he suggests with no pleasure that his analysis has been "repeatedly confirmed". Hence, the spectacular rise of ISIS is not seen as being created in part by UK and US foreign policy but rather by "that bad version of Islamic belief that somehow takes hold of Muslim minds" (p291).

Regardless of the failures of the past decade, our governments continue to plough on down a path that can only end in catastrophe. In spring 2015 the Prevent agenda, which had been a central part of New Labour's "CONTEST" anti-extremism strategy and continued under the coalition and Tory governments, was placed on a statutory footing. Public institutions such as schools, colleges and universities are now required to spy on and report anyone "at risk of radicalisation". A new counter-extremism bill is intended to target anybody who expresses "vocal or active opposition to our fundamental values, including democracy, the rule of law, individual liberty and the mutual respect and tolerance of different faiths and beliefs". Although the strategy purportedly promotes inclusion, it took no account of the views of key Muslim organisations and representatives. Its proposals will simply stoke up Islamophobia.

As I write these words, the government is pressing ahead with military action in Syria. This will simply make the world more dangerous and, in all probability, ensure that there are violent reprisals in Britain. In such troubled times, analyses such as that presented by Kundnani could not be more important.

Everything moves

Rob Jackson

Antonio Gramsci (edited and translated by Derek Boothman), **A Great and Terrible World: The Pre-Prison Letters, 1908-1926** *(Lawrence and Wishart, 2014), £25*

The Italian revolutionary Antonio Gramsci is widely acknowledged, even beyond the left, as one of the most important thinkers of the 20th century. This collection gathers together around 200 of his letters ranging from his school days in Sardinia, through joining the socialist movement at university, as an international communist leader in the early 1920s, right up until the moment of his arrest and imprisonment by Benito Mussolini's fascist regime in 1926. It presents a fascinating narrative that makes much detail about Gramsci's pre-prison life available to English-speaking readers, including some recently discovered correspondence published here for the first time.

Gramsci's early letters to his family are filled with requests for money and, despite frequent ill health, reports of his promising academic results. The latter earned him a scholarship to study modern philology (a precursor of linguistics) in Turin, where he developed a passion for language and the study of dialects that would continue to manifest itself even in the final pages of his now-famous *Prison Notebooks*. However, inspired by the upsurge in struggle following the Russian Revolution, Gramsci's increasing political commitment led him to abandon his studies for revolutionary journalism.

These letters document the emerging concepts of Gramsci's Marxism, which do not simply appear "full-blown" in the *Prison Notebooks*, but can be seen developing in dialogue with both his personal and political relations. They highlight the importance that Gramsci placed on education in building political organisation, even taking some cues from the well-organised religious schools of the Catholic Church. However, Gramsci conceives education as the creation of a collective critical culture, not as scholastic instruction. In a letter from 1918, Gramsci explains a scheme he initiated among young workers in the Turin socialist movement, the Club for Moral Life. These discussion groups aimed to help young socialists develop the habits of research, of "disciplined and methodical reading, to the simple and calm exposition of their convictions" (p100). He would return to this project in 1924, designing correspondence schools for the Communist Party of Italy (PCI) while in exile from fascism in Vienna.

Editor and translator Derek Boothman skilfully places the bewildering array of characters and events that populate Gramsci's letters in their historical context with a detailed yet readable introduction. Due to gaps in the correspondence, we get only a fleeting glimpse of the *biennio rosso*, the two red years (1919-20). This period marked the high point of the revolutionary wave in Italy following the First World War. Readers who are new to Gramsci's life may therefore wish to supplement this volume by reading about his engagement with the militant factory council movement in Turin through the revolutionary newspaper *L'Ordine Nuovo, New Order* (see for example, Megan Trudell's article "Gramsci: the Turin years" in *International Socialism 114*).

The influence of these formative experiences is ever-present in Gramsci's subsequent letters, which cover his time as a leader of the young Communist Party of Italy. The PCI was born in difficult conditions, splitting with the Italian Socialist

Party in 1921 as the wave of militancy receded and the fascist movement was on the rise. Gramsci travelled to Moscow as a delegate of the Communist International (Comintern), and his time there had a profound effect on him. The severe blows inflicted by fascism on the working class movement in Italy made many activists deeply pessimistic. Gramsci acknowledged these defeats, but pointed his comrades towards "the daily demonstration that I witnessed in Russia of a people creating a new life for itself, new patterns of behaviour, new relationships, new ways of thinking and posing all life's problems" (p271).

Gramsci had initially subordinated himself within the PCI to the intransigent faction led by the "talented and energetic" leader Amadeo Bordiga. This group advocated abstaining from elections and called for an immediate break with bourgeois democracy. But Gramsci later argued against the left grouping of Bordiga, saying that the PCI could not assume the attitude of "misunderstood geniuses". Gramsci and his comrades had learnt "how deeply rooted the traditions of social democracy are and how difficult it is to destroy the residues of the past through simple ideological polemics" (p158). From December 1923, Gramsci moved to Vienna in order to reorientate the PCI towards the united front strategy proposed by the Comintern.

These letters bear witness to Gramsci's struggle with Bordiga, patiently winning over key leaders to a new perspective of broadening the basis for mass political activity and building the independent leadership capacities of the working class movement. The distinguishing feature of Gramsci's conception of "Marxism as developed in Leninism", was not an intransigent and fixed ideological position that sets up a firewall against reformism, but rather "an organic and systematic body of organisational principles and tactical stances" (p168).

Activists can draw inspiration from the revolutionary determination of Gramsci as he reorganises the PCI, with some success, under harsh conditions of clandestinity. Sadly, Gramsci's political activity was cut short in 1926 by the fascist prison sentence that would ultimately lead to his death. The depth of his commitment resonates even in his most personal letters. Gramsci wonders to his partner Jul'ka Schucht, whether it is possible to have a passion for struggle without love: "would it not have sterilised and reduced to a pure intellectual fact, to a pure mathematical calculation, my nature of being a revolutionary?" (p247) The apt title, "A great and terrible world", is one of the most frequent refrains in the letters between Gramsci and Jul'ka. It is a line from Kim by Rudyard Kipling, one of Gramsci's favourite authors.

The collection also includes Gramsci's famous letter of 1926 to the Russian Communist Party criticising the handling of Leon Trotsky and the internal opposition by Stalin and the majority of the leadership. Gramsci's letter emphasises that "your duties as Russian militants can and must be carried out within the framework of the interests of the international proletariat" (p373). Palmiro Togliatti from the PCI reproached Gramsci for this criticism. In his reply, Gramsci presciently warned Togliatti that: "the whole of your reasoning is vitiated by 'bureaucratism'" (p380).

This collection is highly recommended for those studying Gramsci and activists alike. Boothman's translation and editorial apparatus are impressive in their forensic detail without interrupting the flow of the letters. The letters provide a painfully honest window into the highs and lows of the upheavals in Western Europe following the First World War.

Gramsci's legacy is the experience of building a mass revolutionary organisation, and the possibility of achieving this under the most challenging conditions. Even in the darkest moments, Gramsci's vivid imagination sparks with the hope for a new civilisation free from the horrors of fascism and capitalism. Yet, he disdains utopian stances, and his strategy is always rooted in the "real relations of conflicting forces" (p287), which must be realised through the hard work and discipline of revolutionary organisation.

Genomes: Just how important are they?
Terry Sullivan

John Parrington, **The Deeper Genome: Why There is More to the Human Genome than Meets the Eye** *(Oxford University Press, 2015), £18.99*

John Parrington has written a lively and engaging popular science book about the history of genetics or what is increasingly referred to as "genomics".

The history starts towards the end of the 19th century with Gregor Mendel who first showed, in pea plants, that characteristics like height and colour can be passed to offspring according to precise mathematical rules. Mendel's work implied that for sexually reproducing organisms there are two copies of what would become known as genes, one inherited from the father and one from the mother. In "dominant" situations only one copy of a gene variant is needed to help produce the characteristic whilst in "recessive" situations two copies are required.

If characteristics like height and colour can be passed on to offspring how do genes help produce these characteristics? A key insight was provided by Jacques Monod and Francis Jacob who began their research around the start of the Second World War. Monod and Jacob argued that there are in fact two types of genes: "structural" genes and "regulatory" ones. Structural genes "code" for ribonucleic acid or RNA which has a similar structure to deoxyribonucleic acid or DNA. RNA in turn produces proteins including enzymes. Regulatory genes "code" for RNA whose protein products act as switches to turn these structural genes on or off. It should be noted that recent research paints an even more complex picture than this distinction suggests and this is in part the source of the "deeper" genome of the book's title.

Perhaps the most familiar part of the history conveyed in the book is Francis Crick's and Jim Watson's discovery of the double helix structure of DNA in the early 1950s. Although the contribution of Rosalind Franklin was overlooked at the time she played a key role in solving the problem of how the molecule was able to replicate. As their full names suggest, both DNA and RNA are nucleic acids, the subunits of which—nucleotides—come in four varieties, defined by the bases. The four bases of DNA are: adenine, cystosine, guanine and thymine. The key insight Crick and Watson proposed was that the two strands of the double helix are held together by an attraction between adenine and thymine on the one hand and guanine and cystosine on the other. When the strands split apart during cell division they form the template for another mirror-image strand to be formed. The importance of the aforementioned discoveries is shown by the seemingly never ending flow of Nobel Prize winners that Parrington mentions.

In the 1960s Roy Bitten and David Kohne made the surprising discovery that over half of the genome of a mouse is made up of sequences that do not code for proteins. It was not at all clear what if anything they did do. This seemed to lead to the picture of islands of genes in a sea of repetitive sequences or "junk" DNA. This also raised the question of why our bodies would spend vital energy replicating and storing something with no apparent function.

More recently, the Human Genome Project set out to map the 3 billion or so nucleotides in the human genome. This was and still remains the largest and most costly biological project ever known. It was completed to much fanfare in 2003. Another aim of the multi-billion pound project was to work out the number of genes humans have. This was a surprisingly small 22,000 (a common estimate before the start of the project was 100,000). Even more surprising is the fact that grapes have over 30,000! Among other things, this clearly shows that genes alone cannot account for the differences between humans and other organisms.

In 2012 the Encyclopedia of DNA Elements or ENCODE was published. Its aim was to provide detailed information about each gene and its relationship to the rest of the genome. Perhaps ENCODE's most surprising claim was that as much as 80 percent of what had been considered to be "junk" DNA actually had an important function. Parrington is clearly excited by the findings of ENCODE but he is equally clear that those findings have not been universally accepted. For example, one critic lambasted the claims of ENCODE as "absurd", its statistics "horrible" and that it was "the work of people who know nothing about evolutionary biology" (p4).

Much of the history contained in the book will be familiar to those with an interest in biology. However, everyone will learn something new. For example, not only does Parrington tell us that Monod was jointly responsible for the distinction between regulatory and structural genes (as noted above), we also learn that while he was carrying out this work he was active in the French Resistance, eventually becoming its chief of staff. Perhaps even more amazing is that Monod helped smuggle the dissident scientist Agnes Ullman out of Hungary following her support for the failed Hungarian uprising.

Francis Crick, one of the discoverers of the double-helical structure of DNA, famously contended that life is a one-way flow of information from DNA to RNA to protein, something he dubbed the "central dogma of molecular biology". An interesting aspect of the book is Parrington's contention that this is not in fact always the case. For example, it turns out that the position on a chromosome of some genes is not fixed but rather highly mobile. Furthermore, the source of some gene's mobility is via an RNA intermediary which then turns back into DNA before it reinserts itself into the chromosome. The key point here is that RNA can code for DNA and, as a consequence, the flow of information, contrary to Crick's claim, is not one-way but two-way.

Such findings appear to lead to one of the more unusual parts of the book, Parrington's cautious support for "epigenetics". This is the claim that gene activity may be altered in ways that do not involve changes in the DNA sequence. This is sometimes referred to as "Lamarckism" following the work of French scientist Jean-Baptiste Lamarck, who suggested 200 years ago that the environment directly influences hereditary material. Although Parrington cautiously supports epigenetics as an alternative to Crick's central dogma, sometimes he uses language that seems to support the central dogma and is more in keeping with those who mistakenly hold that genes almost single-handedly make us who we are. For example, he writes of "how our genomes define us" (p4) and that "our human uniqueness must be based on genetic differences between ourselves and other species" (p172).

Parrington's stated aim in the book is to find a middle way between two views. The first, he argues, holds that genes should be treated as abstract units or, little better, as discrete and isolated entities on chromosomes. The second recognises their complex and interconnected nature but holds that we have learnt nothing useful from the Human Genome Project. However, this way of framing the argument suggests that there is only one choice to be made when in fact there are two questions here. First, has the Human Genome Project given us a clearer idea of the nature of genes, the genome they constitute and the causal networks of which they are part? Secondly, have we learnt anything useful from the Human Genome Project about the diseases that afflict us? Parrington is correct that the answer to the first is "yes" but despite being convinced by much in the book I think that the answer to the second is a qualified "no"; qualified because, while much has been learnt, precious little has been achieved in terms of actually fighting disease and saving lives. To see this consider the following quote in Parrington's book from Craig Venter: "We have, in truth, learned nothing from the genome other than probabilities. How does a one or three per cent increased risk for something translate into the clinic? It is useless information" (p152). Venter, as the leader of Celera Genomics's rival efforts to sequence the human genome, would seem to have much to gain from a positive assessment of its importance.

However, overall Parrington has written a very good popular science book that can be read by all with profit. I recommend it.

The Aldermaston generation
Allister Mactaggart

Cal Winslow (ed), **E P Thompson and the Making of the New Left: Essays & Polemics** *(Lawrence & Wishart, 2014)* £15.99

This collection of E P Thompson's writings covers the period from 1956 to 1963, a tumultuous but also highly creative and active period for Thompson as a key organiser in the New Left following the Soviet invasion of Hungary, and the resultant resignation of over 10,000 members from the British Communist Party. The editor, Cal Winslow, has assembled 13 important pieces of Thompson's work from this period as "an appreciation, a tribute by a former student, comrade, and friend" (p307).

Thompson's opening essay, "Through the Smoke of Budapest" of 1956, written as the smoke was literally still in the air, demonstrates his ability to cut through dogma to uncover the core of Stalin's "mechanical idealism" (p44) and brings to the fore key arguments. Thompson's critique of Stalinism as "Leninism turned into stone" (p44) reveals both the strengths and weaknesses of his critique as a disillusioned ex-member of the Communist Party. He understands Stalinism as Leninism "wrested out of context" (p42) but sees some of the faults of Stalin as originating in the work of Lenin, Marx and Engels.

In the following essay, "Socialist Humanism: An Epistle to the Philistines", the base and superstructure model employed by Marx and Engels is considered a "bad and dangerous model" (p57) because Stalin uses it in a mechanical manner. Similarly, Marx's use of the word "reflection", coupled with Stalin's "uncritical acceptance of Lenin's *Materialism and Empirico-Criticism*" (p77), are seen by Thompson as providing Stalin with ambiguities which were then applied in a dangerous, crude manner. Although he does accept that Stalin had missed the subtleties of these thinkers, there is a train of thought that seeks to find fault with them rather than laying it firmly at the door of Stalin and the other "mechanical idealists" in the Soviet regime (and elsewhere), and their misappropriation of Marxist theory.

Thompson seeks to rescue Communism from the inhumanity of dangerous abstractions and to put real people at the forefront of theory and practice. He remains committed to revolution but one grounded in "humanist" values. He states that this is a "moment not only for 'rethinking', but also for '*re-affirmation*'" (p99). The models that Thompson wants to employ are derived from the origins of British Marxism and "its since forgotten fusion with English Romantic socialism" (p9). In "The Communism of William Morris" he thus highlights Morris's moral and aesthetic discoveries as a necessary complement to Marx's. Similarly, in his review of Raymond Williams's book *The Long Revolution*, Thompson takes issue with Williams's definition of culture as "a whole way of life" and contrasts this with his own definition as "a way of conflict" (p204). Thompson considers that Williams's selective defence of "The Tradition" in literature and culture aligns it uncritically with the reactionary ideas of T S Eliot and is, therefore, unhelpful for a socialist intervention in cultural matters.

In the development of the New Left, and the passionate energies unleashed by the "Aldermaston generation", we can see how large groups of people became politically active in response to the events unfolding at the time, and how Thompson and the New Left sought to harness that radicalism. Thompson thereby takes on the arguments by reformists in the Labour Party who argued that "affluence" was leading to an improvement in terms and conditions in society, and the perceived apathy of many people. As he points out, "apathy is a symptom as much as it is a cause" (p137) resulting from the Labour movement suffering from problems of ageing and bureaucratisation. As such, he concludes that, "It is because the majority of Labour politicians have ceased to hold any real belief in an alternative to capitalism that their kind of politics has become irrelevant" (pp143-144), a reflection which retains its sting.

Yet the difficulties of seeking to hold together the new breed of radicals becomes clear in how a non-aligned, decentralised, non-hierarchical left, which Thompson proposes as a new model for democratic socialism, can become dissipated by a lack of central organisation. Coupled with this, splits in the board of the *New Left Review* between the "first" New Left and the new editorial board, or the "Team" as Thomson calls them (as shown in the previously unpublished memo "Where are we now?" of April 1963), reveal deep structural and ideological points of dispute between comrades, and between different traditions and trajectories.

For Thompson, detailed archival work, uncovering the importance of largely forgotten "provincial" socialists such as Tom Maguire in Leeds in the late-19th century, provides a means to renew past histories for the present. The final essay in the collection is "The Free-born Englishman", published in the *New Left Review* in 1962 as a chapter from Thompson's major work of the following year, *The Making of the English Working Class*. This essay provides a working model of Thompson's praxis of challenging the "absurd substitutions of historical roles" in other non-Marxist interpretations of history, whereby "the persecuted are seen as forerunners of oppression, and the oppressors as victims of persecution" (p306) and uncovering "elementary truths" (p306), laying the way open for a renewed and re-affirmed tradition of socialism for the forthcoming revolution.

This collection provides detailed insights into the theoretical and practical interventions of a Marxist revolutionary, historian and teacher at a time of great historical significance. They are thus both relevant as historical documents of their time, as well as providing important points of reference and reflection for our own. As Thompson pointed out, "It is never safe to assume that any of our history is altogether dead. It is more often lying there, as a form of stored cultural energy" (p8).

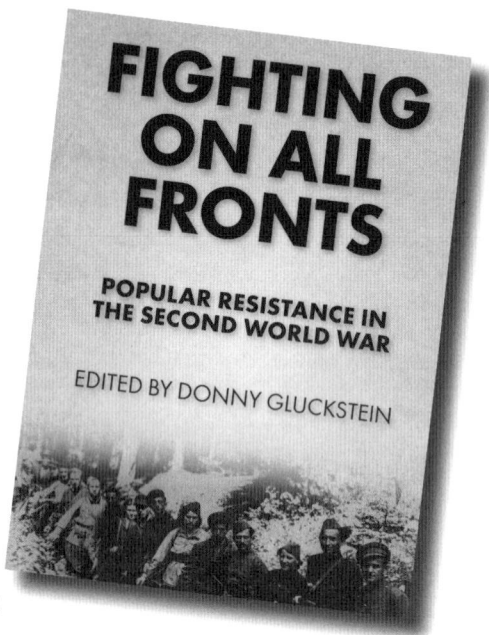

Pick of the quarter

The centenary of the 1916 Easter Rising is fast approaching. The latest issue of the *Irish Marxist Review* commemorates with a special issue. Kieran Allen assesses the myths and reality of the rising, Mary Smith reveals the neglected history of women in the battles for independence, while Conor Kostick applies the same treatment to the role of the working class. Dave Sherry looks at the impact of events in Ireland on the "Red Clydeside" revolt in Glasgow. In his editorial, John Molyneux reflects on the hypocrisy of mainstream Irish politicians who celebrate the events of 100 years ago "with full pomp and circumstance" while at the same time condemning "anyone who protests with the least vigour or militancy today".

The January issue of the *Critical Muslim* journal is titled "Extreme". It features articles by Anne Alexander on ISIS, on class conflict in early Islam by Benedikt Koehler, Islamophobia and US national security by Gordon Blaine Steffey, contemporary art and religious offence by Samir Younés, a review of Arun Kundnani's *The Muslims Are Coming!* by Talat Ahmed and a blistering attack on the extremism of the new atheists by the *Guardian*'s Andrew Brown.

The Socialist History Society has added a new pamphlet to its occasional publication series—on historian Eric Hobsbawm, who died in 2012. The pamphlet is based on the speeches at a conference in 2013 celebrating Hobsbawm's life, it details his extensive contribution to labour history and gives a useful overview of his major works including his tetralogy *The Age of Revolution*, *The Age of Capital*, *The Age of Empire* and *The Age of Extremes*. Hobsbawm was a member of the Communist Party until its demise. Although at times he retreated into academic work rather than party activism (partly due to his criticisms of the party leadership), the pamphlet's authors conclude that his aim as a historian was not merely to indulge in uncovering the minutiae of past events but to understand the past in order to "illuminate the present". Go to www.socialisthistory-society.co.uk

Two issues of *New Left Review* have appeared in the past quarter. The lead article in number II/95 by Wolfgang Streeck offers some commonplaces about the eurozone crisis, though the editors embarrassingly claim that Streeck offers "a landmark critique of Smithian notions of money"—a discussion that relies on Max Weber's treatment of money as an instrument of social struggle and ignores Marx's much more profound exploration of the subject. Elsewhere in the same issue, Neil Davidson's major study of bourgeois revolutions is subjected to nit-picking sectarian criticism. The more recent issue (II/96) opens with an extended editorial by Perry Anderson that surveys the grim plight of the Palestinian people, subjected to a flourishing Fortress Israel that has benefitted from the cowardice and venality of the Fatah leadership. One less palatable consequence—for both the partners Israel and Fatah and their Western backers—is, as Anderson points out, the growing support for a one-state solution.

The issue concludes with a review by John Newsinger, one of *International Socialism*'s most productive contributors, of Janam Mukherjee's new study of one of the greatest crimes of British imperialism, the Bengal Famine of 1943-4. His summary is devastating:

"In order to protect the Raj from a Japanese threat that never materialised, the British state sacrificed the lives of some five million people, the War Cabinet maintaining an attitude of callous indifference. In Churchill's particular case, indifference was strongly tinged with racism. Even [secretary of state for India Leo] Amery, on one occasion, was driven to remark that he couldn't see "much difference between his outlook and Hitler's". As Mukherjee insists, the Bengal Famine was no natural disaster but rather "the direct product of colonial and war-time ideologies and calculations which knowingly exposed the poor of Bengal to annihilation through deprivation"—"a grievous crime was committed in broad daylight", one that is still unacknowledged. The British were far from alone in perpetrating this crime... Indian elites and political leaders were both accessories and beneficiaries, largely unmoved by the suffering in the countryside. Here, Mukherjee highlights a crucial silence in Indian historiography. These classes still rule India—and Pakistan—today".

AC & CR